Banjo FOR DUMMIES

A Wiley Brand

2nd Edition

Banjo
FOR
DUMMIES®
A Wiley Brand

2nd Edition

by Bill Evans

FOR
DUMMIES®
A Wiley Brand

Banjo For Dummies®, 2nd Edition

Published by: **John Wiley & Sons, Inc.,** 111 River Street, Hoboken, NJ 07030-5774, www.wiley.com

Copyright © 2014 by John Wiley & Sons, Inc., Hoboken, New Jersey

Media and software compilation copyright © 2014 by John Wiley & Sons, Inc. All rights reserved.

Published simultaneously in Canada

For general information on our other products and services, please contact our Customer Care Department within the U.S. at 877-762-2974, outside the U.S. at 317-572-3993, or fax 317-572-4002. For technical support, please visit www.wiley.com/techsupport.

Wiley publishes in a variety of print and electronic formats and by print-on-demand. Some material included with standard print versions of this book may not be included in e-books or in print-on-demand. If this book refers to media such as a CD or DVD that is not included in the version you purchased, you may download this material at http://booksupport.wiley.com. For more information about Wiley products, visit www.wiley.com.

Library of Congress Control Number: 2013952435

ISBN 978-1-118-74633-2 (pbk); ISBN 978-1-118-74629-5 (ebk); ISBN 978-1-118-74625-7 (ebk)

Manufactured in the United States of America

10 9 8 7 6 5 4 3 2 1

Contents at a Glance

Table of Contents

Introduction

You just can't get that wild and complex sound out of your head. You thought about trying to play, and you ended up here — with a copy of *Banjo For Dummies* in your hands. It's time to join the hundreds of thousands of other players all over the world who can't get enough of one of the world's most unique and loved instruments. You're ready to play the five-string banjo.

You've probably already come to the realization that no matter what you may have seen on television or in old movies, real banjo players aren't comedic rubes or country bumpkins. They're folks just like you and me from all walks of life who at some point heard the sound of a banjo and said to themselves, "That's for me!"

While the five-string banjo is usually associated with bluegrass, folk, and country music, these days musicians play just about any kind of music on the banjo — from rock to jazz to classical and everything in between. You can use the banjo to accompany songs around a campfire or to play a Bach partita. You can play anything on a five-string banjo. It's time to get started!

About This Book

Banjo For Dummies, 2nd Edition, is your musical road map for wherever you may want to roam in your banjo travels. From choosing the right instrument and accessories to hands-on experience playing bluegrass, old-time, and historical styles, it's all here. This book transports you from the most basic beginners' questions to performing intermediate tunes played in the most popular styles used today. I even sneak in more than a few advanced concepts for those of you who really want to be challenged. You can find clear, step-by-step explanations to each and every technique and discover shortcuts that are especially helpful to the adult student.

In this new edition, you'll find a chapter covering intermediate to advanced clawhammer and old-time fingerpicking styles (Chapter 8) and another new chapter revealing the secrets of how to sound great playing with others using bluegrass accompaniment techniques (Chapter 10). You can also dig deep into bluegrass styles (Chapter 9) and discover the fascinating world of early American banjo (Chapter 11).

With this edition of *Banjo For Dummies,* you can now watch as well as listen. There are over 40 short videos on 24/7 standby online, ready to provide assistance with tuning, hand positions, basic playing techniques, songs, and even changing strings. Need more? Check out the online audio tracks that correspond to techniques and songs presented in the book.

Although I'd like to think that this book makes for a gripping and powerful literary experience, don't worry about reading *Banjo For Dummies* cover to cover. Think of this book instead as a reference work that's designed for you to jump into and out of at any point along the way. Take a look at the table of contents and start at the chapter or section that best matches your ability and interests the most. Don't forget to check out the index at the back of the book for an even more comprehensive listing of topics.

You may notice that you can't find a speck of conventional music notation anywhere in *Banjo For Dummies*. Instead, you find banjo *tablature,* the universal form of written music notation for just about all styles of banjo playing. Tablature is easier to master than regular musical notation and clearly shows you exactly what to do with both hands.

Every now and then, you'll run across information contained in a gray-shaded sidebar. Think of these as rest stops along the banjo superhighway — you can check them out as you're passing through or return to pay a visit later when you have a bit more time to enjoy the scenery.

Within this book, you may note that some web addresses break across two lines of text. If you're reading this book in print and want to visit one of these web pages, simply key in the web address exactly as it's noted in the text, pretending as though the line break doesn't exist. If you're reading this as an e-book, you have it easy — just click the web address to be taken directly to the web page.

Foolish Assumptions

I'm betting that you've picked up this book because you're interested in playing the banjo, but I don't want to assume too much more as I begin this banjo adventure with you. You may or may not own a banjo or have any prior experience on the banjo or any other kind of instrument, and I don't assume you come to this book knowing anything about music. I also don't assume you're interested in one particular style or way of playing the banjo over another (which is why I include more than one).

However, I *do* assume that you're going to be playing a five-string banjo instead of a tenor or plectrum banjo, which are actually different kinds of instruments (see Chapter 1). I also assume that you want to get started quickly and not waste time with unnecessary and overly technical information. If I've described you in one way or another, you've come to the right place.

Icons Used in This Book

In the margins of this book, you can find the following friendly icons to help you recognize different types of information.

This icon highlights the really good information that's not only worthy of your full attention but also likely to be something you'll come back to again and again.

This icon points you to expert advice and time-saving strategies that can make you a better banjo player.

You can consider information attached to this icon to be fun but not essential to playing the banjo. You may find it interesting (I do!), but you can skip over it if you're short on time.

Exercise caution with text marked by this icon in order to protect yourself, your banjo, or your musical reputation!

This icon lets you know that there's an audio track and, in many cases, a video clip that demonstrates the concept, playing technique, or song discussed in the text. Check out these online resources at www.dummies.com/go/banjo to deepen your understanding and speed your progress.

Beyond the Book

In addition to the material in the print or e-book you're reading right now, this product also comes with some online goodies, available for easy access at your first jam session when you suddenly can't remember how to fret a G chord. Check out the eCheat Sheet at www.dummies.com/cheatsheet/banjo for helpful insights and pointers on reading chord diagrams, how to fret the chords you'll use the most, reading banjo tablature, and playing basic right-hand patterns.

You can also discover my list of ten jam session essentials, more practice hints, upgrades to banjo parts, and more at www.dummies.com/extras/banjo.

I've recorded numerous audio tracks and video clips so that you can view and listen to various techniques and songs discussed throughout the book. There's even a video to guide you through changing strings on your banjo. Go to www.dummies.com/go/banjo to download these files.

Where to Go from Here

As a banjo player on a mission, you want to know where, when, and how you can get started. You can always read this book straight through, but the beauty of any *For Dummies* book is that you can direct your own course and dip into chapters as you need them.

As you create your own road map, I can offer you a few suggestions to point you in the right direction:

- ✔ If you need to purchase a banjo or you're interested in an upgrade, head to the buyer's guide in Chapter 13 first.

- ✔ If you're a beginner with banjo in hand, and you want to start playing right away, proceed to Chapters 2 and 3, where you get your banjo in tune and play your first chords.

- ✔ If you're ready to start working on authentic banjo styles, roll up your sleeves and work through Chapters 5, 6, and 7.

- ✔ If you're an experienced player, dig in by checking out intermediate to advanced old-time playing techniques in Chapter 8, more challenging bluegrass techniques in Chapter 9, and early American banjo styles in Chapter 11.

Part I
The Amazing Five-String Banjo

getting started

with

the banjo

web extras Visit www.dummies.com for great free Dummies content online.

In this part...

- Discover the difference between various kinds of banjos and find the right kind of five-string banjo for the music you want to make.

- Nothing sounds worse than an instrument out of tune, so find out everything you need to know about keeping your banjo in tune and sounding sweet.

- Get comfortable sitting and standing with the banjo and find a comfortable left-hand position for fretting chords.

- Read chord diagrams and banjo tablature — they're not as tough to decipher as you may think.

- Play your first few chords, and then make music with easy to play right-hand strumming and picking patterns.

Chapter 1

You Want to Play What?: Banjo Basics

In This Chapter

▶ Connecting to the world-wide banjo community

▶ Getting to know different kinds of banjos

▶ Exploring the banjo and all its parts

▶ Starting on the road to becoming a great player

*B*efore you begin any trip, you probably like to know where you're going. If you're new to the banjo and don't yet own an instrument or if you're wondering about your eventual musical destination, this chapter is definitely the place to start your *Banjo For Dummies* excursion. The key is in the ignition, so put this thing in drive!

In this chapter, you spread out your banjo road map and start planning what I hope will be a wonderful, lifelong musical journey with the five-string banjo. You see what makes the five-string banjo different from other kinds of stringed instruments, and you get to take a look at some of the various kinds of banjos available today. I name the parts of the banjo and preview the musical skills you'll master in this book on the way to becoming a great banjo player.

Getting into Banjo

There's something about the five-string banjo that brings out strong feelings in people. Folks who like the banjo usually *really* like it, sometimes to the mystery, confusion, and even chagrin of those loved ones around them. What is it about this instrument that inspires such passion, and how can you tell if you've been bitten by the banjo bug? This section explores some answers to these questions.

Loving that amazing sound

You know the sound of the banjo when you hear it: the bright, rhythmic waterfall of short, cascading notes that can conjure up just about any emotion (but *happy* is usually the first to come to mind for the typical guy or gal on the street). The banjo is usually associated with folk, country, bluegrass, and old-time music, but these days, you can also hear the instrument in rock, jazz, and even classical settings.

Over the years, I've asked hundreds of amateur and professional players why they initially got interested in the banjo, and the usual answer is "I fell in love with the sound." I think an equal attraction is the lure of hearing a lot of notes compressed into what seems like the smallest of musical spaces. In the hands of a skilled player, the banjo is an instrument that's capable of amazing virtuosity.

Becoming a true believer

Banjo players usually remember well the precise moment in time that they became hooked on the instrument. For me, growing up as a suburban teenager far from significant hills of any kind, that moment arrived when I was watching Roy Clark play banjo on *Hee Haw* and thinking to myself, "If I can somehow sit through this show every week, I think I can eventually learn 'Cripple Creek.'" I didn't especially like country music at that time, and I'd never heard of bluegrass music — but I really loved the sound of the banjo.

Growing up in the 1970s, I could also hear the banjo as a background instrument on hit songs from the Eagles, the Doobie Brothers, Neil Young, and James Taylor. Hearing the banjo in these contexts made me believe that the banjo *must* be cool if those musicians used it on their recordings, despite what my friends thought about this disturbing turn in my musical tastes.

Today, you can hear the sound of the banjo in just about any style of music, short of Gregorian chant (although I bet there's a monk in a monastery somewhere in the world learning "Foggy Mountain Breakdown"). More than ever, the banjo is an integral part of contemporary music, showing up on stage with Mumford & Sons, Taylor Swift, the Avett Brothers, and most of the biggest hat and hair acts in country music.

The path-breaking banjo player Béla Fleck has performed with jazz artists Chick Corea and Marcus Roberts, and he has composed a concerto for banjo and orchestra. The actor/comedian/writer Steve Martin is bringing the banjo to thousands of new listeners who come to his concerts for the jokes but leave humming Steve's original banjo music. In addition, thousands of banjo players come together every year at their favorite bluegrass and old-time music festivals, camps, and workshops to make music together, as they have for many decades.

My own youthful enthusiasm for the banjo evolved into a wonderful, lifelong relationship that's still going strong. I get a joyful feeling every time I play a tune on the banjo. I'm also amazed at how my love for the instrument has opened the door to many new and wonderful experiences (such as graduate school, international touring and teaching, and this book!) and is at the basis of many of my most cherished friendships. When you play the banjo, you're not just playing a musical instrument; you're opening a door to new life experiences, such as the joy you'll experience playing music with others. Even if you never become as obsessed about the banjo as I am, I believe that the banjo can improve your life and make you a happier person if you give it the chance.

There's no doubt about it: The banjo is *hot* right now — and it's time for you to join in on the fun!

Identifying Different Kinds of Banjos

Although the five-string banjo is by far the most popular type of banjo being played today, decades ago the most popular banjos in the first half of the 20th century were four-string tenor and plectrum banjos. These banjos are really different instruments and shouldn't be confused with the five-string banjo. Understanding the differences between banjos is important, because before you begin your adventure, you need to make sure you're traveling with the right kind of equipment.

In the following sections, I compare and contrast the different instruments in the banjo family, so you don't mistake one type of banjo for another.

Five-string banjo: The subject of this book

The short 5th string is what makes the five-string banjo different from other types of banjos and from just about every other instrument in the known universe. Most of the time, you know immediately that you're looking at a five-string banjo when you see a *tuning peg* (a geared mechanism that keeps the string in tune) sticking out almost halfway up the *neck* (the long, narrow piece of wood where you fret strings with the left hand; for more on these terms, see the later section "Knowing the Parts of a Banjo"). This tuning peg holds the 5th string of the banjo (see Figure 1-1).

The 5th string is a crucial distinguishing characteristic of the five-string banjo, both in the instrument's appearance and in the sound of the music. The 5th string is not only shorter than the other four banjo strings, but this string is also the highest in sound (or *pitch*). The 5th string on a banjo lies within easy reach of the right-hand thumb, which you use to play this string in all kinds of banjo music. Having the highest-pitched string next to the string with the lowest pitch is unusual in comparison to how pitches are arranged on the strings of a guitar (as you can see in Figure 1-1), but this is one of the things that makes the banjo sound so great! This characteristic of the banjo is also one part of the instrument's ancient African ancestry (for more on this, see Chapter 11).

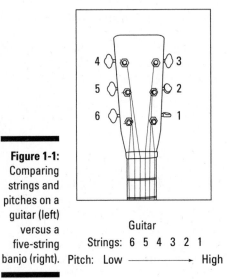
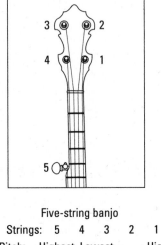

Figure 1-1: Comparing strings and pitches on a guitar (left) versus a five-string banjo (right).

Guitar

Strings: 6 5 4 3 2 1

Pitch: Low —————————→ High

Five-string banjo

Strings: 5   4   3   2   1

Pitch: Highest Lowest ————→High

Illustration by Wiley, Composition Services Graphics

Tenor and plectrum banjos: Look for another book

In the early decades of the 20th century, folks loved the quality of the banjo's sound so much that they attached different kinds of necks to the banjo body to create new instruments with different numbers of strings. These hybrid instruments were tuned and played differently from the five-string banjo.

Tenor and *plectrum* banjos are examples of this phenomenon. These four-stringed instruments are commonly used in traditional jazz, Dixieland, and Irish music. They don't have the short 5th string and are usually played with a flatpick instead of with the fingers. Although these banjos make the same kinds of sounds and look a lot like the five-string banjo, tenor and plectrum banjos use other tunings and playing techniques and are viewed as different instruments by banjo fans.

Don't confuse these tenor and plectrum banjos with the five-string variety. The bodies of these instruments are the same, but the necks reveal the difference (see Figure 1-2). You can't play five-string banjo music on a four-string tenor or plectrum banjo — these instruments aren't interchangeable! You need a five-string banjo to play five-string banjo music.

Figure 1-2: Comparing a five-string (a) and a tenor (b) banjo.

a

b

Photographs courtesy of Elderly Instruments

Banjos of all sorts

In the early decades of the 20th century, America was mad for anything that sounded remotely like a banjo. (Amazing, isn't it? Just like it is today!) Instrument makers took guitar and mandolin necks and attached them to banjo bodies, creating new kinds of instruments of all sizes that had that great banjo sound but could be played using guitar and mandolin techniques.

Banjos with mandolin necks usually have eight strings and are called *mandolin banjos* or *mando-banjos*. These instruments are smaller than most five-string banjos. Banjos with guitar necks have six strings and are called *guitar banjos*. These instruments are perfect for guitar players who want that banjo sound (and maybe are too lazy to actually learn to play the banjo — but you didn't hear that from me!). Guitar banjos have six strings instead of five and can be a bit larger than most five-string banjos.

Today, these more obscure branches of the banjo family tree are seen largely as novelty instruments and, like the tenor and plectrum banjo (see the section "Tenor and plectrum banjos: Look for another book" in this chapter), are considered to be a different kind of instrument than a five-string banjo. Mandolin banjos are played like mandolins, and guitar banjos are played like guitars.

Knowing the Parts of a Banjo

The banjo combines wooden, metal, skin, and/or plastic parts held together by rods, nuts, screws, and brackets to make some of the most incredible and beautiful sounds in the world. You could call the banjo the Frankenstein of musical instruments, but I like to think of it as the *Bionic Woman*. Practically all banjos share a common characteristic of having a replaceable top playing surface made of plastic or animal skin (called the *head*) that's stretched tightly across the body of the banjo (called the *pot*) to form the top of the resonating body of the instrument (see Figure 1-3).

Five-string banjos come in three different basic styles: open-back, resonator, and electric. Musicians select the kind of banjo they play based on their musical style and their personal tastes. Chapter 13 explains the differences between these kinds of banjos, along with tips for making an informed purchase.

In the following sections, you get to know the banjo from head to toe (well, really from the top of the headstock to the bottom of the pot). You also discover how the instrument captures the energy of a plucked string and turns it into that unmistakably great sound that banjo players love. You can refer to Figure 1-4 to see exactly where these parts are located on the banjo.

Looking at the neck

The neck is one of the two main sections of the banjo (the pot being the other; see the section "Checking out the pot"). The *neck* is the long piece of wood that supports the strings and tuners. Necks are usually made of maple, mahogany, or walnut.

To get a better feel for the banjo, take a look at the parts of the banjo neck:

- ✔ **Frets:** The thin, metal bars on the banjo neck that are positioned at precise intervals to give you the various pitches needed when fretting a string. (*Fretting* is what you do when you move a left-hand finger into position behind a fret to change the pitch of a string.) In the world of fretting, you use the term *up the neck* to refer to moving the left hand toward the pot and *down the neck* when you talk about moving the left hand toward the nut and peghead.

- ✔ **Fingerboard:** A thin, flat, wooden strip glued to the neck that holds the frets and is the surface upon which the left hand produces notes and chords.

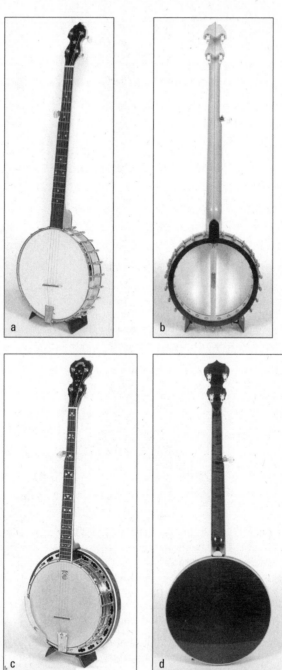

Figure 1-3: Comparing open-back (a and b) and resonator (c and d) five-string banjos.

Photographs courtesy of Elderly Instruments

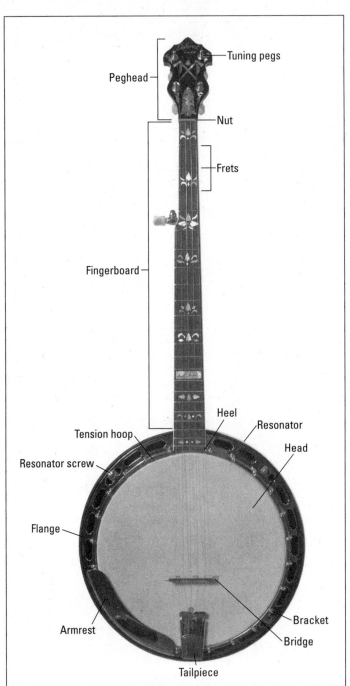

Tuning pegs

Peghead

Nut

Frets

Fingerboard

Heel

Resonator

Tension hoop

Head

Resonator screw

Flange

Armrest

Bracket

Bridge

Tailpiece

Figure 1-4:
The parts of
a banjo.

Photograph courtesy of Gruhn Guitars

- ✔ **Peghead:** Also called the *headstock,* the peghead is the elaborately shaped end of the neck that holds the tuning pegs for the four lower strings of the banjo.

- ✔ **Tuning pegs:** Sometimes called *tuners* or *tuning machines,* these pegs are the devices that raise or lower the pitch of the banjo's strings with a turn of the buttons located on the backside of the peghead. The pegs for strings 1 through 4 are attached to the peghead, while the tuning peg for the 5th string is found on the topside of the neck near the 5th fret.

- ✔ **Nut:** A block of ivory, bone, or plastic that's glued to the end of the fingerboard where the peghead begins. Strings 1 through 4 pass through the grooves in the nut on their way to the shafts of the tuning pegs. The 5th string has its own smaller nut, located near the 5th fret.

- ✔ **Heel:** The name given to the part at the end of the neck that's attached to the pot of the banjo.

- ✔ **Truss rod:** You can't see the truss rod, but it's an important part of most banjo necks. The *truss rod* is an adjustable metal rod that runs down most of the length of the banjo neck in a channel underneath the fingerboard. This rod helps to keep the neck stable and controls the amount of curve in the neck to keep the strings from buzzing when playing. Although some banjos don't have truss rods at all, most banjos have adjustable truss rods, which can be accessed at the peghead by removing the truss rod cover located just above the nut at the peghead. (*Note:* This is a procedure best left to the pros.)

Checking out the pot

The other major section of the banjo (other than the neck; see the preceding section) is the *pot,* the round lower body of the banjo including all of its constituent parts. You can see some of the following parts highlighted in Figure 1-5:

- ✔ **Head:** The head is the plastic or skin membrane that acts as the vibrating top of the banjo. The head is largely responsible for the unique sound of your new favorite instrument.

- ✔ **Rim:** Sometimes called the *shell,* the rim is the circular wooden ring that is the centerpiece of the pot and is made from laminations or blocks of maple or mahogany. A well-made rim is essential to a good-sounding banjo.

- ✔ **Tone ring:** This part of the pot is a metal circular collar that's machined to fit on top of the wooden rim, and the head is stretched tight across its top outer circumference. Tone rings come in a variety of shapes and sizes. Together with the rim, the tone ring provides the fundamental color of the banjo's tone. However, tone rings aren't found on all banjos and having one isn't absolutely necessary to having a good-sounding instrument.

✔ **Brackets:** Sometimes called *hooks,* brackets are ringed around the banjo pot and are responsible for tightening the head via the bracket screws that are attached to each bracket on the underside of most banjos.

✔ **Tension hoop:** Sometimes called the *stretcher band,* this circular metal ring fits over the outside edge of the banjo head and helps to uniformly stretch the head down across the top of the tone ring as the brackets are tightened.

✔ **Bridge:** The bridge transmits the vibrations of the strings to the head. Bridges range in size from 5/8 inch to 3/4 inch. They are movable, but are held fast to the banjo head by the tension of the strings.

✔ **Tailpiece:** This part holds the strings on the pot end of the banjo. Many tailpieces are adjustable in various ways that can subtly affect overall banjo tone.

✔ **Armrest:** The armrest is attached to the pot of the banjo and extends over the top of the banjo head to make right-hand playing more comfortable while simultaneously protecting the head.

✔ **Coordinating rods:** Seen only from the back of the banjo, these rods are attached at opposite ends of the rim, parallel to the banjo strings. The primary function of the coordinating rods is to keep the neck securely attached to the pot. However, they can also be used to make slight adjustments to the height of the strings off of the fingerboard (called *string action*). Some banjos have only one coordinating rod, and many open-back banjos have what's called a *dowel stick* instead of a coordinating rod.

✔ **Resonator:** The bowl-shaped piece of wood that's attached to many banjos, especially those used in bluegrass music, is the resonator. The resonator projects the sound out and away from the instrument. It's usually constructed from the same kind of wood as the banjo neck. Open-back banjos don't have resonators (see Chapter 13 for more on the types of banjos).

✔ **Resonator screws:** Three or four resonator screws keep the resonator attached to the rest of the banjo pot.

✔ **Flange:** The flange is a circular metal piece connecting the pot to the resonator that helps to keep the resonator in place.

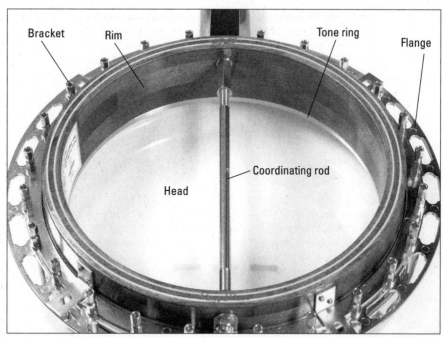

Photograph by Anne Hamersky

Figure 1-5:
The banjo
pot (as seen
from the
back).

Picking up string vibrations

When you strike a banjo string with a right-hand finger or thumb, the string
starts to move back and forth. These vibrations move through the bridge
(a piece of wood positioned on the banjo head) to the banjo head, which
amplifies that sound. Banjo players frequently refer to right-hand playing as
picking the banjo. You can read more about authentic right-hand banjo
picking techniques in Chapter 5.

The *pitch* of any string (its sound as measured by how high or low it is) is
determined by how much tension or tightness is in each string and how long
or short it is. The tighter or shorter the string, the higher its pitch. You can
change the pitch of a string in two ways:

✔ **Turn the tuning pegs.** A twist of a tuning peg in one direction or the
other raises or lowers the pitch of a string. The direction is different for
each string. (For more on tuning, check out Chapter 2.)

✔ **Fret the strings.** When you *fret* a string, you place a left-hand finger
behind one of the 22 frets found on the fingerboard of the neck. As you
fret, you're shortening the length of the string and raising its pitch.
An *open* string is one that is unfretted in the left hand. A fretted string
sounds higher in pitch compared to an open string or to that same
string fretted on a lower fret (a lower fret is one that is farther away from
the banjo body). For more on fretting with the left hand, see Chapter 3.

Becoming a Banjo Player

If the banjo is the first stringed instrument you've ever attempted to play,
it may seem as if you have a million things to remember at this first stage.
Everything feels so new and unfamiliar. Don't get discouraged! Banjo players
tend to be perfectionists, so be careful not to let your desire to play things
correctly overwhelm your love for playing (and remember that everyone
learns from his or her mistakes — even banjo players). Having fun with the
banjo is more important than playing everything perfectly.

When you want to become more proficient on the banjo, you can't find a
substitute for time actually spent playing the banjo — the more you play, the
faster you progress. Focus on one new skill at a time, and don't spend too
much time on the Internet finding out what everyone else thinks about this
or that aspect of banjo playing. Just *play* (and check out Chapter 16 for more
great practice suggestions). After you've gained a few basic skills, find other
musicians at your ability level to play with as soon as possible. Playing with
others will significantly speed up your progress.

In the following sections, I present just a few of the skills you should strive
to master as a banjo player (and as you make your way through *Banjo For
Dummies*).

Making wise purchase choices

These days, new players can find good starter banjos that are affordable and
easy to play. The crucial first step in your purchase is finding an acoustic
specialty store that really knows banjos and actually *likes* banjo players. And
as you shop, keep in mind that your choice of instrument should be based
mostly upon the kind of music you want to play (and, of course, how much
money you have to spend).

I cover everything you need to know about what to look for in banjos and
playing accessories and how to find them in Chapters 13 and 14.

Tuning and holding your banjo

Keeping your instrument in tune is something that you practice each time you play — and an absolutely essential skill when playing music with others. Tuning your banjo can be frustrating at first, but with careful listening to compare one pitch with another and some trial and error, you can have this skill mastered in no time.

After you're in tune, you want to adopt a comfortable playing position for both sitting or standing. You have a lot of individual options in this regard. Just remember not to raise the neck too high and try using a strap. If you follow these two suggestions, you'll be well on your way to finding your personal comfort zone.

I cover getting your banjo in tune in Chapter 2. Check out Chapter 3 to help you get comfortable holding the banjo and fitting the strap.

Fretting chords with the left hand

A *chord* is three or more notes sounded together. Chords support a melody and are the building blocks for accompanying other musicians. The best way to begin your playing adventures is to become familiar with well-used chords such as G, C, and D7. A comfortable left-hand position makes forming these chords much more fun. Let your thumb touch the top of the back of the banjo neck, relax your shoulder and elbow into your body, and be sure you're using the tips of your fingers to press the strings just behind the frets — now you're in business.

In Chapter 3, you can dig deeper into finding a comfortable left-hand position and get used to fretting chords up and down the banjo neck.

Playing authentic right- and left-hand patterns

Coordinating right-hand picking techniques with the left-hand work of making chords and creating new notes is a full-time job for banjo players! Mastering exercises that isolate what each hand does by itself lays the foundation for making great banjo music with both hands together.

In Chapters 5, 6, 8, and 9, you take a look at these techniques, because you need them in clawhammer and bluegrass banjo to create melodies and to play with others in jam sessions.

Practicing some real tunes

The real fun begins when you utilize your technique to play melodies on the instrument in authentic banjo styles. Melody notes can usually be organized as a group of notes, called a *scale*. Finding melody notes in a song becomes easier after you've mastered a few scales on the banjo neck, so I recommend that you start with the scales I outline in Chapter 4.

After you get the feel for the scales, you can use the right- and left-hand techniques you master to capture as many melody notes as you can and create arrangements that sound good on the instrument.

In Chapters 7, 8, and 9, you can play beginner and more advanced versions of tunes in clawhammer, old-time fingerpicking, and traditional and contemporary bluegrass styles. Chapter 11 explores early banjo styles from the 19th and early 20th centuries. The online audio examples allow you to hear me play musical examples from this book, and now you can check out video online for the most important exercises and tunes presented. We banjo players have to stick together, and I'm there for you, online 24/7!

Jamming in good company

Banjo players love to make music with other musicians — guitarists, fiddlers, mandolin and dobro players, and bassists. When you're playing your banjo with others, remember to play in a way that enhances the sound of the total group. Active listening and playing in good rhythm play a big role in your efforts to make other musicians sound their best.

In Chapters 4, 10, and 12, I discuss the unique techniques and skills you need to accompany other pickers and singers on familiar bluegrass and old-time tunes in informal jam sessions. I also cover some of the unspoken ground rules of jam etiquette to make your transition into group playing go smoothly.

Meeting other banjo lovers

You may be amazed at how many opportunities you have to share your enthusiasm for the banjo with other like-minded players. From finding a teacher to attending a workshop, camp, or festival, you can have more fun with the instrument and become a better player faster by connecting with others who share your enthusiasm for the banjo. As a new player, don't wait until you've already acquired some playing skills before seeking help from others. You'll become a better player much more quickly by seeking out help at the very beginning of your banjo adventure. In Chapter 12, I talk about the world of banjo that lies beyond your doorstep.

 Camps and workshops are often designed for all levels of students. If you already play, you can recharge your banjo-picking batteries at a regional camp or workshop where you can hang out with the banjo stars, make many new friends, and come away with new playing ideas that will keep your hands busy for months to come.

Keeping your banjo sounding great

Banjos are much more adjustable than other stringed instruments such as the guitar or bass. However, you don't have to become an accomplished, all-knowing, instrument-repair person to keep your instrument in top shape.

 Keeping fresh strings on your instrument is the most important thing you can do to keep your banjo running right. After a few weeks or months of playing, your strings will inevitably become harder to tune — or they may even break. Keep an extra set of strings handy in your case along with a small pair of wire cutters, and you'll be ready for all contingencies!

You may also want to check out all the movable parts on your banjo every couple of months. For example, keeping the head tight keeps your banjo sounding bright and loud, and checking to see that the bridge is in just the right place on the banjo head keeps your fretted notes in tune. I cover everything you need to know about these topics, as well as determining when you need to seek out professional advice, in Chapter 15.

Chapter 2

Tuning Your Banjo

. . . .

In This Chapter

▶ Sizing up strings and frets for G tuning

▶ Tuning your banjo by ear: Relative tuning

▶ Using a tuner or another instrument: Reference tuning

▶ Access the audio tracks and video clips at www.dummies.com/go/banjo

. . . .

Question: "What's the difference between a banjo and a motorcycle?"

Answer: "You can tune a motorcycle."

This unfortunate but frequently recited banjo joke speaks to a greater truth: The banjo can be one of the most difficult and frustrating of all stringed instruments to tune. One of the first steps to becoming a great player is getting tuned in and staying that way throughout a practice or playing session.

With just a bit of practice, using this section as a guide, you can master this all-important but sometimes elusive skill, making it possible for you to play at home without driving your loved ones insane. And when it's time to play with other musicians in a jam session, they'll be so grateful that you took the time to figure out how to tune your banjo that they just might let you play "Cripple Creek" with them twice at a slow speed.

To tune the banjo, you raise or lower the amount of tension of each string to match the sound of another banjo string or to match a reference note provided by another instrument or an electronic tuner. You adjust each string by turning its corresponding tuning peg. In this section, you get familiar with several different methods to tune your banjo, so you have absolutely no excuse but to tune in and pick on!

Like all other elements of banjo playing, tuning is a skill that gets easier with practice and the passage of time. Being able to distinguish one note from another isn't a mysterious psychic ability that you either are or aren't born with — tuning is a learned skill. Keep actively listening to how the sounds of the strings change as you turn the pegs. Don't be afraid to ask others for advice if you're unsure about whether a string is in tune, even when playing with others in a jam session. Other musicians want you to be in tune just as much as you want to be!

G Tuning: Getting Your Strings in Order

Although banjo players use a variety of tunings to play different kinds of songs and to create different moods on their instrument, the most frequently used *tuning* is called G tuning (which is also the type of tuning that's used in most of this book with the exception of many of the old-time tunes covered in Chapter 8). With this tuning, the five open strings of the banjo are tuned to the notes of a G major chord (a *chord* is a collection of three or more notes played together; I talk more about chords in Chapter 3).

Here are the pitches used for each string in G tuning:

> 5th string: G
>
> 4th string: D
>
> 3rd string: G
>
> 2nd string: B
>
> 1st string: D

Note that only three different pitches are used in G tuning: G, B, and D. These three notes make up the G major chord. The 1st-string D and 5th-string G are one octave higher in pitch than their 4th- and 3rd-string counterparts. Your ears hear the two D notes and the two G notes as being essentially the same, but you can also hear that the 1st and 5th strings are higher in pitch. Musicians long ago decided to assign the same letter name to pitches that you hear in this way, but they also recognized that the two D's and the two G's aren't *exactly* the same pitch. They're one *octave* apart, with the octave being the point where that same note is repeated again but at a higher pitch.

Figure 2-1 shows the pitches of each string in G tuning along with a fretboard image summarizing the relative tuning relationships between the strings (which I cover in the next section). You can check out Audio Track 1 to hear the pitch of each banjo string in G tuning.

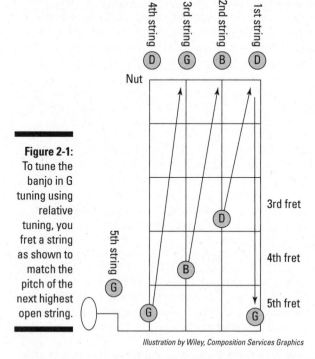

Figure 2-1:
To tune the banjo in G tuning using relative tuning, you fret a string as shown to match the pitch of the next highest open string.

Illustration by Wiley, Composition Services Graphics

Relative Tuning: Tuning the Banjo to Itself

Relative tuning involves using one string as a reference to tune the other strings of your banjo. That string doesn't really have to be in tune with any outside source, because in this case, you're just getting the banjo strings in tune with one another so that you can play by yourself.

With each new string you tune in relative tuning, you then fret that string to create a new reference note that you use to tune the next highest string. Relative tuning is the most useful way to tune the banjo, because you need nothing but your banjo and your ears to get your instrument in tune. You have a banjo; now you can get to work on training your ears!

Even pro players follow up on their initial pass at relative tuning by trying different pairs of strings to hear what they sound like together and tuning the adjacent pairs of strings a second time. If one or more strings are severely out of tune to begin with, you definitely need to repeat the processes I describe in the following sections once or twice until the banjo is in good tune.

When tuning from low to high, you begin with the lowest-pitched 4th string and work your way up to the 5th string, the highest-pitched string. Using the following instructions, you tune the remaining four strings up from the 4th string, using the left-hand middle finger to fret each reference note. For now, try striking (or *picking*) each string with a downward motion of your right-hand thumb. You can watch me demonstrate relative tuning from low to high in Video Clip 1. I name and play all the open strings on the banjo in G tuning.

When you're comparing the pitches of two strings as you work through the following steps, your goal is to match the pitch of the open string to the fretted string that you pick. If the open string sounds higher in pitch, that string is *sharp,* and you want to adjust the tuning peg for that string in the direction that brings its pitch down (usually clockwise for the 3rd and 4th strings; counterclockwise for the 1st and 2nd strings). If the open string is lower in pitch, that string is *flat;* in this case, you rotate the peg in the direction that causes the pitch of the string to rise (usually counterclockwise for the 3rd and 4th strings; clockwise for the 1st and 2nd strings).

1. **Pick the 4th string fretted at the 5th fret and compare its pitch to the open 3rd string.**

   You may need to strike the fretted 4th string first, wait a moment to hear its pitch, and then strike the 3rd string to listen to its pitch. Does the 3rd string (the second note you play) sound higher or lower than the 4th string? Try singing the two pitches to *feel* whether the pitch rises or falls.

2. **Using the tuning peg, adjust the pitch of the 3rd string up or down until it matches the pitch of the fretted 4th string.**

   When the pitches of the two strings match each other, the 4th and 3rd strings of your banjo are in tune.

3. **Pick the 3rd string fretted at the 4th fret and match the open 2nd string to this sound.**

   After these strings sound the same, you have the 4th, 3rd, and 2nd strings of your banjo in tune.

4. **Pick the 2nd string fretted at the 3rd fret and tune the open 1st string to this sound.**

5. **Pick the 1st string fretted at the 5th fret and tune the open 5th string to this sound.**

   Remember that the 5th string is the short string on your banjo that's located on the opposite side of your neck from the 1st string. Some banjos have 5th-string tuning pegs that are difficult to turn without causing wild fluctuations in pitch. Don't worry if it takes a bit more time to get the 5th string in tune.

Even if you follow my instructions carefully, I'm sure that you may discover the following frustrations when tuning the banjo in this way (but don't "fret" — you aren't alone):

- ✔ **Your reference point is always a fretted string when tuning from a lower- to a higher-pitched string.** You need to lift the left hand up to adjust the tuning peg of the string you're attempting to tune and then fret it again on the lower string to play the reference pitch.

- ✔ **If you make a slight error at the beginning of this process, that mistake is exaggerated as you proceed to try and tune the rest of the strings.** You may have to start all over.

If you're having difficulty determining whether a string is sharp or flat, tune it down until the string is obviously below the pitch of your reference note. Then gradually bring the string you're trying to get in tune up in pitch to match the reference note.

Reference Tuning: Getting a Little Outside Help

Relative tuning is great when you're playing by yourself or for quickly touching up a string or two in the middle of a practice session. However, when playing with others (or with the audio tracks and video clips that accompany this book, available at `www.dummies.com/go/banjo`), you need to get accustomed to tuning your banjo using one or more outside reference notes as provided by an electronic tuner or another instrument. I explain how to tune by using reference notes in the following sections.

If you're practicing on your own, the source of your reference pitches doesn't matter; the important thing is to have the banjo in tune with itself. If you're playing with others, everyone should use the same reference pitch, whether it comes from an electronic tuner or an instrument.

Using an electronic tuner

Tuners provide a reference point for you to tune individual strings one at a time. These days, a tuner is pretty much an essential accessory to carry with you wherever you take your banjo. When you play a string, the tuner "hears" the note and gives an indication of the note's pitch by showing a letter name for the note closest to it in pitch, with an accompanying ♯ (sharp) or ♭ (flat) sign, if needed (for instance, if the note you're playing is closest to an F♯ in pitch, the tuner reads F♯). The tuner also indicates whether your string is sharp (too high) or flat (too low) in relation to your reference note via a meter or a row of small LED lights. (Check out Chapter 14 for a discussion of how tuners work and of the different types of tuners currently available.) An electronic clip-on tuner is shown in Figure 2-2.

If the string is significantly out of tune, the tuner may assign an alphabet letter that isn't a G, B, or D (check out the section on G tuning a few pages back in this chapter for the skinny on the notes used in this tuning). I've been avoiding it up to now, but so you aren't thrown off by these various letters, you should know the following order of notes in music:

G / G♯ *or* A♭ / A / A♯ *or* B♭ / B / C / C♯ *or* D♭ / D / D♯ *or* E♭ / E / F / F♯ *or* G♭ / G

Figure 2-2:
Using an electronic clip-on tuner makes tuning easier.

Photograph courtesy of Elderly Instruments

Here are a few tidbits of info that may help you better understand this series of notes and how they relate to tuning your banjo:

- ✔ **Equivalent notes:** You may notice that some notes in the preceding series have an *or* between them. Without getting too boring, just remember that a G♯ is the same pitch as an A♭, an A♯ is the same as a B♭, and so on. These equivalent notes are found at the same fret on your fingerboard.

- ✔ **Pitch:** As you move to the right in the order of notes, you're naming higher-pitched notes; as you move to the left, the notes are lower pitched.

- ✔ **Half versus whole steps:** If you move one note in either direction (for instance, going from a C♯ or D♭ note to a D note), you move a *half step.* If you move two notes in either direction (for instance, going from an F to a G or from a C to a D), you move a *whole step.*

A half-step movement corresponds to a change of one fret up or down on your banjo fingerboard, and a whole step equals a movement of two frets from one note to the next. For example, if you're playing an open string and you want to move up a half step, you fret the 1st fret of that same string. If you want to move up a whole step from an open string, you fret the 2nd fret.

To use an electronic tuner, you turn the tuning pegs until the readout matches the note that string should match. For example, if you're trying to tune your 3rd string to a G and the tuner gives you an F♯ reading, you know from the preceding order of notes that your 3rd string is far enough below a G pitch that the tuner hears the note as an F♯ — the pitch that's one half step below G.

To get your 3rd string in tune, continue striking the 3rd string with the right hand and slowly turn the tuning peg to raise the string's pitch. At some point, the tuner's readout should change from an F♯ to a G note, but at this point the tuner tells you that your 3rd string is a *flat* G note instead of a *sharp* F♯. Continue raising the pitch of the string until the tuner indicates that the string is exactly in tune to a G note. You use the same process for each of the strings, raising or lowering their pitches until the tuner indicates that you've reached the desired note.

Don't strike the strings too hard when using an electronic tuner. A light touch is best for the tuner to give the most reliable reading. Also, the meter on some tuners shifts slightly to the left or right as it responds to ever-so-slight changes in pitch that occur as a string continues to vibrate. If this happens to you, tune the string to the pitch that the indicator "sits on" for the majority of the time that the tuner is registering its pitch. This approximation gets you close enough to do a touch-up on that string by using relative-tuning techniques (see the previous section on this topic for instructions).

Tuning with an electronic tuner at a jam session

When musicians come together to make music, they first take some time to make sure that their instruments are in tune with one another before they start to play. Just before a jam session begins, you may see musicians off in different corners or with their backs turned momentarily from the main group, as they get in tune by using electronic clip-on tuners (see the preceding section for the how-to). In this case, the participants use the reference notes provided by their tuners to get as closely in tune with each other as they can. (If the participants have their backs turned because they're talking to their agents, you might have found an advanced jam session!)

Don't hesitate to borrow another musician's tuner whenever you need one in a group session. Believe me — everyone wants you to be in tune just as much as you do!

If your jam session is taking place outside, as often happens at a music festival, chances are good that all the instruments will gradually drift out of absolute tuning in reaction to the sun, the humidity, and warm temperatures. If you're joining a jam session that's already in progress, the musicians may be in tune with each other but not with your tuner. In these situations, get a reference pitch from another instrumentalist and tune your banjo to that instrument using the guidelines in the next section.

Using another instrument as a reference

If you don't have an electronic tuner or you want to be in tune with others in a jam session, you can use pitches from other instruments to get your banjo where it needs to be. In general, ask another musician to play a certain note on her instrument. Then, try to get your string to match that pitch by turning the tuning pegs. After tuning each open string to the corresponding note, you can then double-check your tuning by using relative tuning techniques (see the section on this topic earlier in this chapter).

Here's how you can use various instruments to tune your banjo:

- **Guitar or dobro:** The 4th (D), 3rd (G), and 2nd (B) strings of the guitar are tuned to the same pitches as the corresponding strings in G tuning on the banjo (see the section on G tuning earlier in this chapter for more info). The dobro's top four strings are tuned to the same pitches as the top four strings on your banjo, so if someone in your jam session is playing one of these instruments, ask to use his pitches as reference points for you to tune your banjo — as long as that person is also in tune, that is!

  I usually try to tune my 3rd-string G first, and then I move down in pitch to tune the 4th string and up to tune the 2nd, 1st, and 5th strings. When I have a break in between songs, I ask the guitar or dobro player to play a 3rd string open, or the fretted equivalent if she has a capo on, so I can make sure my banjo is in tune with the other instruments. If I'm out of tune, I make adjustments on each string until my strings' pitches match the pitches on the guitar or dobro.

- **Piano:** If you have a piano or an electronic keyboard around the house, that's another great source for getting reference notes to tune your banjo. Tune each banjo string to the corresponding piano note (see Figure 2-3).

- **Fiddle or mandolin:** If you're playing music with just a fiddler or a mandolin player, you can still get in tune with her by asking for her G note. A fiddle is tuned to the same pitches as a mandolin. The open G note on these instruments is the same as your 5th-string G pitch but is an octave higher in pitch than your 3rd-string G.

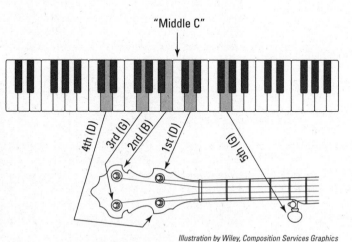

Figure 2-3: Piano notes and their corresponding strings on the banjo.

Illustration by Wiley, Composition Services Graphics

However, you can still use this note to tune your G string, and then you can tune your remaining strings using relative tuning techniques (see the section "Relative Tuning: Tuning the Banjo to Itself" earlier in this chapter for more help). Or, you can ask for the other pitches you need to get the other strings in tune.

The tone of the other instrumentalist's notes is going to be different than the notes on the banjo, but remember that you're comparing the pitch of each note, not the tone. When in doubt about your own tuning, don't hesitate to ask another musician for help.

Promote world peace: Use a banjo mute!

If you're one of those folks who lives in a crowded household or a college dorm, or if you have to catch your practice time late at night or very early in the morning, you need to find a way to ramp down the volume of your banjo. Try these quick solutions to temporarily tame your savage banjo beast:

✔ **Place a mute on the bridge.** A *banjo mute* fits onto the top of your banjo bridge and soaks up the musical energy that the bridge normally transmits from a vibrating string to the banjo head. (See photo a in the accompanying figure.) Mutes dramatically reduce your banjo's volume and can change the tone quite a bit too, lending a sweet sustaining sound to your banjo that makes it sound almost like a harpsichord. You can buy a banjo mute at an acoustic specialty store (but don't let them talk you into believing that a ball-peen hammer is a real mute — that's a more permanent solution!). In lieu of a store-bought mute, you can

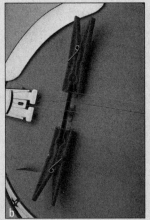

Photographs by Anne Hamersky

also use a couple of clothespins, snapped to either end of the bridge (as shown in photo b). This solution works just about as well!

- ✔ **Just stuff it!** Cram a hand towel or a T-shirt into the back of the banjo, in the space between the head and the closest coordinating rod or the dowel stick (take a look at photo c). If your banjo has a resonator, you need to remove it first to get to the back of your instrument. The more firmly you position the cloth against the underside of the head, the more it absorbs the energy of the head and the quieter your banjo becomes.

Chapter 3

Starting to Play: Fretting and Strumming

In This Chapter

▶ Understanding banjo terms

▶ Sitting and standing with the banjo

▶ Using the left hand to fret chords

▶ Playing the G, D7, and C chords

▶ Understanding chord diagrams and chord progressions

▶ Access the audio tracks and video clips at www.dummies.com/go/banjo

*Y*ou've brought your new banjo home and cleared a corner of the house to practice, far enough out of the way to avoid disturbing the unbelievers in your household. As you sit down and open the case, that wonderful new banjo smell fills the room, and you're no doubt thinking that this instrument is about the most beautiful thing you've ever seen in your entire life. Go ahead and savor this moment! Pat yourself on the back for taking the plunge and making the commitment to become a banjo player. But now what? Where do you begin? Now that you're a banjo *owner,* what are the first steps on the road to becoming an actual banjo *player?*

This chapter answers these questions. Get started by attaching a strap on your banjo so you can play both sitting and standing. Next, put your left hand to work, find a comfortable hand position, and then really get down to business positioning your fingers to fret the G, C, and D7 chords. Finally, combine fretting chords with some mighty right-hand strumming to play your first, honest-to-goodness song. You're going to be amazed at how quickly you can make great-sounding music.

Talking Banjo Talk

Many folks prepare for a trip to a foreign country by practicing a few phrases in the language that's spoken there. Playing the banjo is very much the same kind of adventure — it's great to know banjo speak before you start to make banjo music. Plus, you may find *Banjo For Dummies* a little clearer if you know some of the basic terms I use throughout this book.

Although that banjo-playing kid in the *Deliverance* movie didn't talk very much, it's still helpful to familiarize yourself with the following basic banjo terms:

- **Left hand:** When I give you any instructions regarding the left hand, I'm referring to the hand you use to push the strings against the fingerboard to make chords (you do this with the tips of your fingers, of course, not the entire hand). You also use the left-hand fingers to create new notes on the banjo by using slides, hammer-ons, pull-offs, and chokes (slide on over to Chapter 6 to discover more about these special techniques). If you're a left-handed banjo player playing a banjo especially made for left-handed players, you make these same moves with your right hand.

- **Right hand:** The right hand is the hand that strikes the banjo strings. In *Banjo For Dummies,* you first use the right-hand thumb to strum across all the banjo strings, but soon enough you utilize techniques where the right-hand thumb and the index and middle fingers each play a different role in producing authentic right-hand banjo styles (you can find these techniques in Chapter 5). If you're playing a left-handed banjo, you use your left hand to make these moves.

- **Frets:** The raised metal strips that run along the top surface of your banjo fingerboard underneath and perpendicular to your strings are the frets. Most banjos have 22 frets with each fret assigned a number. The 1st fret is the fret that's closest to the nut and the 22nd fret is located the closest to the banjo head.

- **Fretting:** The act of pushing one or more left-hand fingers against the fingerboard just behind a fret to shorten the length of a string is called *fretting.* Fretting changes the sound (or *pitch*) of a note. The shorter the length of a string, the higher that string's pitch — and the higher up the neck you're fretting. (For more on fretting, you can check out the section "Fretting with the Left Hand" later in this chapter.)

- **Open:** You call an unfretted string an open string. Later in this chapter, you're introduced to *tablature,* the written form of banjo music. In tablature, an open string is indicated with the number 0.

- **Strings:** Yeah, I know you know what strings are. But banjo players are so methodical that they assign numbers to each string so they can talk about them more easily. Remembering the order of strings as expressed through these numbers is crucial to understanding banjo tablature and interpreting a *chord diagram,* which is a representation of how a chord is fretted.

Left-handed but not left out!

If you're left-handed, playing the banjo creates a unique challenge. Unlike a guitar or mandolin, you can't just flip the banjo around and switch hands to play because the shorter 5th string tuning peg will no longer be positioned as it should be on the top of the banjo neck. If you already own a right-handed banjo, try playing it in the right-handed way for a couple of weeks and see how it goes. On the other hand, if you don't yet own a banjo or if you're experiencing a great deal of frustration trying to play in that strange right-handed way, pay a visit to your nearest full-service acoustic instrument store and try out a left-handed instrument. I guarantee that after you try both kinds of banjos, you will know very quickly which kind will be best for you.

Full disclosure: I'm left-handed but I learned to play right-handed. However, I've taught several left-handed students who wouldn't play any other way than with a left-handed instrument.

The 5th string is the short string on your banjo. If you're holding the instrument in a playing position (see the following section, "Positioning Body and Banjo"), the 5th string is the string that is the closest as you look down at the strings. From the 5th string, the strings are then numbered 4, 3, 2, 1 across the banjo. The 1st string is the farthest away from you as you look down on the instrument.

✔ **Sharp and flat:** You use these terms in reference to getting the banjo in tune. If a note you're playing on your banjo is *sharp*, its pitch is higher than the note you're trying to tune to; if its pitch is lower, your banjo note is *flat*.

Positioning Body and Banjo

It's time to take the banjo out of its case and get ready to play! Picking up a banjo and trying to play for the first time may seem a little awkward if you don't know how to hold or position the instrument. To get the most enjoyment out of your practice time and to be ready for anything when playing with others, you should be comfortable both sitting and standing while playing the banjo. In either case, being as relaxed as possible is a good idea.

So how are you supposed to play in these positions with ease? Take a deep breath and don't worry — this section gives you the foundation you need to comfortably strike a convincing banjo-player pose.

If you've never played banjo before, you may not be quite ready for all the advice in this section. You may need to first become comfortable with your left- and right-hand positions on the banjo, which I discuss later in this chapter and in Chapter 5. After you have a good grasp on your hand positions, feel free to come back to this section and devote a bit of time again to finding a comfortable posture sitting and standing with the banjo.

Strapping on your banjo

You've probably already discovered that banjos can be heavy. Even if you have a more lightweight, open-back banjo, the distribution of weight on your banjo may very well be uneven, with much of the mass at the peghead concentrated where the four tuning pegs are located. (Where's the peghead, you ask? Flip back to Chapter 1 to check out banjo parts.)

Take a moment and sit in a chair with your banjo in a playing position, with the pot of the banjo resting on your legs and the neck extending to your left at about a 45-degree angle. Hold the pot of the banjo against your body, with just a slight angle so you can more easily see the banjo fingerboard and head. If you remove your left hand as a support, does the neck move downward? If so, start using a strap even when sitting. You need the left hand free to fret chords, not to support the weight of the banjo neck.

Find a real banjo strap — not a guitar strap — to use on your instrument. Both kinds of straps look pretty much the same except for what's at either end. Most banjo straps have hooks, ties, or screws at both ends that you use to attach the strap to the banjo pot. A guitar strap more often has just holes punched into the leather or plastic at either end and nothing else, providing no way to easily attach it to the banjo.

Getting used to holding the banjo and working with the strap is a bit like breaking in a brand new pair of shoes — it takes a bit of time, but soon enough everything fits like a glove. The following sections provide all you need to know to fit the strap on the banjo and the banjo on you.

Attaching the strap

Some inexpensive banjos have hooks on the banjo body that are designed to hold a strap. However, these hooks usually aren't located in a position that provides the most comfortable support. Many players attach the strap to brackets located underneath the neck and the tailpiece of the banjo, as shown in Figure 3-1. This position seems to provide a good deal of support and control, but you want to experiment by using different strap lengths and brackets to see what feels right to you.

If you attach the strap to the banjo in this way, you shouldn't have to remove it when you need to put the banjo away in its case. Try wrapping the strap around the banjo pot, making sure that the top of your case still closes easily (see Figure 3-2).

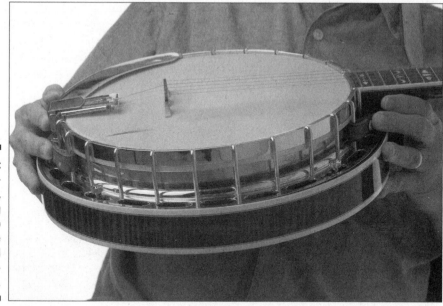

Figure 3-1:
For a comfortable fit, try attaching the strap below the neck and the tailpiece.

Photograph by Anne Hamersky

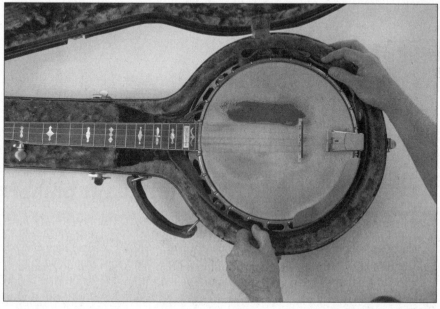

Figure 3-2:
Getting the strap out of the way when it's time to put the banjo in its case.

Photograph by Anne Hamersky

Fitting the strap

Although some players wear the strap across the right shoulder, most players adjust the length of the strap so that it wraps over the left shoulder, around the back, and underneath the right arm. You can see both options in Figure 3-3.

Figure 3-3: Two different ways to wear a strap.

Photographs by Anne Hamersky

As you fit the strap to the banjo, you need to properly adjust its length. The length of your strap determines the vertical placement of the banjo in relation to your body. Although you won't find any hard-and-fast rules, I like to have just enough length to the strap so that when I sit down I can divide the weight of the banjo between my shoulder and my knees.

After you've found a strap position that seems to work when sitting, try standing up with the banjo to see how the banjo feels in relation to your hands. You need to use the same strap length for both sitting and standing, so experiment to find a strap fit that works well for both situations.

Making three or four adjustments as you try to find the right strap position for your banjo isn't unusual. You may have to take the strap off the banjo each time to adjust its length until you find what feels just right. This is a minor hassle, but after the strap is set, you won't have to worry about it anymore and you'll be better able to find comfortable hand positions for playing.

Sitting down to play

How you hold your banjo while sitting down is determined by how much you need to see the banjo fingerboard while you're playing. Some players use the position dots on the top side of the banjo neck to keep track of where they are on the banjo neck and don't actually look at the fingerboard directly at all, but most players prefer to actually see what their flying fretting fingers are doing.

Another aspect of finding a comfortable playing posture is to experiment with different neck angles (the banjo neck that is, not *your* neck!). New players are often so concerned with seeing the fingerboard that they raise the neck to bring it closer to their eyes. Too much of this can lead to some technique problems in both the left and right hands. My advice is to angle the neck such that the peghead is no higher than eye level.

You also want to find a chair around the house that allows you to comfortably sit upright, provides you with some back support (if you need it), and allows your arms to move freely (no recliners allowed!). When I'm playing around the house, I like to use an adjustable office chair with the side arms removed. As you sit, position the banjo so that you're able to see the fingerboard and the banjo head, but don't let the banjo be so low in your lap that you have to reach far around the neck to fret with the left hand.

After you've actually started to play banjo, take a look at photos of some of your favorite players and experiment with different neck angles to see what works the best for you. Figure 3-4 shows three different ways of holding the banjo while sitting. Note that the middle player, Jody, rests the banjo on his right thigh and doesn't need a strap at all. Erin (left) and yours truly (right) prefer straps on our heavier resonator banjos.

Figure 3-4:
Erin (a),
Jody (b),
and Bill
(c) show
three dif-
ferent ways
to enjoy
playing the
banjo while
sitting.

Photographs by Anne Hamersky

Standing with your banjo

The key to being comfortable while standing with the banjo is to adopt a position that's similar to the position you use when sitting. If you've found a good sitting position (see the preceding section), stand up with the banjo and watch what happens. Try adjusting the strap length so that you have little to no change in the position of the banjo for both your sitting and standing positions.

Note also the relationship of your hands to the instrument as you both sit and stand. You want these positions to be as close as possible to one another whether you're up or down. Keep your arms relaxed and your elbows bent while standing and remember not to raise the peghead above eye level. Your left hand should easily be able to fret at any point along the banjo fingerboard, and your right hand should have easy access for striking the strings.

Figure 3-5 shows three different ways of standing while playing banjo. Erin (a) holds the banjo a little lower and off to the side of her body. Jody (b) angles

---

Don't let "Dunlap's disease" get you down

If you're in the prime years of your life like me, you may suffer from Dunlap's disease. What's that, you innocently ask? Well, Dunlap's disease is when your belly is so big that it "done laps" over your belt! If you suffer from this common malady, you may prefer to position the banjo a bit to the right side of your body, whether sitting or standing (see the section "Standing with your banjo"). Many players position the banjo squarely on their right thigh and may not need a strap to support the banjo at all while sitting. When standing with a strap, you want to position the banjo in a similar way at the right side of your body. If you're a Dunlapper, don't be afraid to move your banjo around until you find a position that's comfortable for you.

---

the banjo neck a little higher and holds the banjo a bit more off to the side, while yours truly (c) holds the banjo higher on the body and more out in front. All are fine ways to take a stand for better playing.

Figure 3-5: Erin (a), Jody (b), and Bill (c) use straps for standing while playing and hold their banjos slightly differently.

Photographs by Anne Hamersky

I spend almost all my time practicing sitting down and even though I've been playing for over 35 years, I still have to make a subtle mental adjustment every time I stand up to play. A day or two before a performance, I devote a share of my practice time to playing standing up so that I'll feel more comfortable playing with others on stage. At a festival, you spend a good deal of your time standing in a circle of musicians at jam sessions, so practicing while standing up is a great idea every now and then (and don't forget to bring a comfortable pair of shoes!).

Fretting with the Left Hand

The left hand's job is to change the pitches of the banjo strings to get all the notes you need for chords and melodies. The left hand accomplishes this task by pressing the tips of the fingers against the fingerboard just behind a fret, as needed, to shorten the length of a string and make its pitch higher. This technique is called *fretting*.

Fretting individual strings and chords on the banjo is a breeze after you've adopted these simple tips for finding a comfortable left-hand position on your banjo neck. Here's a step-by-step guide:

1. **Rest your left hand on your leg and totally release all body tension from your hand and arm, just as if you were asleep (see Figure 3-6a).**

   Your hand should assume a relaxed shape in which all the fingers are slightly bent in toward your palm (I know for some of you, it's difficult to relax. I'm from Berkeley, California, so just think of this as the California portion of the lesson and chill!).

2. **Keeping the wrist relaxed but straight, place the left-hand thumb on the upper part of the back of the banjo neck, opposite the space between the 1st and 2nd frets (see Figure 3-6b).**

   Remember not to support the weight of the neck with the left hand or pull down on the neck with your thumb. And keep chillin'! The hand and fingers should stay relaxed, as in Step 1.

3. **Relax your shoulder, arm, and elbow, bringing your elbow down and in toward your body.**

   This should move your hand forward in front of the banjo neck, maximizing the angle that your fingers will use to fret the strings.

4. **Move your left-hand middle finger just behind the 2nd fret of the 3rd string and push down on the string, fretting it with the tip of your finger (see Figure 3-6c).**

   Don't fret on top of the 2nd fret but position the finger as close behind the fret as you can. Try to maintain a vertical position with the fretting finger so that the adjacent strings are able to ring freely.

5. **Try playing the 3rd string with the thumb of your right hand.**

   The goal is to get a clear, ringing sound out of the note you've just fretted, with no buzzing.

If the new note sounds good, congratulations! You've accomplished the first necessary task to becoming a great banjo player, and you're now officially playing the banjo!

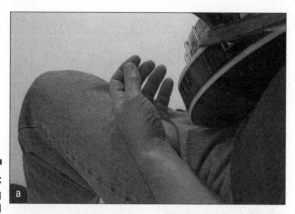

Figure 3-6:
Getting
a good
left-hand
position:
Relaxing the
left hand (a),
positioning
the thumb
to get ready
to fret (b),
and fretting
the 3rd
string at the
2nd fret (c).

Photographs by Anne Hamersky

Now lift up the fretting finger and play the open (or unfretted) 3rd string with your right-hand thumb. As you lift the fretting finger, don't bring it too far up above the string; position your finger just above the string so that you're ready to fret again. Now fret the 3rd string again at the 2nd fret and strike the string with the right-hand thumb to check for clarity. Alternate between the open and fretted positions until the movement of your left-hand finger becomes second nature.

Remaining relaxed while fretting is important, so every now and then, do a quick mental check to make sure your arm, elbow, and hand are as comfortable as possible. Creating tension by using too much pressure with the left-hand fingers when fretting isn't unusual for new players. You want to use as much fretting pressure as it takes, but no more.

You can find out just how much pressure you need by placing a finger in a fretted position, just barely touching the string. Now gradually apply more pressure on the string with the left-hand finger, striking it repeatedly with the right hand as you go. You literally hear the sound come into focus as you fret. After you've passed the threshold where the sound is clear, note how much pressure you're using with the left-hand finger. If you're like most people, you may be surprised at how little effort it takes to cleanly fret with the left-hand fingers. The goal is to use just as much pressure as you need to get a clear fretted sound, but no more.

Watch Video Clip 2 to see how I put these fretting tips into action, and if you want to check out some more advanced left-hand techniques such as the slide, hammer-on, pull-off, and choke, turn to Chapter 6 with your right hand as soon as possible.

Fingering G, D7, and C Chords

The first time you discover how to fret a chord on your banjo is a very big moment in your burgeoning playing career. Whether you're blazing through a banjo breakdown or accompanying a campfire singer, chords are essential to playing the banjo. In this section, you master the three basic chords used in thousands of songs. If the world suddenly seems like a much better place after you've successfully fretted each of the chords in this section, that's a good indication that you were born to be a banjo player.

After you've mastered each chord by itself, try moving from one chord to the next, in any order that strikes your fancy. Strum with a downward right-hand thumb motion across all five strings a few times for each new chord and strive for a clear, ringing sound from each string for all three chords. This stuff is pretty exciting, isn't it? You'll put these chords to use later in this chapter.

Try to keep the tips of your left-hand fingers close to the neck and pointed towards the fingerboard at all times as you move from one chord to the next. At first, you may have to move one left-hand fretting finger at a time as you work the different chord fingerings into your motor memory. However, in the long run, fretting all the strings you need for a chord at the same time is more efficient. After you've mastered this skill, you can switch between chords with greater speed and accuracy.

The G chord: Real easy

Although people very seldom associate the banjo with Zen, you really *don't* have to fret anything at all to play the G chord, grasshopper! A G chord is just the sound of your right hand strumming the open strings in G tuning (see Chapter 2 for more tuning info). You could use your left hand to wave to your adoring fans, but I think it may be a little early for these kinds of grand gestures.

The D7 chord: A little harder

For the D7 chord, you place your middle finger just behind the 2nd fret of the 3rd string and your index finger behind the 1st fret of the 2nd string. Try strumming down across all five strings with your right-hand thumb, starting with the 5th string and striking each note down to the 1st string. Try a slow strum to check the accuracy of your fretting on each individual string, but then don't be afraid to go wild with some fast strumming to strut your stuff!

The C chord: More challenging still

The C chord is a bit harder than the D7 chord (see the preceding section) because you use one more left-hand finger to fret this chord. Here, the left-hand index frets the 2nd string, 1st fret — just as with the D7 chord. However, now you move your middle finger to the 4th string, 2nd fret, and you also need to fret the 1st string at the 2nd fret. Be careful that you fret the 4th and 2nd strings with enough of a vertical angle with your left-hand fingers so you don't block the sound of the open 3rd string.

Your hand should look something like Figure 3-7 when you fret the D7 and C chords.

Seeing is believing, so if you're having trouble figuring out how to fret these chords, take a look at Video Clip 2, where I provide left-hand technique tips and show you how to fret the C and D7 chords.

Figure 3-7: Here's how your hand looks fretting the D7 (a) and C (b) chords. Note the position of the thumb.

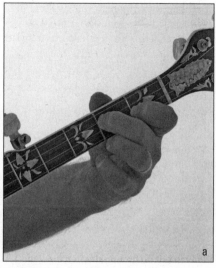

Photographs by Anne Hamersky

Checking Out Chord Diagrams

Looking for an easy way to remember how to fret a chord with your left-hand fingers? A *chord diagram* not only communicates which strings are fretted for a particular chord but also where on the fingerboard you put those fingers and which left-hand finger you use to fret each string.

Chord diagrams aren't the same as banjo *tablature,* which is the written form of banjo music that I explain in Chapter 4. Chord diagrams show you *how* to fret a chord with the left hand, but they don't tell you *what* to play with it. However, when you play with others, you use chords all the time. Chords are also the basic building blocks of just about every melody, and the following sections help you get comfortable reading chord diagrams.

Reading a chord diagram

If you're already familiar with reading chord diagrams for the guitar, you'll find that banjo players use the same system. If you turn your banjo around so that the fingerboard faces you, that's how the banjo neck is represented in a chord diagram (check out Figure 3-8 to more fully break down the parts of a chord diagram):

- ✔ From left to right, the vertical lines represent the 4th, 3rd, 2nd, and 1st strings on your banjo. Most banjo chord diagrams don't include the 5th string, because you rarely fret it, especially when you're just beginning to play.

- ✔ The top horizontal line represents the banjo nut. The *nut* is what guides the strings from the fingerboard to the peghead. One way to think of the nut is as a "0" fret, because your banjo strings are open at this location on the neck.

- ✔ The second line from the top stands for your banjo's 1st fret, and the line below that represents the 2nd fret, and so on.

- ✔ The black dots that appear on the vertical string lines indicate behind what fret and on what strings you should fret.

- ✔ The letters located underneath the chord diagram indicate the left-hand finger you use to fret each string. For the left hand, I = index finger; M = middle finger; R = ring finger; and P (or sometimes L) = pinkie (or little) finger. Some books use the numbers 1 through 4 to represent the left-hand fingers in the same way.

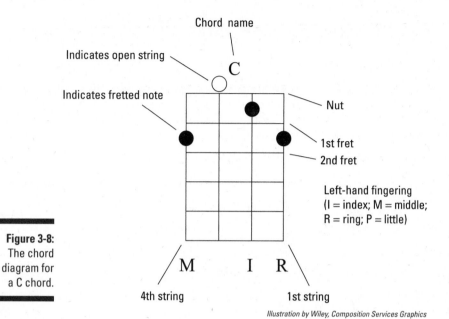

Chord name

Indicates open string

Indicates fretted note

Nut

1st fret

2nd fret

Left-hand fingering
(I = index; M = middle;
R = ring; P = little)

Figure 3-8:
The chord
diagram for
a C chord.

M I R

4th string   1st string

Illustration by Wiley, Composition Services Graphics

Check out the chord diagrams for G, D7, and C chords in Figure 3-9. Of course, there are lots of other chords you can play on the banjo, and Appendix A has most of them. My advice is to tackle just one or two new chords at a time, practicing them when they appear in a new song. Don't try to learn them all at once without playing a song where you can put them to good use.

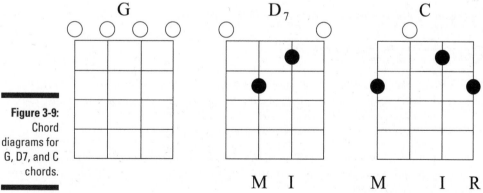

Figure 3-9:
Chord
diagrams for
G, D7, and C
chords.

Illustration by Wiley, Composition Services Graphics

Interpreting up-the-neck chord diagrams

As you become more proficient, you can fret chords all up and down the neck of your banjo. To represent a chord that's played above the 5th fret, a chord diagram includes a number that usually appears to the right of the diagram — either next to the top fret line or adjacent to the uppermost fretted note in the chord. This number indicates exactly where you need to position your left hand on the banjo neck (see Figure 3-10).

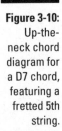

Figure 3-10:
Up-the-neck chord diagram for a D7 chord, featuring a fretted 5th string.

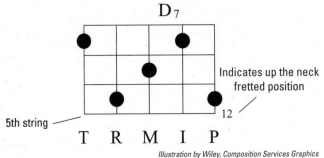

Illustration by Wiley, Composition Services Graphics

If you need to fret the 5th string as part of a chord, a fifth vertical line is added to the left side of the chord diagram to represent this string. The 5th string is often fretted up the neck with the left-hand thumb, which is represented with the letter *T* in a chord diagram.

Chord Progressions: Playing Your First Song

The *chord progression* of a song is the part of your musical road map that indicates what chords you play, in what sequence these chords occur, and how long each chord lasts before you move on to play the next one as you play a song. Although you can find about as many different chord progressions as you can songs, you can count on some predictability in how chords follow one another in most songs you play on the banjo. This makes figuring out and remembering new chord progressions much easier as you encounter them in new songs.

Many songs use only the G, C, and D7 chords (which are covered in the earlier section "Fingering G, D7, and C Chords"). However, the more chords you know, the more quickly you can play along with new songs.

Familiarize yourself with the chord progression of a new song just as soon as you begin to work on it. The chord progression not only lays out the form of the piece, but also provides the foundation you use later on for playing (and remembering!) the melody and for improvising. The chord progression is also what keeps everyone on the same page as you play a song with others in a jam session. In this situation, everyone plays through the chord progression repeatedly until all the players agree that it's time for the song to come to an end.

When you're working through a chord progression, try strumming with an even downward motion of your thumb across all five strings of the banjo, striking all five strings in an even sweeping motion with the thumb. In the next few chapters, you find more interesting things to play as you accompany a tune, but for now, strumming is just fine! You're working on the crucial new skill of changing chords in the left hand without losing the beat as you strum with the right hand. This takes a lot of coordination! If you don't get it at first, take your time and keep trying. You can do it.

It's time to strum along with a song that just about everybody knows, "She'll Be Comin' Round the Mountain." Figure 3-11 shows the lyrics with slash marks indicating where each right hand strum is played. Above the lyrics are the chords you'll fret along the way. Check out my strumming and singing on Video Clip 3 and Audio Track 2 and just jump right in and play along. The sooner you memorize the chord progression and pull your eyes away from the printed page, the quicker you'll feel like you're really playing music. Listen to how the chord changes relate to the melody as you get used to strumming and changing chords smoothly.

/   /   /   /   /   /   /

G

She'll be comin' round the mountain when she comes,

/   /   /   /   /   /   /   /

D7

She'll be comin' round the mountain when she comes,

/   /   /   /   /   /   /   /

G   C

Figure 3-11: She'll be comin' round the mountain, she'll be comin' round the mountain
Strum along
to "She'll
Be Comin'
Round the
Mountain."

/   /   /   /   /   /   /   /

D7   G

She'll be comin' round the mountain when she comes.

Most new players find that the trickiest part of strumming along to a song like "She'll Be Comin' Round the Mountain" is going from the G to the C chords smoothly without interrupting the steady flow of the right-hand strums. If you run into this same problem, try switching back and forth over and over again between the G and C chords until you've mastered this transition.

Chapter 4

Playing by the Rules: Songs and Tablature

*I*f you've worked through Chapters 2 and 3, your banjo is in tune (at least most of the time) and you're blazing new musical trails with the all-important G, C, and D7 chords. You've even strummed through the chord progression of an entire song.

With this chapter, you begin uncovering the mysteries of how music works by taking a look at the basic building blocks of a song: rhythm, melody, and scales. Then you take a look at *tablature,* the written form of music for the banjo, and begin to use this tool to more quickly understand new songs. Along the way, you explore major scales on the banjo and locate and play a few simple melodies by ear. I also introduce you to a versatile right-hand picking technique called the pinch pattern, and give you some tips on participating in jam sessions. You have a lot of work to do, so get out your banjo and get started!

The basic knowledge and skills covered in this chapter prepare you for more exciting adventures to come with clawhammer and bluegrass style banjo, the two most popular ways of playing in the world today. You can return to this chapter each time you work on a new song or technique if you ever feel the need to brush up on these concepts.

Breaking Down the Parts of a Song

How is it that some banjo players can play along with just about any song that comes up, even something that they've never heard before? I can tell you from personal experience that you aren't simply born with this skill — it's something that's nurtured. Songs are like road maps, and if you can follow the signposts correctly, you can make your way through just about any bluegrass or old-time tune. The more songs you learn, the more you can get around Banjo Town without a GPS.

Although every song has something that makes it different from any other song (even if it's just the title!), most bluegrass and old-time pieces share many of the same underlying musical characteristics. If you understand how songs are put together, you have a much easier time getting started down the road to becoming a great banjo player.

Songs are made up of rhythm, chord progressions, melodies, and scales (for a review of chord progressions, turn back to Chapter 3). Rhythm gives life to music and it's the best place to start an exploration of the inner workings of making music on the banjo.

Feeling the rhythm

One of the things that separates music from random noise is that time is organized (in some way) within a piece of music. When talking about music, *rhythm* can refer to several different things: You can refer to the rhythm of a particular musician or band (as in "That banjo player really plays with a lot of drive!" or "I think those guys' rhythm needs some work!") or the rhythm of a particular piece of music ("I like that song — it's got a great groove!"). For now, I use the word *rhythm* to refer collectively to all the different aspects of music that have to do with time and duration.

The most important aspect of playing the banjo well — both as a beginner and as an advanced player — is to play with good rhythm. Although your biggest worry at first may be about fretting chords and hitting the right strings (see Chapters 3 and 5 on these topics), you eventually want to put a lot of effort into playing a song all the way through in a steady rhythm without stopping — no matter what! Playing without stopping is especially important when playing music with others or playing along with the audio tracks that accompany this book. If you start to work on this skill right now at the earliest stages of your playing, you can soon be comfortable playing songs with others, even as a beginner.

Rhythm is something that everyone is born with — it's in the steady pulse of your heartbeat and in the measured cadence of your steps as you walk. If you can keep a steady beat or pulse by tapping your foot or clapping your hands, you've got rhythm. You can apply that natural sense of rhythm to playing songs on the banjo.

On the other hand, finding the rhythm in music may not be natural for everyone. If you struggle finding the rhythm of a song, you can break down the elements of rhythm, and you can practice to keep pace with any song. I get you started in the following sections by introducing a few key terms you need to know. However, I'm with Pete Seeger, who once wrote that he's willing to learn just enough formal music to get by as long as it doesn't hurt his banjo playing. I will only cover a few terms that all musicians use to talk about rhythm in music — and I guarantee you won't lose any self-respect as a banjo player in the process.

To count or not to count: It's all in your head

Have you ever watched the feet of your favorite musicians while they're playing on stage or in a jam session? Even though they may actually be *playing* in perfect time together, musicians often don't tap their feet in the same rhythm or even in a way that has any discernible relationship to the beat of the music.

What's with that? The answer lies in the fact that what you're seeing in all the fancy irregular footwork isn't necessarily how a musician is keeping time. Musicians often count out the rhythm just before starting a piece to give the other players an idea of the tempo, but after a song has started and everyone is playing along, most musicians rely on their internal sense of rhythm by listening to what's happening around them while simultaneously keeping track of the rhythm in their heads. Most musicians don't keep an actual count going after a song has started, but they do actively keep track of the tempo and where the beat falls.

Although most people (and even beginning banjo players) can establish a consistent beat in their heads, keeping that beat going while trying to play banjo is usually more difficult. That's when a good outside source for keeping the beat can come in handy. A *metronome,* a device that keeps an audible steady beat for you, is a great way to play in good rhythm when practicing by yourself (see Chapter 14 for a discussion of how to play with the metronome).

However, when playing with others, keeping good time is everyone's shared responsibility. Listening and adjusting to the rhythm of the other musicians as you play is just as important as — if not more important than — following the beat you've established in your head. Keep one ear on what others are playing and the other one on your own picking, and you'll soon be playing all your music in good time!

Beats, tempo, and meter

I use the term *beat* to refer to a musical unit of measure. To understand what a beat is, try singing one of your favorite songs and tapping your foot in rhythm to your singing. For example, the song "Will the Circle Be Unbroken" sounds like this (try tapping your foot with each capitalized syllable and tap indication): "WILL the CIR-CLE [tap] BE un-BRO-KEN [tap], BY and BY LORD BY [tap] and BY [tap] [tap]." Each foot tap is a beat. In all the music you play, each beat is equal in duration to every other beat.

The idea of playing along with a steady beat is central to good banjo playing. The word *tempo* refers to how fast you're tapping (or clapping or playing) that beat. Although classical musicians use a lot of fancy Italian words such as *presto, largo,* and *fusilli* to refer to different tempos (okay, fusilli is actually the name of a pasta), banjo players use terminology such as *slow, medium fast, fast, real fast,* and *really, really fast.* Most of the time, banjo players actually just start playing at whatever tempo feels right, and everyone else joins in when they've grabbed hold of that steady beat.

You can organize beats into groups of two, three, or four beats for most banjo music (and if you're playing Irish music, you sometimes group beats into units of six and even nine beats). Musicians use the word *meter* to refer to any recurring cycle of beats.

Time signatures, measures, and downbeats

A *time signature* indicates the meter and the kind of count you use for a particular song. The time signature usually appears at the very beginning of a written piece of music and is shown as two numbers positioned one on top of the other (like a fraction without the horizontal line). As you can see in Figure 4-1, the top number in the time signature indicates the number of beats in a cycle, while the bottom number stands for the kind of note that equals one beat.

Top number = how many beats are in one measure

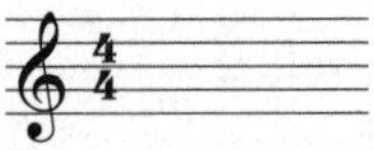

Figure 4-1:
4/4 time
signature.

Bottom number = what type of note gets one beat

Illustration by Wiley, Composition Services Graphics

4/4 time (spoken "four-four time") is the meter used most frequently in printed music for bluegrass and old-time banjo music. With this time signature, you have four beats in each cycle and a quarter note equals one beat (I discuss note values a little later in this chapter). The count that goes along with this time signature is "one-two-three-four, one-two-three-four," and so on. Waltz-time banjo music is in 3/4 time with three beats per cycle and a quarter note signifying one beat. The count that goes with 3/4 time is "one-two-three, one-two-three."

A *measure* (or *bar*) marks off a single rhythmic cycle. In written music, a measure is indicated by a vertical line that extends through the staff. In banjo tablature, the *staff* consists of five horizontal lines that represent the five strings of your banjo (more on reading tablature later in this chapter).

The first beat of each measure is called the *downbeat.* The downbeat of each measure is usually emphasized when counting but isn't necessarily played louder. The initial *downbeat* (the first beat of the first full measure of a song) is an important moment when you're playing with other musicians, because that's usually the time when the other players join in. When it comes time to change chords in a song, you most often (but not always) move to the new chord on a downbeat of a new measure.

Take a look at "She'll Be Comin' Round the Mountain" in Tab 4-1. This song appears in Chapter 3, where you strum across the strings with the right hand while fretting chords with the left hand. This time, there's more detail expressed in the music: Consider a tab staff, a time signature and measures in

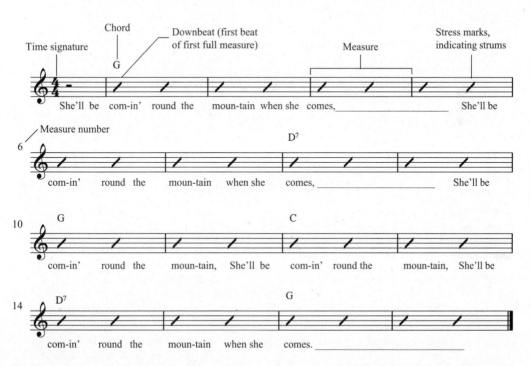

Tab 4-1: Understanding rhythm indications and strumming chords to "She'll Be Comin' Round the Mountain."

addition to the chord progression (indicated above the staff) and the song's lyrics (indicated below the staff).

The time signature to this piece is 4/4, which means that every measure has four beats. This piece has 16 measures all together. The chord progression to "She'll Be Comin' Round the Mountain" consists of six measures of G, two measures of D7, two measures of G, two measures of C, two measures of D7, and two measures of G.

Note that in this particular tune, the chords change at the start of a new measure. I've also added a label to show where the downbeat occurs. Note that you don't start "She'll Be Comin' Round the Mountain" on this downbeat. Your first strum and your singing begin at beat three of the preceding measure. This happens a lot when beginning a song, so no need to worry!

Changing chords quickly

Most new players find that the hardest part of strumming along to a song like "She'll Be Comin' Round the Mountain" is going from the G to the C chords smoothly without interrupting the right-hand strums. When you run into difficulties at a particular point in any song, try to isolate that problem and practice it over and over again.

For example, you can practice moving back and forth between just the G and C chords by creating an exercise where you shift from one chord to the other with each right-hand strum. You aren't playing the entire song at this point, but you're working on that "problem" moment in the song, where you have to fret the C chord, by practicing this move over and over again. In the long run, you save a lot of time and energy by focusing on problem areas rather than playing through the entire tune and slowing down at the trouble spots.

Smooth sailing

Trying to get the feel for a new song isn't always the easiest of tasks; however, here are a few practice tips that you can use when you begin any new song:

✔ Don't worry about speed when learning a new song; just try to keep the strums steady and fret each chord as cleanly as you can (for more on fretting, see Chapter 3).

✔ Listen to the audio track first to get an idea of what the song or technique is supposed to sound like; then try practicing it on your own. Finally, try playing along with the audio track.

✔ Try to memorize the chord progression as quickly as you can. This will free up your visual attention to look at your amazing left-hand fretting maneuvers instead of your eyes being tied to the written music.

✔ Don't worry about singing while you're playing — but if you eventually feel comfortable doing this, by all means go for it!

Keep the tips of your left-hand fingers pointed toward the banjo fingerboard even if you aren't using them at that moment to fret. When playing the G chord, you can position the left-hand fingers you use for the C chord just above their fretted positions, a technique called *ghosting*. These fingers are then ready to move into position and push down (or *fret*) the strings behind the appropriate fret (Figure 4-2 shows how to ghost and fret a chord). Even when you aren't fretting anything at all in the left hand, it's still a good idea to keep the tips of your left-hand fingers pointed toward the fingerboard. You can be sure that you'll need them sooner or later!

Figure 4-2:
Ghosting
the C chord
(a) and fret-
ting the C
chord (b).

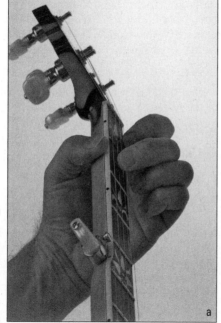
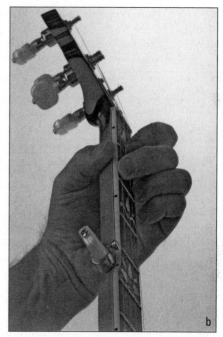

Photograph by Anne Hamersky

Finding the melody

As unbelievable as it may sound, you can find folks out there who think that all banjo music sounds alike. They even assert that you can tell one tune apart from another only by its title (yes, a banjo joke is in here somewhere). I believe that our mission as banjo players should be to dispel this cultural misunderstanding by trying to play as much of the melody as possible in each song we play while still trying to make it sound like good banjo music. Because the melody of each tune is unique, each banjo version of a song also has the potential to be different.

A well-played banjo solo consists of a melody, but a lot more is usually going on as well. You may also hear the cascade of rolling notes that accompanies a bluegrass banjo solo or the percussive and syncopated brush and 5th-string techniques clawhammer players use. The real wonder of banjo music is how the melody can be expressed *inside* and *through* these techniques.

When you figure out a tab arrangement from a book (like this one, for instance), the melody is already provided for you, but bringing out that melody as you play the song so a listener can recognize it is still up to you. With more playing experience, you can work up your own arrangements from scratch. In this case, you have to locate the melody notes on your banjo on your own and combine the melody with the left- and right-hand techniques that you know can make your arrangement sound like good banjo music. Either way, knowing how to bring out the melody of a song is a must.

Because melodies are made up of a series of notes that can be organized into a scale, understanding just a little bit about scales can be a big help in finding the melody notes to any song on your banjo (yes, this is a bit of formal music theory, but I promise that you'll be a better banjo player for it). Armed with your scalar knowledge, you also have the opportunity to play a few tunes in the following sections.

Starting with the scale

The first step in working up a banjo solo is to locate the melody notes of the tune on your fingerboard. Unless you're moving straight to avant-garde modern classical music (in which case, this may not be the right *For Dummies* book for you), the majority of the melodies you encounter are made up of just a few notes. If these notes are grouped from low to high, they almost always form a scale.

You can begin a scale on any string or on any fret of the banjo. *Scales* are made up of a select group of notes on the banjo fingerboard, and different types of scales group notes in different ways. Melodies can start at the beginning, in the middle, or at the end of a scale.

Many advanced players, especially those interested in jazz on the banjo, take the time to locate the notes of a particular scale in every position and on each string of the banjo and learn all kinds of scales appropriate to this style of music. So if you're interested in playing jazz on the banjo, you better get to know your scales.

The *major* scale is the most commonly used scale in much of the music of the Western world as well as a great deal of banjo music (after all, the banjo is a part of both country and western music, right?). Most people have the sound of the major scale thoroughly ingrained into their musical subconscious from years of hearing and singing this scale in all kinds of songs. Do you remember Julie Andrews singing "Do Re Mi" from *The Sound of Music* soundtrack? Okay, maybe you *don't* want to remember this, but at any rate, that song is all about the major scale.

To get started with playing melodies on the banjo, all you really need to know for now is how to construct a major scale. In the following sections, I show you how to do just that.

Scaling one string: Discovering the G-major and D-major scales

You can create a major scale on any note on the fretboard by following the formula in this section. The first note of the major scale indicates what kind of major scale you're playing.

For example, because many of the melodies you'll be playing use the notes found on the G-major scale, you can discover how to build a major scale by starting on the open 3rd string, which just happens to be a G note. You then travel up the 3rd string, finding all the notes of the G major scale (do-re-mi-fa-so-la-ti-do!) as you climb up the neck of the banjo.

To uncover a G-major scale, begin by picking up your banjo and following these steps:

1. **Play the 3rd string open, and as you hear the sound of this note on the banjo, try singing the same note.**

   Think of this note as the first note, or the "do" of a major scale. You can also think of this note as the first note in the melody "Frère Jacques."

2. **Sing what you think the second note of the major scale should be, using the syllable "re."**

   You can also think of this note as the second note in the melody "Frère Jacques."

3. **Find this second note on your 3rd string.**

   Because it's a higher note than the first note of the scale, you need to fret this string. Compare what you're singing (and hearing in your head) to the sound of the fretted string. You can find a match for the second note of the G-major scale, the "re" note, at the 2nd fret.

4. **Sing "do" and "re" again, but now also continue up the scale by sing-ing "mi," the third note of the G-major scale.**

   This note is also the third note in the melody of your ol' buddy "Frère Jacques."

5. **Find this "mi" note on the 3rd string.**

   The match is at the 4th fret of the 3rd string.

6. **Try singing the next note in the scale, the "fa" note, and try finding this note on the 3rd string.**

   This *isn't* the next note in "Frère Jacques," by the way! You can find this note at the 5th fret, only one fret up from the "mi" note.

If you continue singing the rest of the notes of the major scale (so-la-ti-do) in this way and match the corresponding notes on the banjo's 3rd string to your singing, you end up with the scale in Figure 4-3 as it ascends up the banjo's 3rd string. And if you can't sing, Figure 4-3 shows you the notes, which you can also hear on Audio Track 3.

Figure 4-3:
Finding the G-major scale on the 3rd string.

Strings	⌐2 frets⌐	⌐2 frets⌐	⌐1 fret⌐	⌐2 frets⌐	⌐2 frets⌐	⌐2 frets⌐	⌐1 fret⌐
1st/D							
2nd/B							
3rd/G — G	A	B	C	D	E	F♯	G
4th/D							
	Nut	3Fr			7Fr	10Fr	12Fr
				5th/G			

Scale steps	do	re	mi	fa	so	la	ti	do
	1	2	3	4	5	6	7	8

Illustration by Wiley, Composition Services Graphics

As you can see in Figure 4-3, the names of the musical notes in a G-major scale are G-A-B-C-D-E-F♯-G. However, when you're playing the banjo, you rarely think about the actual names of the notes — you don't have enough time to worry about them! Banjo players more often think about the distances between the notes in a scale, as measured by the number of frets between one note and the next and the sounds that they hear as they move from one note to another. When you think of the G-major scale in this way, the pattern shown in Figure 4-3 emerges.

Banjo players just love to play songs that use the G-major scale, but sooner or later you also have to find your way around other scales. D major is another popular key for music played on the banjo. Using the same formula for finding a G-major scale, you can discover the D-major scale by starting on your open 4th string D and choosing the ascending notes. If you do it correctly, you end up playing a D-major scale, as shown in Figure 4-4. You can also listen to Audio Track 4 to hear me play the D major scale.

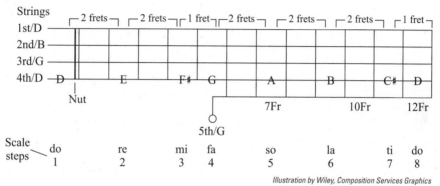

Figure 4-4: Finding the D-major scale on the 4th string.

Illustration by Wiley, Composition Services Graphics

Bringing more than one string into play: The G-major scale

As you can probably guess, when you play melodies on the banjo, you don't usually run up and down just one string. It's more economical to play the higher notes of the scale on the 2nd and 1st strings and the lower scale notes on the 3rd string. This limits the movement of the left hand to the lower frets of the banjo and makes it a lot easier to quickly find the correct melody note.

Figure 4-5 provides a road map to the G-major scale as you can find it on the 3rd, 2nd, and 1st strings of your banjo.

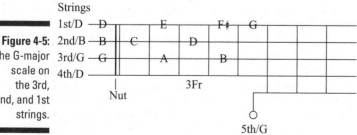

Figure 4-5: The G-major scale on the 3rd, 2nd, and 1st strings.

Illustration by Wiley, Composition Services Graphics

However, melodies often go below the starting point of the G-major scale, using notes found on the 4th string. You can now add these 4th-string notes to get the full picture of where you can find the notes of the G-major scale, using all four strings on the lower frets of your banjo. Be sure to note that by starting on the open 4th-string D, you're still playing a G-major scale, but you're now catching some of the lower scale notes that you use when playing melodies that use this scale. Check out Figure 4-6 and listen to Audio Track 5 to hear me play the G-major scale.

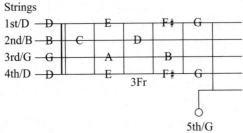

Figure 4-6:
The G-major scale on all four strings.

Illustration by Wiley, Composition Services Graphics

Although knowing the names of all the notes on the fingerboard of your banjo is an impressive feat (the kind of information that can certainly win you new friends at the next banjo players' cocktail party), this same info can be found in Appendix A in this book! Remembering this kind of information isn't crucial right now. Focus instead on knowing where the notes of the G-major scale are located on the lower frets of your banjo and learn to hear the *sounds* of these notes.

Trying out a tune (or two)

After you've found the notes of the G-major scale on the lower frets of the banjo (see the preceding section), it's now time to work out some melodies by using this scale. Keep in mind that all the open, unfretted strings on your banjo in this tuning are also notes in the G-major scale.

With your banjo at the ready, try finding the melody of "Frère Jacques" by ear, starting on the open third string G of your banjo and playing both open and fretted strings as needed to capture each melody note. This is an ear training exercise, so find the notes in whatever way you can. Use any left-hand finger as needed to fret a melody note and strike each note with a downward movement of your right-hand thumb. If you get desperate, you can compare your version with mine by listening to Audio Track 6 (and it's always a good idea to check out whether we're playing the same song!).

"Frère Jacques" shows the relationship between a melody and its scale: All of this song's melody notes are in the G-major scale. After playing this song, you can probably see how becoming familiar with this scale can make figuring out a melody on the banjo much easier.

Because you don't have much chance of hearing "Frère Jacques" at a jam session, you can try something a little closer to home with "She'll Be Comin' Round the Mountain." Challenge yourself once again and make an attempt to figure out the melody first by using your ears in a trial-by-error approach. This exercise trains your ears and brain to locate the melody by using your familiarity with the G-major scale on the banjo neck. Here's a hint to help you get started: Play the open 4th string, and then the 4th string at the 2nd fret, followed by four hits on the open 3rd string. These are the first notes of the tune (as in *She'll be com-in' round the...*). Now try to find the rest of "She'll Be Comin' Round the Mountain" on your fretboard, using your memory of the melody or my sensitively beautiful rendition on Audio Track 7 to guide you.

Don't expect to get all the melody notes perfectly the first time around. As you experiment, you can learn from your mistakes, so don't be afraid to make them!

Try playing your version of the melody to a loved one and see whether she can guess what song you're playing. Did she hear "She'll Be Comin' Round the Mountain"? I hope so, but if not, that's okay too. You're just getting started with this process, and coordinating your brain, hands, and ears to figure out a melody and play it without stopping may take a while.

Finding the melody by ear is the first step towards working up a great banjo solo. Remember to let your ear be your guide and keep in mind that not all songs use the G-major scale. After you've figured out the basic melody, you can then use it as your foundation to work up a more "banjoistic" version of the tune.

Reading Tablature

Tablature (or *tab* for short) is the written form of music for the banjo. Although tablature uses quite a few elements that are also found in conventional music notation, tab imparts information that's specific to the banjo, such as what string you play and whether that string is open or fretted. Tablature is a part of almost every instructional book and CD set. And although tab never replaces being able to play by ear, it enables you to cover ground more quickly when learning a new piece of music and allows you to double-check what you've learned by ear. Therefore, it's a great idea to take a little time to get acquainted with reading tablature in the following sections.

Finding notes

The big difference between banjo tablature and standard music notation is that although both use five horizontal lines on the staff, the lines on the banjo tab staff represent the five strings of your banjo. The top line corresponds to the banjo's 1st string and the bottom line represents the banjo's 5th string, with the second, third, and fourth lines from the top standing for the 2nd, 3rd, and 4th strings on your banjo (see Tab 4-2).

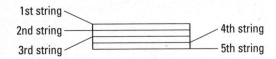

Tab 4-2: The five lines on the banjo tab staff represent the five banjo strings.

Need help in remembering which tab lines stand for which banjo strings? Note that the visual orientation of the strings on the tab staff is the same as what you see as you look down on the strings while playing. From this point of view, the 1st string is the string that is farthest away (and is "on the top" of the tab staff) and the 5th string is the closest (and "on the bottom" of the tab staff).

In banjo tablature, you also see numbers on each line. These numbers represent the notes you play, as shown in Tab 4-3. The line that the number sits on indicates which string you play and the numeric value tells whether to play an open (unfretted, indicated with "0") or fretted string.

Tab 4-3: Numbers on the tab staff lines show open and fretted notes.

And Tab 4-4 displays what the G, C, and D7 chords look like in tablature. The *b* below the tab staff indicates a right-hand brush.

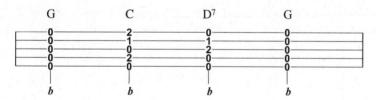

Tab 4-4: Tablature for G, C, and D7 chords.

Tracking down the rhythm

Banjo tablature expresses rhythm in much the same way as it's read in conventional music notation, in terms of measures and time signatures (see the section "Feeling the rhythm" earlier in this chapter for more info). Banjo players typically think of a single measure of tab in 4/4 time as a rhythmic space that's waiting to be filled by a maximum of eight notes (or an equivalent combination of fewer notes with longer duration).

Each note on the tab staff has a stem attached that indicates the duration of the note. The three note values that you encounter most frequently in banjo tablature are the quarter note, the eighth note, and the sixteenth note.

Each of these notes has a vertical line, called the *stem,* extending down from the note. An eighth note has either a curled or horizontal line attached to the bottom of the stem, while the sixteenth note has two horizontal lines. These lines are called *flags* and distinguish one rhythmic value from another on the tab page. Each note value also has a corresponding *rest* sign, which indicates a corresponding number of beats where no note is played. Tab 4-5 shows these three note values with their corresponding rests as they appear on a tab staff.

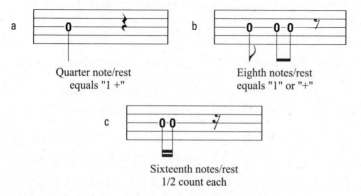

Tab 4-5: Quarter, eighth, and sixteenth notes and rests in banjo tab.

Determining the value of a note in tablature is just like using grade-school fractions: Two sixteenth notes take up the same amount of musical space or time as one eighth note, and two eighth notes occupy the same amount of space as one quarter note. A measure in 4/4 time needs to be filled with the equivalent of four quarter notes. Tab 4-6 shows just a few of the many rhythmic combinations that meet this requirement.

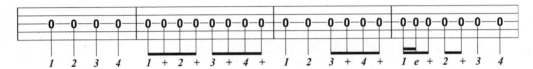

Tab 4-6: Combining quarter, eighth, and sixteenth notes (Audio Track 8).

In the beginning, it may be helpful to count out loud (or in your head) "1 and 2 and 3 and 4 and" for each measure of 4/4 time as you play through a piece, letting each note last for its appropriate rhythmic duration. For example, if you're counting along in the example in Tab 4-6, you can see that an eighth note takes up the space of one count (either a number or an "and"), while a quarter note takes up the space of two counts (a number *and* an "and"). And playing along with Audio Track 8 is an even better way to internalize these rhythms.

Playing Pinch Patterns

After you have a feel for how to figure out the notes and rhythm in tab (see the preceding section), you're ready to put all this musical knowledge to work by getting acquainted with the *pinch pattern*. The pinch pattern gets its name from the right-hand motion you use to play the strings. With the pinch pattern, you strike the strings with a downward motion with the thumb and with an upward motion with the right-hand index and middle fingers all at the same time. In other words, you're *pinching* the banjo strings with your right hand!

The pinch pattern is great for beginning players to use when following chord progressions and accompanying songs. For now, you can play this pattern without any fingerpicks on your hands, and you don't need to worry too much about your right-hand position (I cover that more thoroughly in Chapter 5).

Here's a step-by-step guide to playing a pinch pattern for an open G chord (all strings are unfretted):

1. **Pick the 3rd string with a downward motion of the thumb.**

2. **Strike the 5th string with the thumb, the 2nd string with the index finger, and the 1st string with the middle, playing all three strings at the same time.**

   You should hear the sound of three notes together. Remember that the pinch pattern always uses a downward motion with the right-hand thumb and an upward motion with the index and middle fingers every time you pick a string.

3. **Pick the fourth string with the thumb.**

4. **Repeat Step 2 by playing the 5th, 2nd, and 1st strings simultaneously with the thumb, index, and middle fingers.**

You can see in Tab 4-7 what the pinch pattern looks like in tablature for the G, C, and D7 chords. Also, be sure to listen to Audio Track 9 and watch Video Clip 4 to hear and see the pinch pattern in action on these same chords. In the example, *t* stands for the right-hand thumb, *i* for index finger, and *m* for middle finger.

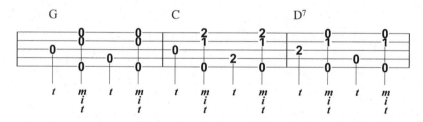

Tab 4-7: Playing the pinch pattern with G, C, and D7 chords (Audio Track 9).

Note that the numbers on the tab staff change with each new chord in Tab 4-7, but that the right-hand picking pattern remains the same in each measure. As you read through any banjo tab, don't forget to follow the chord progression as you play. More often than not, if you fret the chord that's indicated above the tab staff, then you also have the fretted positions you need to match what the tab staff line numbers indicate to play. For instance, in Tab 4-7, you see a C chord above the tab staff. The lines on the tab staff (remember, these lines stand for the strings of your banjo) indicate that you need to fret the 1st string at the 2nd fret, the 2nd string at the 1st fret, and the 4th string at the 4th fret. If you fret all three of these strings at the same time at the beginning of the second measure, following the C-chord indication that you see above the staff, you're also fretting everything that's indicated on the tab staff for this measure.

Now try playing the pinch pattern as an accompaniment for three great tunes: "She'll Be Comin' Round the Mountain" (Tab 4-8 and Audio Track 10), "Worried Man Blues" (Tab 4-9, Video Clip 5, and Audio Track 11), and "Man of Constant Sorrow" (Tab 4-10 and Audio Track 12). Check out Chapter 3 if you need to get more familiar with fretting the G, C, and D7 chords. If you're comfortable playing the pinch pattern, you may not need to look at the tab at all to play these tunes along with the audio tracks.

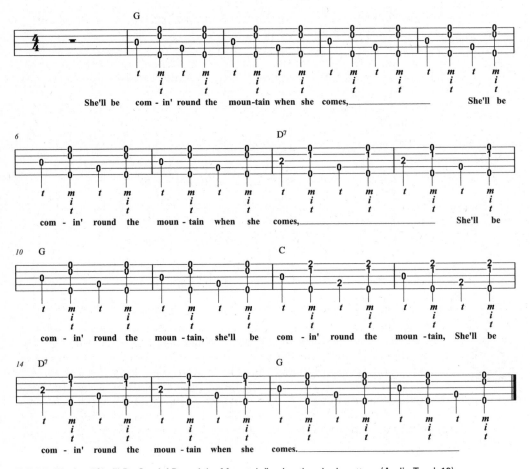

Tab 4-8: Playing "She'll Be Comin' Round the Mountain" using the pinch pattern (Audio Track 10).

Tab 4-9: Playing "Worried Man Blues" using the pinch pattern (Audio Track 11).

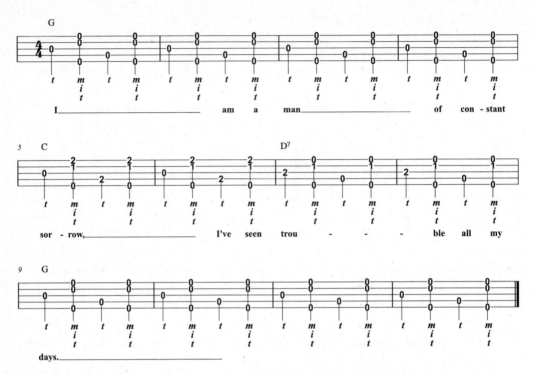

Tab 4-10: Playing "Man of Constant Sorrow" using the pinch pattern (Audio Track 12).

Being a Great Team Player

One of the primary reasons that many people want to learn to play the banjo is to have fun making music with others in bands and in jam sessions. There's nothing quite like a banjo, guitar, mandolin, fiddles, and bass grooving along to an old, lonesome-sounding ballad or burning up a hot, fast instrumental. At a music festival, seeing amateur musicians who have never played together before open up their cases, take out their instruments, and start playing tunes together as if they've been doing it for years isn't unusual. Musicians call these impromptu get-togethers *jam sessions.*

Musicians can play together in such a spontaneous way because they share a similar repertoire of songs and have internalized and put into practice some rules for effective group music-making. If you listen closely to a great bluegrass or old-time band performance, you can hear that the roles of the different instruments seem to change from one moment to the next. At times, the banjo is out front and the center of attention; other times, the banjo is very much in the background; and then you recognize those moments when the banjo is somewhere in between these two extremes. When playing with others, you assume different musical roles with your banjo as you play a song from beginning to end.

In this section, I talk about some of the most important rules for playing with a group and discuss how you can put them to use as a brand-new banjo player.

Perhaps the two most important aspects of playing with others are to maintain a great rhythmic groove that makes the band sound good and to control your volume. The easiest way to achieve good rhythm is to play simple things well. Your right hand not only controls your volume, but also communicates the heart and soul of your playing. Simplicity and drive in your playing creates musical space for others to play their best and for you to express your own emotions most powerfully. A successful jam session is one in which all musicians feel that they're successfully contributing to the overall sound of the group.

Lead playing: Shining the spotlight on yourself

Lead playing has to do with those times when you're the center of attention in your band or during a jam session. If you're playing a well-known banjo instrumental like "Cripple Creek" or "Foggy Mountain Breakdown," you'll probably start the song by setting the tempo and playing all the way through the tune one time before handing off the lead to the next willing instrumentalist. If you kick off an instrumental, you're most likely to be the last one to play it as well, so have some kind of ending ready if you choose (or *call*) the tune in a jam session.

If you're playing a song with vocals, you may get the chance to play a banjo solo only once during the tune, either at the very beginning of the song or after a chorus. That's okay! You can have just as much fun in vocal tunes by playing banjo backup and singing your heart out on the choruses!

When you play lead (also called *taking a solo* or *break*), you call on everything you know as a banjo player to make your playing sound its best. At first, successfully playing a short, memorized arrangement of a song is enough of an accomplishment. As you become a more skilled player, you rely on the chord progression of the song to create new ways of playing a solo right on the spot (this creative process is called *improvisation*). Musicians spend an entire lifetime becoming great improvisers, so don't necessarily expect this to happen to you for a little while. The best journeys with the banjo are taken one step at a time!

When playing a solo, playing at full volume is fine, but don't forget to keep track of the rhythm of those around you as you play. Because banjo players play so many notes in comparison to the other players in the band, you may find yourself tending to push the tempo when you get excited (which usually occurs when you're playing lead). Racing away from the rest of the band is easy if you aren't careful, so as you're shredding through a great solo, keep an ear on the ongoing rhythm of the song and try your best to play in good time!

If you can't hear the other instrumentalists when they're playing lead, you're probably playing with too much force. In this case, reduce your volume until you can hear what everyone else is playing. By doing this, you can enjoy what others are playing a lot more, and in turn, others will enjoy playing music with you!

Backup playing: Allowing others to stand out

For every moment that you're the star of the show, you'll have many more occasions when you give it everything you've got to make those around you sound *their* best. *Backup playing* includes all the different techniques that a banjo player uses to accompany others and is perhaps the highest achievement of great banjo playing.

Because the banjo can so easily overpower other instruments during a jam session or in a band, a simple chording technique is sometimes the best way to allow others to be easily heard, especially if a singer is singing quietly or if you're playing backup to a guitar or mandolin solo (which never seem to be able to pick up as much volume as the beloved banjo). Bluegrass musicians call this chording technique *vamping,* which you can check out in Chapter 10.

At other times, you want to keep a steady flow of notes going with the banjo, changing chords at the same time as other musicians. With this kind of backup (which sounds especially good when accompanying a singer or a fiddle solo), you're keeping the energy flowing by doing what the banjo does best with roll patterns and basic accompaniment techniques. To read more about these ideas, you can flip over to Chapters 5 and 9.

Part II
Let's Pick! Basic Banjo Techniques

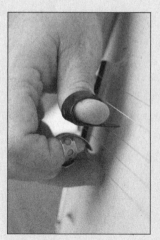 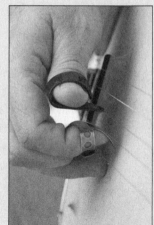 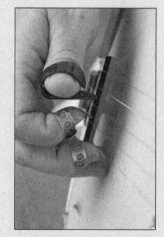

Working up your own versions of songs just got a lot easier! Discover how to match melody notes to bluegrass roll patterns to create your own great music at www.dummies.com/extras/banjo.

In this part...

- ✔ Start with right-hand positions, and try out authentic picking patterns for clawhammer and bluegrass style.

- ✔ Add depth and interest to your sound by incorporating left-hand techniques — slides, hammer-ons, pull-offs, and chokes.

- ✔ Find melody notes on the banjo and play them using clawhammer or bluegrass techniques.

- ✔ Coordinate both hands to play full songs in clawhammer and bluegrass styles.

Chapter 5

Getting Right with the Right Hand

In This Chapter

▶ Getting authentic banjo sounds with the right hand

▶ Understanding the right-hand basics of clawhammer and bluegrass techniques

▶ Accompanying songs in clawhammer and bluegrass styles

▶ Access the audio tracks and video clips at www.dummies.com/go/banjo

*H*ere's one of the most important things that you'll read in this book: The key to becoming a great banjo player is to get your right hand together. Your right hand (or more accurately, your picking hand for all you left-handed players in the house) conveys your rhythm, expresses your mood, captures your tone, and gives the drive to your playing that makes you and those around you want to *move*. In this chapter, you unleash the power of your right hand and make some bona fide (or, for you city slickers, stylistically accurate) banjo sounds.

The two most popular banjo playing styles in the world today are *clawhammer* (also called *frailing*) and *bluegrass*. Each of these styles uses a different right-hand position as well as a different way of striking the strings. Although most players tend to specialize in either one or the other style, I'm excited for you to try both approaches right from the start. However, before you just jump in and start making a racket, it's a good idea to take a look at what the right hand does in clawhammer and bluegrass banjo. Get ready to position your picking hand on the banjo and start striking your fingers against the strings just like you will when you really know what you're doing.

These right-hand techniques are unique to the banjo and sound different from what you would hear on instruments like the guitar and mandolin. You'll notice an immediate difference in your playing after just a few minutes of practice with these patterns. After you become comfortable with the exercises in this chapter, you can put your new skills to work by playing along with two tunes. You'll be well on your way to becoming a good banjo player!

Whether it's clawhammer or bluegrass, playing the banjo makes you part of a living and ever-evolving musical tradition. Each new generation of players, amateur and professional alike, makes its own unique contribution. Now it's time for *you* to start making your contribution by getting out your banjo and practicing the right-hand basics of clawhammer and bluegrass banjo.

Clawhammer and Bluegrass: Down-Picking and Up-Picking

When you're talking about the banjo, the terms *clawhammer* and *bluegrass* refer to two different ways of striking the strings of your banjo with the right hand. Here are the crucial differences:

- **Clawhammer** technique is sometimes called a *down-picking* approach to banjo playing because the right-hand fingers strike the strings in a downward motion. Clawhammer is the older of these two ways of playing the banjo, with historical roots that can be traced back several centuries to the African ancestry of the banjo (for more on these historical roots, check out Chapter 11).

- **Bluegrass** is known as an *up-picking* approach, because the right-hand index and middle fingers strike the strings in an upward motion, with the right-hand fingers moving in towards the palm of your right hand and the thumb moving in a downward direction. North Carolina banjo player Earl Scruggs is largely responsible for creating the bluegrass banjo style, bringing it to national attention in the late 1940s and early 1950s.

Within easy reach of the right-hand thumb, the 5th string is a big part of what makes banjo music sound unique, and both the clawhammer and bluegrass styles focus a lot of attention on this high-pitched string. As you work through this chapter, take note of how the 5th string is used in each style and also how the melody of a song is played, and you'll be well on your way to understanding what banjo music is all about.

Clawhammer Right-Hand Basics

Clawhammer banjo combines melody and rhythm in a way that makes people want to get up and dance. This playing style sounds unlike anything else in American music! The exact origin of the word *clawhammer* is unknown. However, the term seems to describe the desired shape of the right-hand thumb when playing this technique — mimicking the "claw" of the top part of a standard nail hammer (hence clawhammer).

Other musicians relate the term to the hammer-like downward move-ment that's used to strike the strings. Many West African–type banjos (see Figure 5-1) have been played in similar ways for centuries, but the specific rhythms, techniques, and sounds of clawhammer banjo were developed in the southern United States from the mid-19th to the early-20th centuries. When you play clawhammer banjo, you're connecting to a very deep current of musical world history!

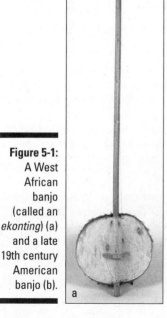

Figure 5-1: A West African banjo (called an *ekonting*) (a) and a late 19th century American banjo (b).

Photographs courtesy of Elderly Instruments

Finding a good right-hand position

Good right-hand technique is the most important aspect of clawhammer playing. Finding a comfortable and stable right-hand position to enable your fingers and thumb to do their work is the first step toward this goal. Check out Video Clip 6 and follow this step-by-step guide to finding a position that works for you:

1. **With your palm and wrist parallel to the banjo head, grab the top of the 5th string with your right-hand thumb over the banjo head, not too far from where the neck joins the banjo pot.**

2. **While still holding the thumb against the 5th string, bring your right-hand fingers into your hand and make a fist; relax the fingers just a bit, keeping them flexed at such an angle that the fingernails are parallel to the banjo head and the fingers are no more than one or two inches above the strings.**

   Your hand should now look like the hand in Figure 5-2a.

3. **Play the 3rd string by moving down and across it with your right-hand index finger, moving the hand from the wrist (see Figure 5-2b).**

   Strike the string with enough downward force so that your index finger comes to rest against the 2nd string (as shown in Figure 5-2c). Some players also use their forearm in addition to their wrist to get a more forceful hand motion. Note that the right-hand thumb stays in contact with the 5th string throughout this exercise.

Your fingers should maintain the same position as your hand moves down to allow the index finger to strike the string — don't let the fingers flip out as they meet the strings. The fingers need to stay fairly stiff so that the index finger can provide resistance against the string, but you don't want to be *too* tense. Likewise, keep the wrist unlocked but not actually loose. The more you practice the techniques in this chapter, the more you can get the hang of playing clawhammer style with the "loose stiffness" that you need to get a good sound.

Figure 5-2:
Resting the right-hand thumb against the 5th string (a); striking the 3rd string with the right-hand index finger (b); letting the finger come to rest against the 2nd string (c).

Photographs by Anne Hamersky

Playing your first clawhammer notes

After you've found a good hand position (see the preceding section), it's time to try a few exercises to get used to striking the strings in the clawhammer style. Clawhammer is very much an individualized approach to banjo playing. Even the best players play in a personalized way, doing what works best for them.

Although I set some general guidelines for you here, experiment with different ways of doing things to see what works best for you. Seek out other players for advice whenever you can, but do what sounds good and feels the most natural to you.

You can work up to playing the basic clawhammer strum by first getting comfortable striking individual notes. For the exercises in the following sections, I suggest you use the right-hand index finger for playing melody notes (as indicated with the small letter *i* underneath each note in the banjo tab). However, the right-hand middle finger is an option preferred by many players. Try playing both ways and do what feels best to you.

Here are some tips for developing good right-hand clawhammer technique:

✔ Having your finger knock the head after striking the 1st string is okay (the *head* is the round, white, top surface of the banjo; for more on banjo parts, check out Chapter 1). Remember, clawhammer is a percussive and rhythmic approach to playing the banjo. Don't be afraid to make some noise!

✔ Most players use their index or middle fingernails to get a good clawhammer sound. In lieu of fingernails, you can use fingerpicks as extensions of the fingernails, but be sure to place the pick so that it covers the nail, not the pad of the finger as in bluegrass technique (see the section "Choosing and fitting thumbpicks and fingerpicks" later in this chapter). Some players, including Steve Martin, use artificial fingernails while others, like Riley Bagus, trim and shape regular plastic fingerpicks until they feel comfortable on the finger.

Try playing without picks first to see what kind of sound you get, and then play with picks or use artificial fingernails if you think yours aren't long enough to get enough contact with the strings or if you aren't getting a clear and forceful sound.

✔ Remember that your finger is moving both *down* into the string and *down* toward the floor. Work toward developing a quick, decisive movement from the wrist that keeps your hand in control.

✔ When your index or middle finger plays the 2nd, 3rd, or 4th string, it usually comes to rest against the next-highest string.

✔ Some players bend their thumb at the joint to get that "claw" effect of hooking the finger underneath the strings. Other players extend the thumb outward. Again, try both and see which works best for you.

Melody-note exercises

Try playing individual notes on the 1st, 2nd, 3rd, and 4th strings with your right-hand index or middle finger (see Tab 5-1 and Audio Track 13). As you slowly play these individual notes, focus on your hand position and technique. Are you moving from the wrist? Are you practicing with good economy of motion (no swooping right hand like guitar player Pete Townshend)? Does your finger maintain its bent shape when it meets the string?

Tab 5-1: Clawhammer right-hand melody note exercise 1 (Audio Track 13).

As you get more comfortable with this first melody-note exercise, try playing different strings in succession in whatever order comes to mind. Tab 5-2 (Audio Track 14) shows some examples.

Tab 5-2: Clawhammer right-hand melody note exercise 2 (Audio Track 14).

Brush exercise

The brush follows the melody note in basic clawhammer banjo technique. In banjo tab, the right-hand indication for the brush is the letter *b,* found below the corresponding notes in the tab staff.

With the brush, you get to choose which right-hand finger (or fingers) to use and how many strings to strike, but you don't have to decide exactly how you're going to do the brush right now. Just keep trying different combinations and in time, you'll decide upon the way that works best for you. However, if you aren't sure where to start, first try brushing across the top two or three strings with just the middle finger by itself. Next, add the ring finger, using both fingers to brush across the top strings. Now try the index finger by itself.

All part of the old-time way

Clawhammer banjo is also known as frailing, rapping, or banging on the banjo. In the mid-19th century, this way of playing was called *stroke style* in banjo instructional manuals. These terms are all strange to use to describe a way of playing a musical instrument, but in this case, they're good ones because they all describe what the right hand is doing when playing the banjo in this way.

Clawhammer banjo is also frequently called old-time banjo, but these terms aren't synonymous.

Old-time refers to a wide variety of folk-based, non-bluegrass banjo techniques. Record companies in the 1920s used the term *old-time* as a descriptive label on 78 rpm recordings to refer to songs or artists with some kind of rural connection. The term stuck, and today *old-time* applies to a wide variety of string band music with guitars, fiddles, mandolins, and banjos. Clawhammer is one type of old-time banjo playing, but other ways of playing banjo are also called old-time by the musicians who play them.

Whatever fingers you use, try striking just the 1st string alone for the brush. Then try the top two, top three, and finally all four strings (that is, excluding the 5th string) with any combination of right-hand index and middle fingers. Although the brush is most commonly played across the top two or three strings (all four is uncommon), you need to get used to the feel and sound you get with each brush. Don't forget to maintain a consistent, bent-finger shape as you hit the strings. Try playing Tab 5-3 and listen to Audio Track 15.

Tab 5-3: Clawhammer right-hand brush exercise (Audio Track 15).

5th-string exercise

After you have a good feel for the brush (see the preceding section) try combining the brush with the 5th string. This time, as you play the brush with a downward motion of either the index or middle fingers, remember to bring the thumb against the 5th string as you complete the brush (as shown in Figure 5-3a). You're now ready to play the 5th string with a downward and sideways motion from the thumb. Don't be afraid to really snap this note with your right-hand thumb, raising the right hand ever so slightly above the strings after the thumb has done its work (see Figure 5-3b).

Figure 5-3: Bringing the thumb to rest against the 5th string (a); raising the hand off of the banjo head (b).

Photographs by Anne Hamersky

Listen to Audio Track 16 and try the exercise in Tab 5-4.

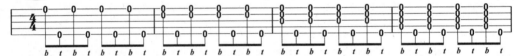

Tab 5-4: Clawhammer right-hand brush and 5th-string exercise (Audio Track 16).

Putting it all together: Melody note + brush + 5th string

If you combine the three movements from the preceding sections, you get the basic clawhammer right-hand technique. The first note that you hit is the melody note, played on either the 1st, 2nd, 3rd, or 4th string. This step is followed by the brush and ends with the thumb striking the 5th string. The first note lasts twice as long as the brush and 5th-string notes.

Players often describe the rhythm that they're going for like this: BUM-dit-ty/ BUM-dit-ty, with the emphasis on the "BUM" (sorry, no offense intended, but what did you expect? This is the banjo after all!). Tab 5-5 shows what this rhythm looks like, and you can hear it on Audio Track 17.

Tab 5-5: Basic clawhammer technique exercise 1 (Audio Track 17).

Each measure begins with a different melody-note string, so try practicing one measure over and over again before going on to the next. When you're comfortable starting with any of the four strings, you can then begin to mix up the melody notes, as shown in Tab 5-6 (Audio Track 18).

Tab 5-6: Basic clawhammer technique exercise 2 (Audio Track 18).

To go one step further, you can try the basic clawhammer technique with the G, C, and D7 chords (see Tab 5-7, which is Audio Track 19). Although I suggest that you use particular index melody notes for each chord, try as many different string options as you can, from 1st to 4th, on each beat. (You need all of these choices when you play melodies in Chapter 7.)

Tab 5-7: Using clawhammer technique for the G, C, and D7 chords (Audio Track 19).

Using clawhammer banjo as accompaniment

Basic clawhammer technique is great to use as an accompaniment to all kinds of songs.

The first note that you strike in basic clawhammer technique (which I call the *melody note* in the previous sections) is dependent on the chord that you're playing (more on this in Chapter 7).

For now, follow the guide in Tab 5-7 in choosing the melody notes for the G, C, and D7 chords and play along to the following tunes in Tab 5-8 (Audio Track 20 and Video Clip 7) and Tab 5-9 (Audio Track 21).

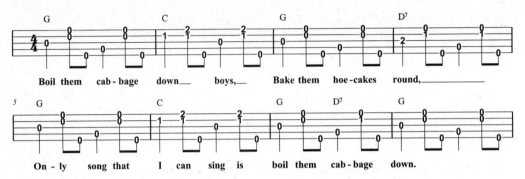

Tab 5-8: "Boil Them Cabbage Down" with clawhammer accompaniment (Audio Track 20 and Video Clip 7).

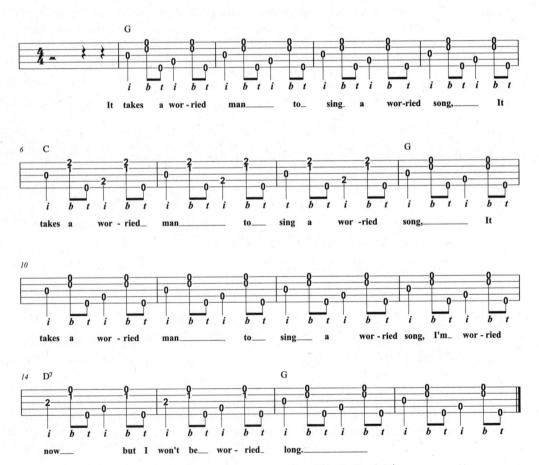

Tab 5-9: "Worried Man Blues" with clawhammer accompaniment (Audio Track 21).

Bluegrass Right-Hand Basics

Bluegrass-style banjo originated with the innovations of Earl Scruggs, who burst upon the national scene in the mid-1940s. The bluegrass style is characterized by a flurry of fast, brilliant-sounding notes and is the sound behind all-time banjo classics such as Scruggs' "Foggy Mountain Breakdown" and "Dueling Banjos." Although this way of playing the banjo is at the foundation of the bluegrass style, banjo players such as Béla Fleck, Alison Brown, Jens Kruger, and Noam Pilkelny have used this approach as a starting point for incredible musical journeys into classical, jazz, and rock styles.

Bluegrass banjo playing uses the thumb, index finger, and middle fingers of the right hand and (for this reason) is sometimes called *three-finger picking*. Because banjo players always go for the shortest description, the term *three-finger picking* has stuck over the years even though it would be more accurate to call it a "thumb and two-finger" style.

Just like when you're figuring out how to play clawhammer banjo (see "Clawhammer Right-Hand Basics," earlier in this chapter), the biggest challenge with the bluegrass style is getting a comfortable right-hand position that enables you to play clearly and quickly. And because bluegrass banjo players use picks on their thumbs and index and middle fingers, part of being able to play bluegrass comfortably is finding the right picks. The following sections help you select and fit the picks you need and find a right-hand playing position that works well for you.

Before Earl, 19th-century musicians played the banjo by using fingerpicking techniques borrowed from the guitar. Later, early 20th-century rural musicians, such as Uncle Dave Macon and Charlie Poole, featured simplified (at least compared to Earl's!) two- and three-finger picking techniques on their early country recordings.

Choosing and fitting thumbpicks and fingerpicks

Bluegrass banjo players use metal fingerpicks on their right-hand index and middle fingers and a plastic thumbpick on their thumb. Initially, you may find that getting used to the feel of these picks is a struggle. It may feel like you're wearing a coat of armor over the ends of your fingers, and you may hear a lot of scratchy sounds when you first start to play. However, just about everyone gets used to the feel of the picks after a few weeks, and you'll appreciate the extra volume, speed, and drive that the picks lend to your playing.

A visit to a music store can reveal numerous kinds of picks available for the thumb and fingers. In the following sections, I describe what you want to look for when you're picking up some picks.

The thumbpick

A *thumbpick* consists of a flat striking surface and a bent section that wraps the pick around the thumb. Most players prefer thumbpicks made from plastic, but a few players prefer the fit and sound of a metal thumbpick. Increasingly, many bluegrass players are using thumbpicks with a polymer blade attached to a metal band. In any case, choose a thumbpick that fits as snugly as possible, with the blade facing in toward your right-hand fingers.

Don't mistake a thumbpick for the more common flatpick, which is a pick used by guitarists and mandolin players. A *flatpick* is held in the right hand by the thumb *and* fingers. You can see the difference between the two in Figure 5-4. Don't be afraid to ask a music store employee or fellow musician to lead you in the direction of the thumbpicks.

Figure 5-4: Comparing a flatpick (left) and a thumbpick (right).

Photograph courtesy of Elderly Instruments

Thumbpicks come in different sizes, thicknesses, and striking surface *(blade)* angles (see Figure 5-5), so try as many different brands as you can to see what feels most comfortable to you. If you're like most players, you'll end up trying many different kinds of thumbpicks, and your preferences will change as time goes on, which is perfectly fine. As in so many other aspects of banjo playing, you can't find one right answer. However, many professional players prefer a thumbpick that isn't too thin and doesn't have too short of a blade.

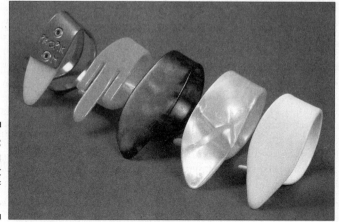

Figure 5-5:
Comparing different kinds of thumbpicks.

Photograph courtesy of Elderly Instruments

As you fit the thumbpick onto your thumb, don't push it too far up your thumb — about halfway between the first joint and the end of your thumb is about right for most players (you can check out this placement in Figure 5-6).

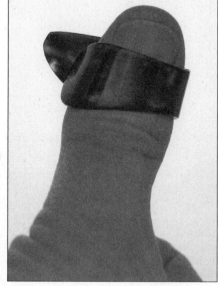

Figure 5-6:
Proper placement of a thumb-pick on the right-hand thumb.

Photograph by Anne Hamersky

TIP

If your thumb is too small for your favorite pick to fit tightly, don't be afraid to add surgical or duct tape to the inside of the pick to make it fit more snugly. Some players even place their thumbpick in boiling water for a few seconds to soften the plastic. You can then shape the pick to fit tighter after carefully removing the pick from the water. (Just don't fetch the pick out of the water with your hands!)

TIP

At prices around $1 to $4, plastic thumbpicks aren't expensive, so go ahead and purchase a bunch of different kinds to see which one suits your playing best. Look for thumbpicks by Dunlop, Golden Gate, National, Propik, and Zookies, among others, for good sound and playability. Blue Chip is the Rolls Royce of the premiere polymer-based thumbpicks, and if you're willing to spend the big bucks (around $35 each), you'll be picking in style.

The fingerpick

Like thumbpicks, metal *fingerpicks* consist of a blade-shaped striking surface joined to a collar that holds the fingerpick around the end of the finger. You want to fit the picks on your index and middle fingers so that the striking surface is on the opposite side of your hand from your fingernail (as shown in Figure 5-7).

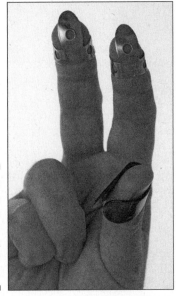

Figure 5-7:
Fitting the fingerpicks on the right-hand index and middle fingers.

Photograph by Anne Hamersky

You can find many different kinds of fingerpicks on the market today (you can have a look at a few of them in Figure 5-8). They vary in size and thickness and also in metal composition. Some fingerpicks have more of a curved striking surface while others have a flat blade. Some have holes in them and others don't. Experiment with different fingerpicks to see which ones fit the most comfortably and — most importantly — sound the best to you.

Fingerpicks range in price from $3 a pair to $35 for a pair of handcrafted, stainless-steel picks. Look for metal fingerpicks from Propik, National, Dunlop, Showcase 41, and Sammy Shelor, among others, for the tone preferred by bluegrass players.

Figure 5-8:
Comparing
different
kinds of
fingerpicks.

Photograph by Anne Hamersky

You need to bend the fingerpicks to get a good fit, because they don't usually come straight from the store ready to use without modification. Here's how you do it (also see Video Clip 8):

1. **Place the pick on the end of your finger with the collar placed between the end of the finger and the first joint.**

   Don't place the collar at the joint itself because that's too far up the finger.

2. **Grasp either side of the collar with your left-hand thumb and index finger and squeeze it so that the fit is snug but not too tight on the end of your finger.**

   Remember that you want the blade of the pick extending just past the end of your finger. If your pick fits well, you can stop here, but most players also like to bend the blade back a bit to match the natural curve of the end of the finger, which I explain in the next step.

3. **If your pick isn't too heavy, you should be able to successfully bend the blade by pushing down on the pick against a tabletop or another hard surface (as shown in Figure 5-9).**

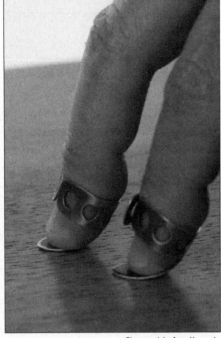

Photograph by Anne Hamersky

Figure 5-9:
Adjusting the bend of the finger-pick blade by pushing on a tabletop.

One last modification that some players make to their fingerpicks is that they fit the pick on the finger at a slight angle, so that when the finger strikes the banjo string, the pick meets the string at a straighter, or more parallel, angle. This modification can result in a fuller, more-pleasing tone as well as added volume. You don't need to worry about this right now, but you may want to try angling the fingerpick as you gain more experience playing.

Acquiring a good right-hand position

I bet that one of the main reasons you love bluegrass banjo music is that it's so incredibly fast and loud. Me too! In order to play at those tempos that approach the speed of sound, you need to find a right-hand position that provides a stable foundation for the thumb and fingers to do all that unimaginably rapid picking.

Relaxation is key to great right-hand bluegrass technique, so remember to constantly check for tension from your shoulder to your fingertips as you work through the following steps to find a comfortable right-hand position (also refer to Video Clip 9).

Getting set

Here's a quick way to get your right hand set in a good bluegrass playing position. I've used this method successfully with hundreds of players, and it can work for you too. Try the following steps while sitting comfortably in a chair without arms, with your feet resting on the floor (for info on the parts of the banjo I mention in this section, see Chapter 1):

1. **Relax your right arm and hand, letting the arm dangle loosely at the side of your body (see Figure 5-10a).**

2. **Bring the right hand up, resting it on your right leg and keeping your arm relaxed (see Figure 5-10b).**

   Note the position of your right hand: When the hand is fully relaxed, it should assume a cupped position with all the finger joints slightly bent.

3. **Place your right forearm against the armrest (or against the side of the banjo, if your instrument doesn't have an armrest), positioning the right hand to be over and above the banjo strings (see Figure 5-10c).**

   You don't want to position your right hand either too high or too low in relation to the strings. If your right-hand ring and pinky fingers are touching the banjo strings, your right hand is positioned too high. On the other hand, if you feel you're having to reach in quite a bit to play the 3rd string with your index finger, your hand is probably positioned too low in relation to the strings.

4. **Slide your right forearm back along the armrest until the ring and pinky fingers come to rest on the banjo head close to the bridge, but aren't actually touching it (see Figure 5-10d).**

   By completing Step 4, your right-hand thumb, index, and middle fingers should be set in a good playing position. You may have to move the right elbow out just a bit to allow your fingers to contact the head. As you anchor the right hand with your ring and/or little fingers, arch your wrist slightly so that your wrist and forearm don't touch the banjo head.

An arched wrist is just about essential for getting the right-hand fingers in a good position for playing close to the bridge. However, falling into the bad habit of bending the wrist in the opposite direction, toward the banjo head, is a common problem with many new players. This way of playing only adds tension to your right hand, forearm, and shoulder, and makes it difficult for the thumb to easily reach all the strings that it needs to play.

Some players arch their wrists just a little and others a lot. You can work out the fine details of your wrist arch as you continue to practice. For now, try to remember to keep at least a bit of an arch in the wrist, and you'll be fine!

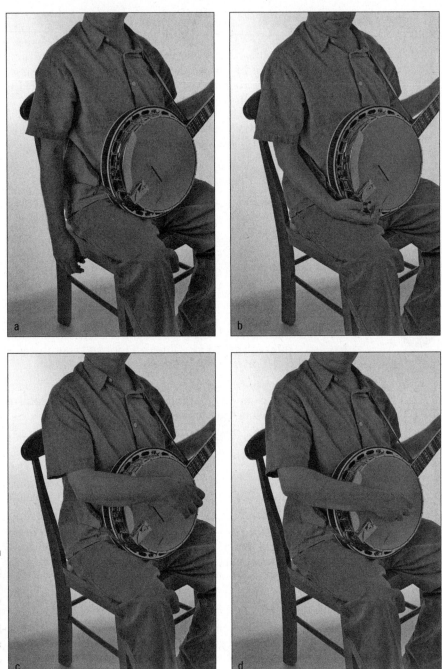

Figure 5-10:
Follow these steps to find a good right-hand bluegrass position.

Photographs by Anne Hamersky

Putting your thumb and fingers to good use

With your hand positioned over the strings and ready to play (see the preceding section), you're ready to take a look at how the thumb and fingers actually strike the strings in bluegrass style:

✔ The thumb is the most active of the three striking fingers, and you need it to be in position to play the 5th, 4th, 3rd, and 2nd strings as needed.

✔ Your index finger plays the 3rd and 2nd strings.

✔ Your middle finger plays the 1st string.

Refer back to that cupped hand position that you used in Step 2 in the preceding section to set your right hand on the banjo head. That's your starting point as you begin to play. Working from this relaxed position, you want to strike the strings by sweeping the thumb across the strings, using the joint that's closest to the hand. If your wrist is arched, the thumb should move across each string, rising up only very slightly in order to avoid hitting the adjacent string with your thumb.

Now try playing the 5th through the 2nd strings with your thumb, playing each string four times slowly in succession before moving on to the next string, as indicated in Tab 5-10, which is Audio Track 22. Listen carefully to the result. Does the note ring clearly? Is there enough volume? Is your hand relaxed as you pick the string with the thumb? If so, good work!

Tab 5-10: Right-hand thumb bluegrass exercise (Audio Track 22).

After you have your thumb movement down pat, move on to play notes with the index and middle fingers (be sure to refer to Tab 5-11 and Audio Track 23 as needed). You want to use primarily the first joint — the one that's closest to the hand — to play strings with your index and middle fingers:

1. **Try playing the 3rd and 2nd strings with your index finger and the 1st string with your middle finger.**

   By using mostly the first joint to move the end of the fingerpick across each string, you almost feel as if you're pushing down on the string.

2. **Move the index or middle finger straight toward the palm of your right hand after picking a string.**

3. **After the follow-through in Step 2, simply relax the finger so that it can return to its original position.**

   Don't deliberately sweep your finger outward from your palm.

Tab 5-11: Right-hand index and middle finger bluegrass exercise (Audio Track 23).

I know that these steps can sound quite complicated! However, I'm actually describing in great detail what usually occurs quite naturally after your hand is properly positioned on the banjo head. Don't think too hard about this process. (After all, we *are* banjo players, aren't we?) Go for what feels effortless and natural and for what gives you the best tone and the most volume.

Figure 5-11 shows my hand position when using the right-hand thumb to play the 3rd string, the right-hand index finger to play the 2nd string, and the right-hand middle finger to play the 1st string. If your fingers and hand look close to mine, you're on the right track!

Figure 5-11:
Picking with the right-hand thumb (a), index finger (b), and middle finger (c).

Photographs by Anne Hamersky

Staying relaxed while picking with the right hand is important. If you're moving on to the exercises in the next few sections, try to imagine that your fingers are doing all the work, while your shoulder, arm, wrist, and the top of your hand stay loose and relaxed.

Playing roll patterns

Roll patterns are repeated right-hand sequences of notes that are the basic building blocks for the rippling, fast sound of bluegrass banjo. Whereas guitarists, fiddlers, and mandolin players practice scales, bluegrass banjo

The great debate: One anchor finger or two?

One of the raging controversies in the bluegrass banjo world over the last several decades is whether it's best to anchor the right hand with both the ring and pinky fingers or whether it's alright to anchor with just the pinky finger. Most beginning players have trouble keeping the ring finger anchored on the head, especially when playing a note with the middle right-hand finger. This is because the muscles of these two fingers are interdependent, and playing a string with the middle finger often causes the ring finger to move in tandem with it.

The majority of professional players have figured out how to anchor both the right-hand ring and pinky fingers on the banjo head (see the accompanying photo a), but several outstanding players anchor just the pinky finger (see photo b), letting the ring finger move with the middle finger. I've taught many beginning students to anchor both fingers by urging them to play for a few weeks by using just the ring finger for an anchor. After this finger is trained to stay on the banjo head, having the pinky finger join it is a relatively easy matter. A proper arch to your wrist should really help in training the ring finger to stay on the banjo head.

The bottom line? My advice is to try supporting the right hand by using both fingers if you can, but if it feels better to use just the pinky finger for support, go for it! If you stay relaxed and you find that you're getting a good sound, you can play well either way!

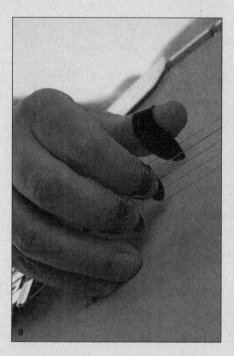

a

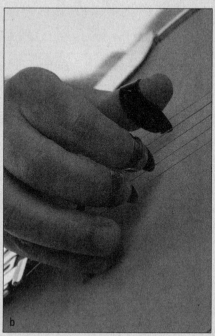

b

Photographs by Anne Hamersky

players work on roll patterns. You can use roll patterns as the foundation for accompanying other players and singers and for playing solos and melodies on the banjo.

Roll patterns are made up of both specific sequences of repeated right-hand finger movements as well as the actual strings that are played (these aren't always the same, because you can play different strings using the same pattern of right-hand fingers). For most songs, roll patterns are made up of repeated phrases of eight notes that are equal in length. You usually don't use the same right-hand finger twice in a row or strike the same string twice in succession when playing a roll pattern.

The alternating thumb roll, the forward-reverse roll, and the forward roll are the basic roll patterns that get you into the fast lane on the bluegrass banjo highway, and I explain them in the following sections.

Alternating thumb roll

The *alternating thumb roll* is sometimes called the *thumb in-and-out roll*. Whatever you call it, the right-hand thumb plays every other note in this eight-note roll, and you alternate using your index and middle fingers in between using your thumb. Note that this roll is actually made up of a four-note sequence that's repeated.

Here are the details on how the alternating thumb roll works:

- ✔ The order in which you use the right-hand thumb and fingers is as follows: thumb, index, thumb, middle, thumb, index, thumb, middle.

- ✔ A common string sequence for this roll is 3rd string, 2nd string, 5th string, 1st string, 4th string, 2nd string, 5th string, 1st string. In tablature, the alternating thumb roll played with the G, C, and D7 chords looks like what you see in Tab 5-12, which is Audio Track 24.

As you play this roll, try to pick each note clearly, making sure that your index and middle fingers are producing enough volume in comparison with the thumb. Play the roll slowly and evenly and try not to stop as you change from the G to the C and to the D7 chords; check out Video Clip 10 to see the alternating thumb roll in action.

Tab 5-12: The alternating thumb roll with G, C, and D7 chords (Audio Track 24).

The forward-reverse roll

The *forward-reverse roll* is a very natural roll for most players to play. You feel the right-hand fingers move in one direction and then double back in the opposite direction as you hear the roll move up and then down in pitch.

- ✔ The order of the right-hand thumb and fingers for this roll is thumb, index, middle, thumb, middle, index, thumb, middle.

- ✔ A typical string sequence is as follows: 3rd string, 2nd string, 1st string, 5th string, 1st string, 2nd string, 3rd string, 1st string.

You can see what the forward-reverse-roll pattern played with the G, C, and D7 chords looks like in tablature in Tab 5-13, which is Audio Track 25 and Video Clip 11.

Tab 5-13: The forward-reverse roll with G, C, and D7 chords (Audio Track 25).

The forward roll

The *forward roll* is the pattern that gives bluegrass banjo its rhythmic and driving sound. This pattern is a bit more difficult than the two rolls in the previous sections because this roll gathers notes into groups of three. You can find several different variations on the forward roll.

Here's a standard way of playing this roll:

- ✔ The order of the right-hand thumb and fingers is thumb, middle, thumb, index, middle, thumb, index, middle.

- ✔ The string sequence for the G and D7 chords is 3rd string, 1st string, 5th string, 3rd string, 1st string, 5th string, 3rd string, 1st string. Note that for the C chord, you substitute the 2nd string for the 3rd string in this series. See Tab 5-14 and listen to Audio Track 26.

Tab 5-14: The forward roll with G, C, and D7 chords (Audio Track 26).

Using bluegrass rolls as accompaniment

A great way to accompany other musicians or a singer is to use the rolls presented in the preceding section interchangeably in a song. Remember that you aren't really trying to play the melody of the song, but you're using the roll patterns to create a flowing accompaniment in the same way that a guitar or mandolin player strums his instrument.

Try accompanying "Boil Them Cabbage Down" (Tab 5-15 and Audio Track 27) by using the alternating thumb, forward-reverse, and forward rolls interchangeably and "Worried Man Blues" (check out Tab 5-16, Audio Track 28, and Video Clip 12) by using just the forward roll.

As you master these arrangements, feel free to mix and match the roll patterns in whatever way sounds good to you. As long as you stay in rhythm and start a new roll pattern on the first beat of each measure, you can't go wrong! If you make a mistake while practicing or playing along with the audio tracks, that's okay. Just stop for a moment and join back in at the beginning of a new roll pattern as soon as you can.

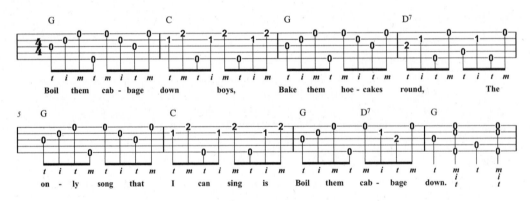

Tab 5-15: Accompanying "Boil Them Cabbage Down" using forward-reverse, forward, and alternating thumb rolls (Audio Track 27).

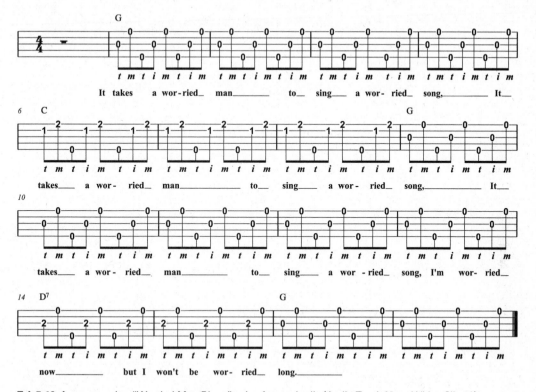

Tab 5-16: Accompanying "Worried Man Blues" using forward rolls (Audio Track 28 and Video Clip 12).

Chapter 6

Sliding, Hammering, and Pulling: Adding the Left Hand

. . . .

In This Chapter

▶ Playing slides, hammer-ons, pull-offs, and chokes

▶ Using left-hand techniques in clawhammer and bluegrass banjo

▶ Access the audio tracks and video clips at `www.dummies.com/go/banjo`

. . . .

*W*hether you're moving up or down the strings while fretting, coming down on the string to create a higher-pitched note, snapping off the string to sound a lower-pitched note, or bending a fretted note up in pitch, the left hand has a lot to say in the world of banjo music. You can hear a big difference in your own playing after you can make the left hand not only talk the talk but also walk the walk!

This chapter introduces you to the left-hand techniques that all banjo players use to make melodies flow more smoothly and sound more interesting and varied. All the techniques in this chapter focus on how the left-hand fingers can create notes that embellish what your right hand is picking. These left-hand techniques are used in both clawhammer and bluegrass banjo, the two most popular ways of playing the banjo (check out Chapter 5 for an introduction to these different right-hand approaches). Combining the left-hand techniques covered in this chapter with basic clawhammer and bluegrass right-hand techniques puts you in control of all the essential elements you need to play real banjo music in either the clawhammer or bluegrass style, and that's something to get excited about!

You don't have to worry about playing the techniques in this chapter on the 5th string. The function of the 5th string in both clawhammer and bluegrass banjo is to provide a steady, high-pitched drone (a *drone* is a repeated pitch; bagpipes typically have low-pitched drone notes while the banjo has a high-pitched drone). Stick to strings 1 through 4 with these left-hand techniques and you'll be picking fine in no time!

As you gain mastery over each new left-hand technique presented in this chapter (the slide, hammer-on, pull-off, and choke), don't forget to have some fun with these ideas as you perfect them. Mix them up and play the different techniques at random to get used to moving from a slide to a hammer-on or a pull-off to a choke on different strings.

Approach the exercises in this chapter as if you're learning the vocabulary of a new language. As you gain more experience in playing, you'll encounter many more new phrases and gain greater skills in how to combine these phrases into meaningful musical expressions. If you've mastered the techniques in this chapter, you're off to a great start in "talking banjo," and you can confidently go on to the next step — learning some actual banjo tunes (which you can do in Chapter 7)!

Slipping into the Slide

You can't find anything quite like the sweeping sound of a well-played slide on the banjo, just like the ones you hear at the beginning of "Cripple Creek." *Slides* add emphasis to a melody note by moving to that note from another pitch. They can add a bluesy feeling to your banjo playing, resembling the sound of the lonesome wind, a baying hound, or even a speeding train.

To play the slide, you use a left-hand finger that's already fretting a string to sound a new note by moving up or down the banjo neck along the same string to a new fret. The left-hand technique you use is the same regardless of the string you're on. However, the frets that you begin and end each slide on vary according to which string you're playing.

In this section, you're introduced to the basic mechanics of the slide (using the 3rd string) and then move on to playing other slides on the 3rd string before going wild with additional slides on the 4th and 1st strings. (I don't include 2nd-string slides because they aren't as common.)

The secret to a good-sounding slide is to maintain enough fretting pressure with the left hand so that the sound isn't cut off.

Getting down the slide: The basics

To play a slide, check out each of the following steps (I use the 3rd string for the sake of example; you play slides on other strings too, starting and stopping at different frets, but you use these basic mechanics for all strings):

1. **Press down (or *fret*) the 3rd string at the 2nd fret with the middle finger of your left hand.**

   I tend to use the middle finger of my left hand for all the slides on all strings in this section, because I feel like I have the most control with this finger. However, depending upon what's happening with your left hand at a particular moment in a song, you may sometimes need to use another left-hand finger to execute a slide. The left-hand index finger is another good choice for any of the slides you encounter in this section.

2. **Pick the 3rd string with your right hand.**

   If you're playing clawhammer, move down across the string with your right-hand index finger (or your middle finger, if you've decided to use this finger for melody notes). If you're picking bluegrass, play the note with the right-hand thumbpick by moving down across the string.

3. **After the note has sounded, slide the left-hand middle finger along the 3rd string from the 2nd fret to the 4th fret.**

   Keep exerting the same amount of pressure with the fretting finger as you originally used to fret the string and stop the finger just behind the 4th fret. You want to hear a continuous sound as your left-hand finger moves from one fret to another.

4. **Keep the left-hand finger fretted at the 4th fret and let the new note ring.**

Congratulations! You've just successfully played your first slide. If you want to review these tips and watch me play this slide, check out Video Clip 13.

Just like you don't need a whole lot of pressure for the left-hand fingers to get a clear sound on a fretted note, you may also find that you don't need to exert much pressure with your fretting finger to get a good sound out of your slides. Experiment to find the least amount of fretting pressure you need to still maintain the ringing sound of the picked note as you slide from one fret to another.

106

Part II: Let's Pick! Basic Banjo Techniques

Trying 3rd-string slides

If you can play a slide on the 3rd string moving from the 2nd to the 4th fret (I show you how in the preceding section), it's time to try two more 3rd-string slides, once again by using the left-hand middle finger.

You can tackle these 3rd-string slides in a few different ways. Both of these slides paint a banjo blues mood:

- ✔ **Slide from the 2nd fret up to the 3rd fret:** You can follow the same basic steps of a slide from the preceding section; just remember that you don't slide all the way to the 4th fret.

- ✔ **Slide from the 3rd fret down to the 2nd fret:** You carry out this slide in the same way as a slide that starts lower and moves higher. You're simply going in a different direction.

In banjo tablature, the *s* indication lets you know that you're supposed to slide. For example, you can see what these three 3rd-string slides look like in banjo tablature in Tab 6-1. For a refresher course on reading tablature, visit Chapter 5 and don't forget to check out Audio Track 29 to hear the sound of the slide. The designation of *i/t* or *i/m* in the following examples indicates that you can play these techniques using different right-hand fingers.

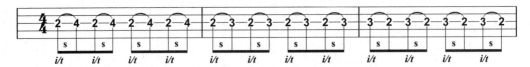

Tab 6-1: Playing 3rd-string slides: 2nd to 4th fret, 2nd to 3rd fret, and 3rd to 2nd fret (Audio Track 29).

Undertaking 4th-string slides

After conquering 3rd-string slides (see the preceding sections), you're ready to move on to the brave new world of the 4th-string slide. The 4th string is the lowest-pitched string on your banjo. If you strike it with some force before you move your left-hand finger for the slide, you can get a booming slide that you can feel all the way into your belly (and this is a good thing, by the way).

The 4th string is thicker and heavier than your 3rd string, so don't be surprised if you have to fret a bit harder with your left-hand finger to sustain the sound of the note with your 4th-string slides.

Follow the basic instructions in the section "Getting down the slide: The basics" presented earlier in this chapter for the mechanics of the slide and don't forget to use your left-hand middle finger to fret the string for the following 4th-string slides (note that both of these slides end at the 5th fret):

- ✔ **Slide from the 4th fret up to the 5th fret:** You don't have far to go on this slide, but remember to apply the appropriate pressure so you can get the sound you're looking for.

- ✔ **Slide from the 2nd fret up to the 5th fret:** Although this slide moves impressively three frets up the neck, other slides cover even more fretted territory. Remember that you don't want to hear all the pitches that lie between the beginning and end points of your slide. Make it a smooth, continuous swoop, and you'll be playing it the way that other banjo players like to hear it.

Check out the tablature for these two 4th-string slides in Tab 6-2, and listen to Audio Track 30.

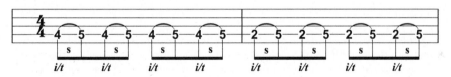

Tab 6-2: Playing 4th-string slides: 4th to 5th fret and 2nd to 5th fret (Audio Track 30).

Focusing on 1st-string slides

You may need some slides on the 1st string every now and then to catch some high melody notes. You may notice that the following 1st-string slides are very similar to the 4th-string slides (you're just on a different string):

- ✔ **Slide from the 4th fret up to the 5th fret:** Because the 1st string is lighter in weight than the 3rd or 4th strings, sustaining the sound of this slide shouldn't take much pressure at all.

- ✔ **Slide from the 2nd fret up to the 5th fret:** You're covering a greater distance with this slide, so use more pressure with the left-hand middle finger to sustain the note.

To get a feel for these 1st-string slides in tablature, take a look at Tab 6-3 and listen to Audio Track 31. It's always good to watch someone execute these kinds of techniques. Take a look at Video Clip 13 to check out my sliding expertise!

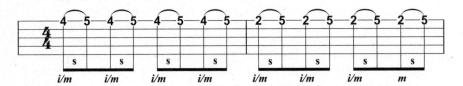

Tab 6-3: Playing 1st-string slides: 4th to 5th fret and 2nd to 5th fret (Audio Track 31).

Nailing the Hammer-On

An aggressive and well-played hammer-on, like you hear at the very beginning of "Foggy Mountain Breakdown," can be one of the most exciting moments in banjo music. This technique lets everyone in the room know you have a banjo, and you know how to use it! Hammer-ons can crack like a whip, their sound hitting you like a hair-raising blast of freezing-cold air. Hammer-ons are an important part of banjo music — and they're a heck of a lot of fun to play.

REMEMBER

With the *hammer-on,* you create a new note with the left-hand fretting finger by bringing it down with some force on a string that's just been played by the right hand. You aren't moving *along* the string as you do with the slide (see the section "Slipping into the Slide"), but you're coming straight *down* on it with the tip of your finger — like a hammer. Like the slide, you use the hammer-on to embellish or emphasize a melody note — the note that's being "hammered on."

You can hammer-on either from an open string to a fretted string or from one fretted string to another, which I show you how to do in the following sections.

Playing open-string hammer-ons

You can get a feel for the open-string (unfretted) hammer-on by following these step-by-step instructions (for the sake of this example, go ahead and begin on the 4th string; you use the same procedure for different strings as well):

1. **Play the 4th string open with either the index finger of the right hand if you're a clawhammer player or the right-hand thumb if you're a bluegrass player.**

2. **Let the note ring for a moment.**

3. **While the open string is still sounding, push the string into a fretted position just behind the 2nd fret with the left-hand middle finger (like a hammer).**

   You need to use enough speed with the left-hand finger so that the sound isn't cut off as your finger moves down to fret the string. You should hear an uninterrupted sound from beginning to end of the hammer-on, just as you do in the slide.

That's all there is to it. You've just played a hammer-on! Now you can try the same hammer-on on the 3rd and 1st strings, moving from the open string to the 2nd fret on either string. Banjo players prefer to use fretted hammer-ons (see the following section) instead of open hammer-ons for the 2nd string, so you don't need to worry about this string right now!

You can check out what these three hammer-ons look like in tablature (the *h* indication tells you to play a hammer-on) by looking at Tab 6-4. Then listen to Audio Track 32. Take a look at Video Clip 14 to review these steps and watch me play an assortment of great hammer-ons on different strings.

Although you use some force to get your hammer-ons sounding right, try not to raise your left-hand finger too high above the fingerboard to achieve this (it's not like you're a baseball pitcher in a windup — after all, it's just a

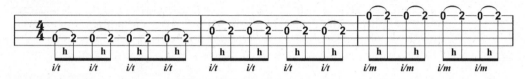

Tab 6-4: Playing 4th-, 3rd-, and 1st-string hammer-ons (Audio Track 32).

hammer-on!). Keep your finger just above where you want to play the hammer-on, with the finger in a position that's fairly close to the banjo fingerboard (see Figure 6-1). When it's time to play the hammer-on, you have more accuracy if your finger has to travel just a short distance to the fingerboard.

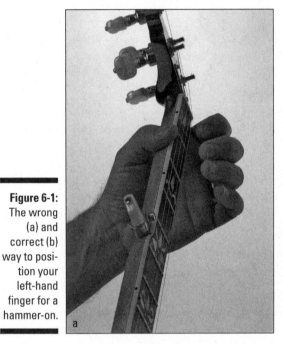
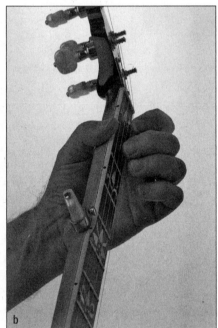

Figure 6-1: The wrong (a) and correct (b) way to position your left-hand finger for a hammer-on.

Photographs by Anne Hamersky

Giving fretted hammer-ons a chance

Fretted hammer-ons are a little trickier than open-string hammer-ons (see the preceding section), because you're coordinating the movements of two left-hand fretting fingers. To get started, try one of the most awesome maneuvers you'll ever play on the banjo: the world-famous "Foggy Mountain Breakdown" 2nd-string hammer-on. Be sure to pay attention to the mechanics because you use this same technique for fretted hammer-ons on other strings:

1. **Fret the 2nd string at the 2nd fret with the index finger of the left hand.**

2. **Play the 2nd string with either the index finger of the right hand (in clawhammer banjo) or the right-hand index finger or thumb (in bluegrass).**

3. **Let the note ring for a moment.**

4. **Bring down the left-hand middle finger just behind the 3rd fret of the 2nd string, using enough force to sound a new note, and hold the middle finger down behind the 3rd fret to let this string ring for a moment also.**

Give yourself a round of applause. You've just played two notes *exactly* like Earl Scruggs plays them — just 99,999 to go! (For more info on Earl Scruggs, check out Chapters 9 and 17.)

When you use this technique in bluegrass, you often play two of these hammer-ons right in a row. Try practicing the fretted hammer-on on the 2nd string many times in succession, keeping the left-hand index finger that's fretting the 2nd fret down the entire time.

Now try this same hammer-on technique on the 3rd and 4th strings, again moving from the 2nd fret to the 3rd fret. (Although you can also play fretted hammer-ons on the 1st string, you don't need to worry about it to play any of the tunes in this book.) Check out the written fretted hammer-ons on the 2nd, 3rd, and 4th strings in Tab 6-5. You can also check out all of these hammer-ons by watching Video Clip 14 and listening to Audio Track 33.

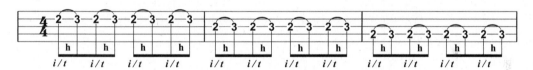

Tab 6-5: Playing fretted hammer-ons on the 2nd, 3rd, and 4th strings (Audio Track 33).

Pulling Off the Pull-Off

Like the hammer-on (see the preceding section), the *pull-off* is another left-hand banjo technique that carries a lot of potential firepower. A pull-off can explode like a firecracker on the Fourth of July, be as mournful as a scorned lover's sigh, or be as rhythmical as a horse's gallop. It's the most percussive of all the left-hand techniques and is generally used to connect a higher melody note to a lower note.

With the pull-off, the left-hand finger is already fretting a note on the banjo fingerboard. You create a new note by giving the string a slight sideways pull or push, either up or down (some folks use the term *push-off* for the latter kind of pull-off, but I use the term *pull-off* in this book to refer to both kinds). As your left-hand finger moves across the string, it snaps off the string, literally sounding a note that can have as much power as a note played by a right-hand finger.

In this section, I show you how you can play pull-offs either from a fretted to an open string or from one fretted note to another on the same string. You can also use the pull-off in a special way that's unique to clawhammer style. Video Clip 15 is your complete guide to pull-offs of all shapes and sizes.

For most folks, pull-offs are a bit trickier than slides or hammer-ons. If you lift straight up off the string with your left-hand fretting finger, you likely won't snap the string with enough force for a strong enough pull-off note. The trick is getting used to the very small sideways movement that's also required of the fretting finger to pluck the string.

Digging into open-string pull-offs

You can start by taking the open-string pull-off step by step (I show you how to do it on the 1st string, but you can use this same technique on the 3rd and 4th strings):

1. **Fret the 1st string at the 2nd fret with the middle finger of your left hand.**

2. **Play the 1st string with your right hand.**

   Use the index finger if you're playing clawhammer or your middle finger if you're playing bluegrass.

3. **Let the fretted note ring for a moment.**

4. **Pull the string with your left-hand finger to sound the open string.**

   Your left-hand finger should move both *sideways* (to pluck the string) and *up*.

Listen to the (hopefully) clear and beautiful sound of the open 1st string!

Banjo players don't use pull-offs often on the 2nd string, but nothing is holding you back from trying this same pull-off on the 3rd and 4th strings, transitioning from the 2nd fret to the open string, just as you did in the steps on the 1st string.

In banjo tablature, the letter *p* lets you know that a pull-off is in your very near future, as you can see in Tab 6-6. Give it a listen on Audio Track 34.

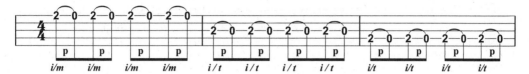

Tab 6-6: Playing open-string pull-offs on the 1st, 3rd, and 4th strings (Audio Track 34).

Mastering fretted pull-offs

In addition to playing a pull-off to an open string (see the preceding section), you can play a pull-off to another fretted note. With fretted pull-offs, you want to make sure that you use your left hand to fret both notes at the same time before executing a pull-off.

The 3rd-string pull-off from the 3rd to the 2nd fret is a defining characteristic of the sound of bluegrass banjo. Here's how you "pull off" a 3rd-string fretted pull-off (be sure to note the technique, because you use this procedure for other strings as well):

1. **Fret the 3rd string at both the 3rd fret with the left-hand middle finger and the 2nd fret with your left-hand index finger (see Figure 6-2a).**

2. **Pull the string, moving both sideways and up, to avoid the 2nd string; as you pull-off with the middle finger, keep the index finger in place on the 2nd fret (see Figure 6-2b).**

3. **Let the new note ring!**

Figure 6-2:
Positioning the fingers for a fretted pull-off (a); position of fingers after playing a fretted pull-off (b).

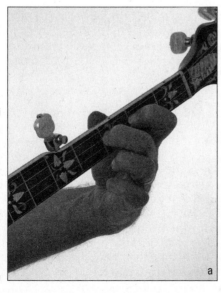

a

b

Photographs by Anne Hamersky

Now try this fretted pull-off on the 1st and 4th strings (using the 2nd string isn't common), pulling off from the 3rd to the 2nd fret as you did on the 3rd string. You can take a gander at the tab for fretted pull-offs on the 3rd, 1st, and 4th strings in Tab 6-7, and listen to Audio Track 35.

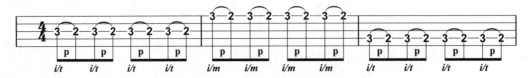

Tab 6-7: Playing fretted pull-offs on the 3rd, 1st, and 4th strings (Audio Track 35).

Sizing up special clawhammer pull-offs

You may want to use the pull-off in a way that's unique to clawhammer banjo. The technique is similar to what you play for an open string pull-off (see the section "Digging into open-string pull-offs" earlier in this chapter), but in this case, you don't play the string with the right hand at all. The sound is created *only* by the left hand moving across the string. This kind of pull-off is played almost always on just the 1st string. Here's a step-by-step guide on how to do this special clawhammer pull-off:

1. **Fret the 1st string at the 2nd fret with the middle finger of your left hand.**

2. **Without striking the string with the right hand, pull off the 1st string with the middle finger of your left hand.**

This pull-off emphasizes just the sound of the open string. Because a note isn't actually fretted, many players simply grab the string with their left-hand finger (without actually bringing their finger all the way down to the fingerboard) and pull down from the 1st string. You can see me demonstrate this special clawhammer pull-off in Video Clip 16.

Bending the Chokes

When you've got a serious case of the blues on the banjo, you're going to be playing some *chokes* on your instrument. This left-hand technique involves pushing or pulling on a fretted note to raise its pitch and then releasing the pressure to lower it back again. A choke is sometimes called a *bend*. (I could have called this section "Choking the Bends," but that sounded even worse than what I came up with, don't you think?) Blues and rock guitarists utilize this technique all the time to imitate the cry of the human voice, but it sounds equally great, if not better, on the banjo too, in my humble opinion. Discover how to play a choke in the following sections.

Playing the Foggy Mountain choke

The classic choke for bluegrass banjo players is once again from Earl Scruggs's "Foggy Mountain Breakdown." The Foggy Mountain choke is way up at the 10th fret of the 2nd string. Here's a step-by-step guide to a Foggy Mountain choke:

1. **Place your left-hand index or middle finger at the 10th fret of the 2nd string (see Figure 6-3a).**

   Using either finger is fine; try both and see which one is strongest for you.

2. **Play the 2nd string with your right-hand index finger.**

3. **While the note is still ringing, push the 2nd string towards the 3rd string with your left-hand finger while still maintaining enough fretting pressure to hear a continuous sound (see Figure 6-3b).**

   This movement is called the *choke*. Remember that the pitch goes up as you choke the string.

Most banjo players like to raise the pitch of this Foggy Mountain choke the equivalent of almost two frets. You have to really bend the string to do this — so much that the left-hand fingernail should come into contact with the 3rd string and push it out of the way.

Figure 6-3: The finger positions before (a) and after (b) playing a Foggy Mountain choke.

Photographs by Anne Hamersky

4. **Release the fretting pressure from the left hand to mute the note and return back to a normal fretted position, but don't lift the left-hand finger up off the string.**

You're now ready to repeat the sequence. Playing two or three chokes in rapid succession in a song isn't unusual, but this requires a lot of concentration! The trick to playing one choke after another smoothly is to release the left-hand fretting pressure when a choke is done while keeping your left-hand finger still touching the second string. This quickly returns the string — and your left-hand finger — back to the starting position and readies you to play another choke.

In tablature, a Foggy Mountain choke is indicated with an upward arrow, as you can see in Tab 6-8.

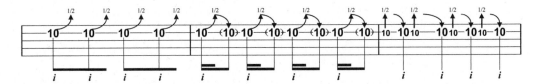

Tab 6-8: Playing chokes on the banjo: Foggy Mountain choke, choke and release, and pre-choke (Audio Track 36).

Experimenting with choke variations

You can also try playing the standard Foggy Mountain choke in almost the same way I describe in the preceding section, but this time, keep *downward* pressure on the string as the finger returns to the normal position. This technique is called a *choke and release.* You should hear the pitch go up with the choke and then come back down again with the release.

Another way to add expression to your playing with chokes is to bend the string *before* striking it with your right hand, and then bring the pitch back down to its normal fretted sound by releasing the choke (but still keeping enough fretting pressure to sound the string!). This technique is called the *pre-choke,* for obvious reasons.

In tablature, a choke and release is indicated with an arched arrow going up and coming back down again, but a pre-choke is indicated with a line going straight up from the note with an arched arrow moving downward, as you can see in Tab 6-8 and hear on Audio Track 36. These different ways of executing the choke on the banjo are tricky, and the best way to get a handle on these techniques is to check out Video Clip 17, where I play more chokes than are legally allowed in several southwestern Virginia counties.

Putting Your Hands Together

The slide, hammer-on, pull-off, and choke are key ingredients to great banjo playing, but it's not until you add these left-hand techniques to right-hand picking that you can really begin to cook. When you coordinate the movements of the right and left hands together, you take a giant leap forward as a banjo player.

In the following sections, I go over a few of the right-hand basics I cover in depth in Chapter 5 to make sure you're ready to move on. Then you begin to put the hands together to play short phrases that are some of the most important building blocks of clawhammer and bluegrass banjo music.

You want to be totally comfortable with the right-hand patterns before adding the left-hand techniques I discuss in this section. This means you should be able to play the right-hand patterns consecutively without stopping *and* without looking at the music. If you're a bluegrass player, you should be able to move from one roll to the next without interruption. If you're playing clawhammer, you want to have enough right-hand control so that your finger can go to whatever first note or melody note you want to play — and actually hit that note a great majority of the time. If you're uncertain about your right-hand skills, you may want to take a moment to go over the info on right-hand patterns for clawhammer and bluegrass banjo, which I cover in Chapter 5.

Make sure that you keep a constant rhythm with your right hand as you add the left-hand techniques. Begin by playing the following exercises slowly, building up speed as you gain confidence. Note that you play all the left-hand techniques relatively quickly, finishing the technique before you play the next note with the right hand. These slides, hammer-ons, pull-offs, and chokes are indicated with either eighth or sixteenth notes in the tab examples. And be sure to listen to the corresponding examples in the audio tracks and watch the noted video clips to internalize the sounds of these rhythms.

Making sure your clawhammer right hand is ready

Try the basic clawhammer right-hand technique (see Tab 6-9), playing strings 4 through 1 for the *melody note* (which is what I call the first note played in the basic pattern). You can hear an example on Audio Track 37.

Tab 6-9: Playing basic clawhammer technique (Audio Track 37).

 Even though the tab indicates that the index finger plays the melody note and the brush, don't forget that you can use either the index or middle finger for these techniques. You can also choose to brush across one, two, or three strings, depending on how you want your playing to sound at that moment.

If you feel like you don't quite have your clawhammer right-hand ready, head back to Chapter 5 for a more detailed explanation of clawhammer right-hand positioning and technique.

Double-checking your bluegrass right-hand skills

Get those fingerpicks on your right-hand thumb, index, and middle fingers and warm up by playing the bluegrass right-hand patterns I introduce in Chapter 5 (and if you didn't know that bluegrass players use picks on their fingers, *definitely* check out Chapter 5 right now before proceeding!).

 Following Tab 6-10 and Audio Track 38, mix it up by playing alternating thumb, forward-reverse, and forward rolls — bluegrass style.

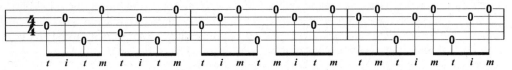

Tab 6-10: Playing the alternating thumb, forward-reverse, and forward rolls in bluegrass style (Audio Track 38).

Joining forces: Using both hands in clawhammer banjo

Banjo players use slides, hammer-ons, pull-offs, and chokes most often to add flavor or draw attention to melody notes. The first note you pick with basic clawhammer right-hand technique usually corresponds to a melody note in the song that you're playing. That's the note that's going to get the royal left-hand treatment.

In the following sections, you get to use all the left-hand embellishments I cover earlier in this chapter together with the basic right-hand clawhammer technique (from Chapter 5), adding up to some remarkable banjo sounds! You discover a lot of new sounds in this section, and Video Clip 18 provides a great overview of these techniques, letting you see and hear me demonstrate each clawhammer style lick.

Clawhammer slides

The 4th-, 3rd-, and 1st-string slides (see the section "Slipping into the Slide" earlier in this chapter) all sound great in clawhammer banjo.

For each of the following examples, you want to execute the left-hand technique just after striking the string with the right hand, finishing the technique before the brush. Practice each individual measure over and over again until it feels comfortable and sounds smooth before moving on to the next measure.

You start by working on integrating the 3rd-string slide into clawhammer technique, because you play this slide most often, and then you move on to playing slides on the 1st and 4th strings.

3rd-string slides

Play the three 3rd-string slides from the section "Trying 3rd-string slides" earlier in this chapter: the 2nd- to 4th-fret slide, the 2nd- to 3rd-fret slide, and the 3rd- to 2nd-fret slide. Follow each slide with an index- or middle-finger brush and a 5th string played by the thumb. (Take a look at Tab 6-11 and listen to Audio Track 39.)

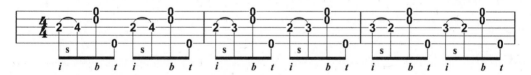

Tab 6-11: Playing 3rd-string slides in clawhammer banjo (Audio Track 39).

1st-string slides

Play the two 1st-string slides I introduce earlier in this chapter: the 4th- to 5th-fret slide and the 2nd- to 5th-fret slide, following each slide with a right-hand brush and the 5th string played by the thumb to get the full clawhammer effect. See Tab 6-12 and listen to Audio Track 40.

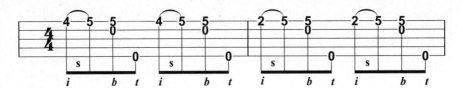

Tab 6-12: Playing 1st-string slides in clawhammer banjo (Audio Track 40).

4th-string slides

The two 4th-string slides use the same fretted positions as the 1st-string slides (see the preceding section), but don't be surprised if you have to fret the 4th string a bit harder to make the notes really ring. See Tab 6-13 and listen to Audio Track 41.

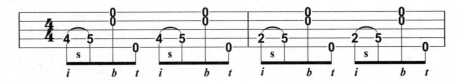

Tab 6-13: Playing 4th-string slides in clawhammer banjo (Audio Track 41).

Clawhammer hammer-ons

If you know how to play a hammer-on, you're now ready to put the hammer-ons to work by integrating this technique into basic right-hand clawhammer playing (flip to the section "Nailing the Hammer-On" earlier in this chapter for a refresher on hammer-ons).

One key to quickly integrating the action of the hands together is to first gain mastery over the skills required from each separate hand. Also, keep the rhythm of what you play with the right hand steady no matter what happens when you add the left hand. You can coordinate the activity of both hands much more quickly if you let the right hand lead the way.

The following exercises group the open hammer-ons together, followed by the fretted hammer-ons.

Open-string hammer-ons

As you play the open-string hammer-ons from Tab 6-14 in the clawhammer style, remember to repeat each individual measure over and over until it sounds good to you, and then move on to the following measure. Your ultimate goal is to play all three measures in succession without catastrophe, much like what you can hear on Audio Track 42.

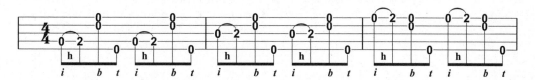

Tab 6-14: Playing open-string hammer-ons in clawhammer banjo (Audio Track 42).

Fretted hammer-ons

Fretted hammer-ons are always a bit tougher to play than open-string hammer-ons, but you can master them with some dedicated practice. Try your hand at the exercise in Tab 6-15, which you can hear on Audio Track 43. With this exercise, you're at least moving from the 2nd to the 3rd fret on each string to ease you in nice and slow.

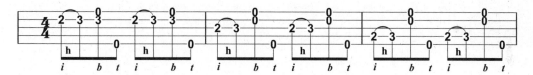

Tab 6-15: Playing fretted hammer-ons in clawhammer banjo (Audio Track 43).

Clawhammer pull-offs

You're probably no stranger to 4th-, 3rd-, and 1st-string pull-offs by now (especially if you went through the section "Pulling Off the Pull-Off" earlier in this chapter). And — you guessed it — the pull-off works perfectly in clawhammer banjo.

Don't forget to make the pull-offs in the following sections really pop by putting some energy behind your left-hand motion. You want to play the pull-off so that it's rhythmically placed exactly between the first melody note and the right-hand brush, as you can see in the accompanying tabs.

4th-string pull-offs

In the clawhammer 4th-string pull-off exercise in Tab 6-16, you play an open-string pull-off followed immediately by a fretted-string pull-off, both on the 4th string. Most players use their left-hand middle finger for both pull-offs. Note that you move the middle finger from the 2nd to the 3rd fret for the second measure of this exercise. Listen to the example on Audio Track 44.

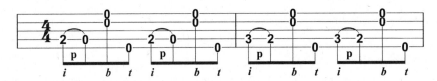

Tab 6-16: Playing 4th-string pull-offs in clawhammer banjo (Audio Track 44).

3rd-string pull-offs

The left-hand fingering for these pull-offs in Tab 6-17 is the same as for the 4th-string variety (from the preceding section). Begin with an open-string pull-off from the 2nd fret to an open string and follow it up with a fretted pull-off that begins at the 3rd fret and ends on the 2nd fret, as you can hear on Audio Track 45.

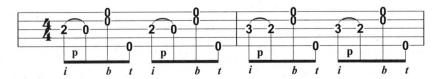

Tab 6-17: Playing 3rd-string pull-offs in clawhammer banjo (Audio Track 45).

1st-string pull-offs

Clawhammer pull-offs work well on the 1st string too. However, don't pull so hard with your left hand as you execute the pull-off that you pull the string off the fingerboard! Give the exercise in Tab 6-18 a try, and listen to the example on Audio Track 46.

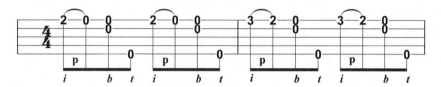

Tab 6-18: Playing 1st-string pull-offs in clawhammer banjo (Audio Track 46).

Special clawhammer pull-off

What's so special about this pull-off? This technique is clawhammer-only — where you pull-off on the 1st string without hitting the string with the right hand first (and that's pretty special). The timing is the same as for all the other pull-offs in this section.

Most players use their left-hand middle finger for this pull-off, positioning it behind the 2nd fret. You can play this pull-off after any initial melody note in clawhammer banjo. In the exercise in Tab 6-19, you use the pull-off while playing melody notes on the 2nd and 3rd strings. Give Audio Track 47 a listen.

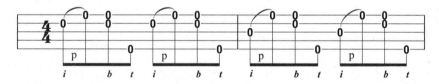

Tab 6-19: Playing the special clawhammer pull-off in clawhammer banjo (Audio Track 47).

Clawhammer choke

Although the Foggy Mountain choke is usually the domain of bluegrass pickers, it's also a very hip thing to play in clawhammer banjo, as you can see as you play along with Tab 6-20. The secret to successfully integrating the choke into right-hand clawhammer technique is to concentrate on keeping the right-hand rhythm steady. Play very slowly at first to maximize the sound of the bending pitch in each stroke and to work into your motor memory the coordination required of the two hands. And it wouldn't hurt to listen to the example on Audio Track 48.

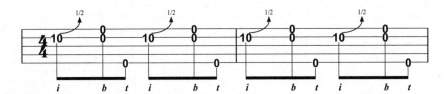

Tab 6-20: Playing the Foggy Mountain choke in clawhammer banjo (Audio Track 48).

Keeping both hands busy in bluegrass banjo

Slides, hammer-ons, pull-offs, and chokes add tremendous excitement to bluegrass banjo music. In the following sections, you can take a look at how some of the left-hand techniques I introduce earlier in this chapter work with the alternating thumb, forward-reverse, and forward rolls from Chapter 5.

Integrating the work of both hands in bluegrass style sets the stage for you to conquer bold new banjo worlds. There's a lot to pick on and fret about as you work through the new techniques presented in the next sections. Don't forget to use the examples provided by the tablature and the accompanying audio tracks as you work to gain mastery of these skills. To double-check your progress, revisit Video Clip 19 as many times as you need to. By watching and listening, you'll arrive at your five-string destination sooner than you would have thought possible!

Bluegrass slides

Remember to keep the rhythm of your right-hand roll notes evenly spaced as you add slides to the bluegrass roll patterns. Play the slide quickly, letting it occupy the rhythmic space of one roll note. If you arrive at your destination fret with the slide just about the time you strike the next string in the roll pattern, you're playing like the pros!

...playing slides in combination with the various ... refresher on how to play a slide, you can refer ...he Slide" earlier in this chapter).

...e the previous sections), having good com-...and techniques separately before you combine ...ore practice, you can turn to Chapter 5 for the ...he sections on the specific left-hand tech-...When you're ready to add the left hand, keep ...ght-hand picking, and it should sound great!

...3rd string, followed by a 2nd- to 5th-fret slide ...ing thumb roll, using Tab 6-21 and Audio ...

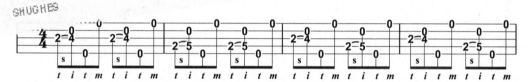

Tab 6-21: Playing slides with the alternating thumb roll (Audio Track 49).

Forward-reverse-roll slides

Try the 3rd-string slide from the preceding section, but at the beginning of a forward-reverse roll. Then follow this with a 4th-string slide that starts at the 2nd fret and ends at the 5th fret. You can use Tab 6-22 as a reference and listen to Audio Track 50 as well.

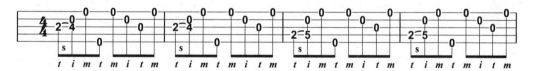

Tab 6-22: Playing slides with the forward-reverse roll (Audio Track 50).

Forward-roll slides

Using left-hand techniques with the forward roll is one of the trickiest blue-grass banjo moves, but it's well worth the effort, giving your playing an authentic and hard-driving sound.

PLAY THIS!

Try playing the forward-roll slides pictured in Tab 6-23. In this exercise, you begin on the 3rd string in measures one and two, playing a 2nd- to 4th-fret slide. For measures three and four, play a 4th-string slide that starts on the 2nd fret and ends on the 5th fret. Note that after playing the 4th-string slide for these last two measures, you finish the roll by playing two 3rd strings with the right-hand index finger. Hear what I mean on Audio Track 51.

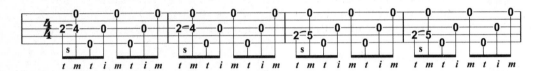

Tab 6-23: Playing slides with the forward roll (Audio Track 51).

Bluegrass hammer-ons

Many bluegrass banjo players place the hammer-on *between* the notes of the roll pattern, especially on slower tempo songs. As the speed of a song increases, you don't have enough time in between your right-hand roll notes to worry about this, and your hammer-on may occur at the same time as you pick the next note in the roll. Both ways of playing the hammer-on are good — as long as you maintain a consistent rhythm in your right hand, that is! You can try out this technique in the following sections.

TIP

Repeat each measure over and over until you've mastered each technique, and then move on to conquer the next measure. Take things one step at a time, and you'll rule your own banjo kingdom in no time!

Alternating-thumb-roll hammer-ons

PLAY THIS!

Try mixing open-string hammer-ons and fretted hammer-ons in this exercise. Begin with open to 2nd-fret hammer-ons on the 3rd and 4th strings before moving to 2nd- to 3rd-fret fretted hammer-ons, using the alternating thumb roll as shown in Tab 6-24 and demonstrated on Audio Track 52.

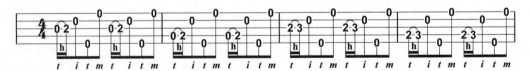

Tab 6-24: Playing hammer-ons with the alternating thumb roll (Audio Track 52).

Forward-reverse-roll hammer-ons

Whatever works in the way of hammer-ons for an alternating thumb roll (see the preceding section) also works for a forward-reverse roll. In this exercise, you play four different hammer-ons: open to 2nd-fret hammer-ons on the 3rd and 4th strings, and 2nd- to 3rd-fret fretted hammer-ons on these same strings. Note how the roll changes in measures two and four to accommodate these 4th-string slides. Jump in and get your feet wet following Tab 6-25 and listening to Audio Track 53.

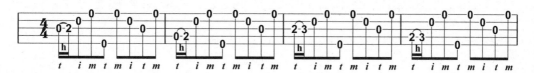

Tab 6-25: Playing hammer-ons with the forward-reverse roll (Audio Track 53).

Forward-roll hammer-ons

Try open and fretted hammer-ons on the 4th, 3rd, and 2nd strings with the forward roll by giving the exercise in Tab 6-26 a go. Note that the strings you play with the right hand change according to which hammer-on you choose to play. In measure one, you begin the forward roll on the 4th string, but in measure two, you start on the 3rd string. In the last two measures, you start the forward roll on the 2nd string. It's all on Audio Track 54.

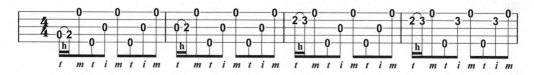

Tab 6-26: Playing hammer-ons with the forward roll (Audio Track 54).

Bluegrass pull-offs

Aggressive, gritty-sounding pull-offs, like you hear master players such as J. D. Crowe and Ron Block play, are a hallmark of traditional bluegrass style. Professional players try to place pull-offs in between the notes of the roll pattern, which requires some quick and precise communication to the left hand. Start slowly with the exercises in the following sections and work up speed as you gain confidence.

Alternating-thumb-roll pull-offs

Try open-string and fretted pull-offs in the bluegrass style by using the alternating thumb roll (see Tab 6-27), paying attention to how the strings you play with the right hand change according to the pull-off that you choose to play with the left hand. Listen to the example on Audio Track 55.

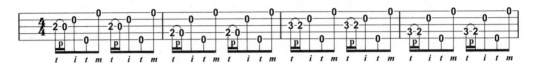

Tab 6-27: Playing pull-offs with the alternating thumb roll (Audio Track 55).

Forward-reverse-roll pull-offs

You can mix things up a bit and start this roll with a 2nd- to 3rd-fret slide on the 3rd string, followed by a 3rd- to 2nd-fret pull-off. (You can use Tab 6-28 and Audio Track 56 as a guide.) Bluegrass players use this phrase frequently. Note that at measures two and four, you can relax by playing the forward-reverse-roll pattern without these left-hand techniques.

Tab 6-28: Playing slides and pull-offs with the forward-reverse roll (Audio Track 56).

Forward-roll pull-offs

You can take that 3rd- to 2nd-string pull-off on the 3rd string and use it in a forward roll, starting the measure with a fretted hammer-on on the 2nd to 3rd fret on the 2nd string, as you can see in Tab 6-29 and hear on Audio Track 57.

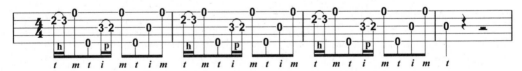

Tab 6-29: Playing hammer-ons and pull-offs with the forward roll (Audio Track 57).

Bluegrass chokes

When combined with the right-hand forward roll, that Foggy Mountain choke can send listeners into paroxysms of wonder and joy (at least I think it's wonder and joy . . . I'm never quite sure, really!). This phrase, which you can see in Tab 6-30 and hear on Audio Track 58 is an intensely idiomatic bluegrass banjo lick. Be sure to apply the left-hand choke each time you strike the 2nd string.

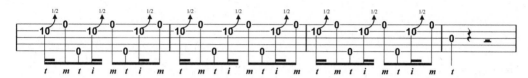

Tab 6-30: Playing chokes with the forward roll (Audio Track 58).

Chapter 7

Working Up Your First Tunes: Clawhammer and Bluegrass

....

In This Chapter

▶ Arranging melodies for clawhammer and bluegrass banjo

▶ Playing four clawhammer and bluegrass tunes

▶ Access the audio tracks and video clips at www.dummies.com/go/banjo

....

*Y*ou've no doubt been waiting for this moment: You're ready to step into the spotlight and play your first songs on the banjo in *both* clawhammer and bluegrass style! If you've worked through the previous few chapters, you're now taking a big leap forward as you move from just playing along with a tune or playing just the melody notes to being able to actually play the tune itself using authentic banjo playing techniques. In time, you'll not only be someone who can accompany others, but you'll also be a soloist (or, in banjo speak, a *picker*).

Clawhammer, which is also known as frailing or old-time banjo, and bluegrass style are the two most popular ways of playing the banjo. While the left-hand playing techniques used for both styles are the same (check out Chapter 6 for an explanation of the essentials of left-hand banjo technique), the right-hand position and the method used to strike the strings in clawhammer and bluegrass style are considerably different.

Clawhammer is sometimes called a down-picking style because the right-hand fingers move down across the banjo strings. Bluegrass is known as an up-picking style because the index and middle fingers of the right hand strike the strings in an upward motion. Check out Chapter 5 for a full explanation of both right-hand playing techniques and get ready to combine the ideas presented in both Chapters 5 and 6 in this chapter.

The beauty and challenge of working up a good solo is integrating the melody with the playing techniques that are unique to clawhammer and bluegrass banjo, which is what I help you tackle in this chapter. I break down the process of working up solos to get you started down the road to creating your own music. You discover how to more easily map out a song on the banjo fingerboard and apply right-hand clawhammer and bluegrass techniques to make melodies come alive. Then you throw in left-hand slides, hammer-ons, and pull-offs to turn your tune into great-sounding banjo music.

I close the chapter by having you play clawhammer and bluegrass versions of five well-known tunes that all banjo players like to play: "Worried Man Blues," "Boil Them Cabbage Down," "Cripple Creek," "Goodbye Liza Jane," and "Ground Hog." You can follow along by watching and listening to the demos at www.dummies.com/go/banjo and by reading the banjo music (called *tablature*) that's in this chapter. You have a lot of ground to cover, so get out your banjo, get in tune, and get started!

Stylin' It: Playing Real Banjo Music

The secret to making great music in both clawhammer and bluegrass styles is to creatively find ways to play songs that use the different fretting and picking techniques that are characteristic of each playing style in such a way that you and your listeners can still hear and identify the melody.

After you feel like you have a handle on finding and playing simple melodies (head back to Chapter 4 for a review of the G and D major scales and finding melodies on the banjo), it's time to add right-hand clawhammer and bluegrass picking techniques to fill in the spaces between the melody notes. As you begin to play honest-to-goodness, authentic-sounding banjo music, the excitement can really begin to kick in (let me hear a resounding "Well, alright!"). So as you make melodies in both the clawhammer and bluegrass styles in the following sections, hold on tight!

Starting with the right hand

As you work up a solo, using either clawhammer or bluegrass right-hand technique, you want to preserve as much of the melody as possible so that your listeners (and you) can keep track of what you're playing. However, you also want to keep the right hand flowing by incorporating the basic clawhammer technique or bluegrass roll patterns with as little interruption in the music as possible. All players experience conflicts between these two goals at times. Listening to and learning from other players and experimentation are the keys to coming up with your own solutions.

Here are a few more tips to keep in mind as you start to work out melodies for clawhammer and bluegrass banjo:

- ✔ **Be flexible with the basic clawhammer technique and the bluegrass rolls and adjust these patterns to play those strings where the melody notes are located.** For example, if the melody is on an open 2nd string, make sure you play that note as part of your bluegrass roll pattern or basic clawhammer technique. Also, use the right-hand techniques to make the solo flow continuously, but don't be afraid to stop and play a few melody notes all by themselves if that's what seems to work best at a given moment.

- ✔ **Although playing those melody notes that occur on the first beat of a chord change is a good idea, don't worry about trying to hit _every_ melody note.** Decide which notes are the most important and see how you can adjust the right-hand patterns to play as many of these notes as possible.

- ✔ **Relate the chord progression to the melody.** For instance, if the song's chord progression moves to a C chord, some of the melody notes will very likely be the same as the fretted notes that are part of the chord you're playing. Fret the full chord first and then go hunting for those melody notes.

- ✔ **Jump at the chance to enhance the melody.** Most melodies have some notes that are held for a relatively long time, alternating with notes that are shorter in duration. Long notes provide a great opportunity to continue playing either the basic clawhammer technique or a bluegrass roll that accentuates that same melody note.

- ✔ **Adjust your playing to the duration of the note.** Maintaining a flowing right-hand technique is more difficult in those passages that contain more melody notes. In these cases, you may have to interrupt your basic right-hand technique to play those notes, and then resume when the melody notes are once again of longer duration.

- ✔ **When playing with others, always try to hold up your end of the rhythm.** Playing in time and changing chords at the proper time are much more important than playing a solo that expresses every melody note but doesn't maintain the correct rhythm or follow the chord progression.

Ready to use these tips in action? In the following sections, you get the chance to add clawhammer and bluegrass right-hand techniques to the melody of "Worried Man Blues" and play two different arrangements of this song. Don't hesitate to use the tab and the video and audio examples together to help speed up the picking process.

Getting a feel for the clawhammer way

Try playing the arrangement of "Worried Man Blues" in Tab 7-1 and on Audio Track 59, using basic clawhammer right-hand technique to capture as many melody notes as possible. You can watch me play this tune in Video Clip 20.

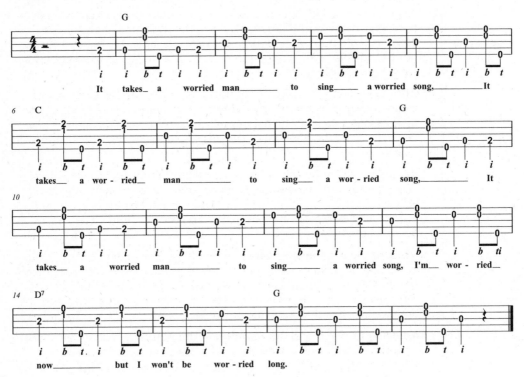

Tab 7-1: Playing "Worried Man Blues" the clawhammer way (Audio Track 59).

Taking on the melody bluegrass style

For some serious melody-making, try "Worried Man Blues" in bluegrass style, using the alternating thumb, forward-reverse and forward rolls and the pinch pattern. You can always find more than one way to capture a melody with bluegrass rolls. The more you experiment with different solutions, the more skilled you become in working out your own arrangements of tunes. But for now, get the feel for a bluegrass melody by following along with my arrangement and listening to Audio Track 60 and watching Video Clip 21.

Note in Tab 7-2 how the melody note often determines which roll works best in each measure. For instance, in the first full measure (at the word "takes" if you're singing the melody "It *takes* a worried man, to sing a worried song"), I play an alternating thumb roll that begins on the open 4th string, because at this initial point in the song, that's the melody note that needs to be played. In the next measure, I use a forward-reverse roll to capture two melody notes:

the open 3rd string (a G note) at the word "man" and a 3rd string fretted at the 2nd fret (an A note) at the word "to." Then in the following measure, I play a forward roll emphasizing the open 2nd string (a B note), followed by another 3rd-string, 2nd-fret A note to get as close as I can to playing each note as if I were singing it. In capturing melodies, feel free to alter the roll patterns to play those strings that match the melody notes you hear in your head.

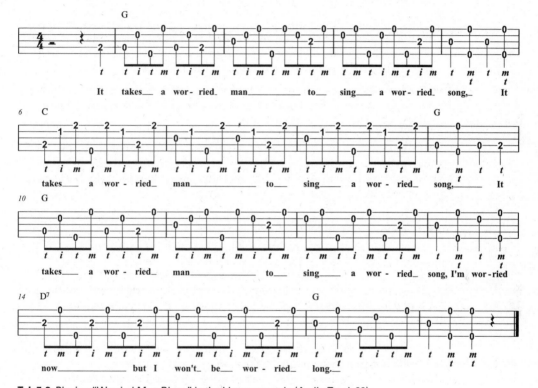

Tab 7-2: Playing "Worried Man Blues" in the bluegrass style (Audio Track 60).

Adding the left hand

After you're comfortable incorporating melody notes into clawhammer and bluegrass right-hand technique (see the preceding section), you can enhance your solos by adding left-hand slides, hammer-ons, pull-offs, and chokes. Because you use these left-hand techniques to draw attention to melody notes, banjo players naturally use them when they need to make a melody note really stand out in a solo.

Here are a few additional guidelines on how to use these left-hand techniques to make the melody really pop:

✔ **If a melody note falls on an open 3rd, 2nd, 1st, or 5th string, that's a good time to play a slide or a hammer-on on a lower string that moves up to the same pitch as the open string.** For example, if the melody note is on an open 3rd string, you can emphasize this same pitch by sliding from the 2nd to the 5th fret on the 4th string.

✔ **If the melody moves down from one open string to the next, try a pull-off or a backward slide on the lower string to facilitate this movement.** For instance, if the melody moves from an open 2nd string to an open 3rd string, try a 3rd- to 2nd-fret pull-off on the 3rd string.

✔ **If a melody needs a bluesy or bent note, call on your left-hand choke.** You can use a choke in much the same way as a slide to make a transition from a lower to a higher note.

I'm still amazed by how adding a bit of left-hand flash can enhance any arrangement. In the following section, you can play two versions of "Worried Man Blues" that both add slides, hammer-ons, and pull-offs to the basic right-hand techniques of clawhammer and bluegrass banjo.

Creating clawhammer melodies

Try the arrangement of "Worried Man Blues" shown in Tab 7-3 and featured on Audio Track 61. In this version, you play slides and hammer-ons to create an even more authentic and exciting clawhammer banjo sound. In banjo tablature, these techniques are indicated by letters below the tab staff: *s* stands for slide and *h* for hammer-on (and when the time comes to play a pull-off, that's indicated with the letter *p*).

Note that the goal isn't to capture each and every melody note that you would sing but to play as many melody notes as you can while playing the basic clawhammer strum as much as possible. (For a review of basic clawhammer techniques, pick your way back to Chapter 5.)

Compare this arrangement with the version presented earlier in Tab 7-1 to explore how these left-hand techniques can add more stylistic impact to an arrangement.

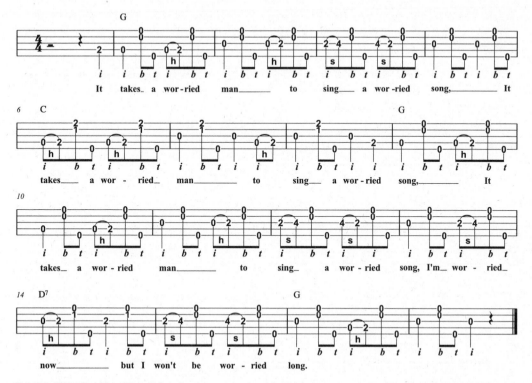

Tab 7-3: "Worried Man Blues" the clawhammer way with slides, hammer-ons, and pull-offs (Audio Track 61).

Playing the bluegrass way

Just as you can add slides, hammer-ons, and pull-offs to clawhammer banjo arrangements, you can also add these same techniques to right-hand roll patterns to create a more genuine bluegrass banjo sound. Give it a try by listening to Audio Track 62 and playing the arrangement of "Worried Man Blues" in Tab 7-4.

Before tackling this bluegrass rendition of "Worried Man Blues," you may want to take a moment and look at the two-hand exercises in Chapter 6 to make sure you're comfortable adding left-hand embellishments to bluegrass roll patterns.

You may notice how incorporating these techniques in bluegrass style makes your playing sound much closer to that of such greats as Earl Scruggs, Sonny Osborne, and J. D. Crowe.

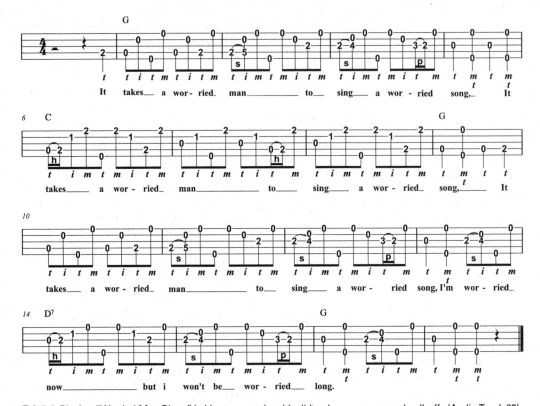

Tab 7-4: Playing "Worried Man Blues" in bluegrass style with slides, hammer-ons, and pull-offs (Audio Track 62).

Tackling a Few More Tunes

This special bonus song section includes arrangements of four banjo favorites in matching clawhammer and bluegrass versions that bring together all the important new skills covered in this chapter.

You have lots of ways to work on these tunes! Take a look at the tabs for each song but also don't forget to listen to the corresponding audio tracks. There's also video for the clawhammer and bluegrass versions of "Cripple Creek" and "Ground Hog," where you can see how both hands work together to create great banjo music. After you're playing each song at a reasonable speed, try playing along with me.

✔ Tab 7-5 and Audio Track 63: Clawhammer arrangement of "Boil Them Cabbage Down"

✔ Tab 7-6 and Audio Track 64: Bluegrass arrangement of "Boil Them Cabbage Down"

✔ Tab 7-7, Audio Track 65, and Video Clip 22: Clawhammer arrangement of "Cripple Creek"

✔ Tab 7-8, Audio Track 66, and Video Clip 23: Bluegrass arrangement of "Cripple Creek"

✔ Tab 7-9 and Audio Track 67: Clawhammer arrangement of "Goodbye Liza Jane"

✔ Tab 7-10 and Audio Track 68: Bluegrass arrangement of "Goodbye Liza Jane"

✔ Tab 7-11, Audio Track 69, and Video Clip 24: Clawhammer arrangement of "Ground Hog"

✔ Tab 7-12, Audio Track 70, and Video Clip 25: Bluegrass arrangement of "Ground Hog"

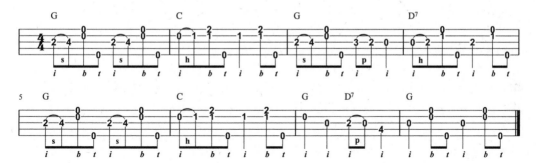

Tab 7-5: Clawhammer arrangement of "Boil Them Cabbage Down" (Audio Track 63).

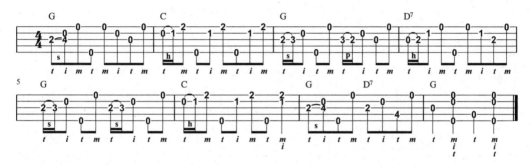

Tab 7-6: Bluegrass arrangement of "Boil Them Cabbage Down" (Audio Track 64).

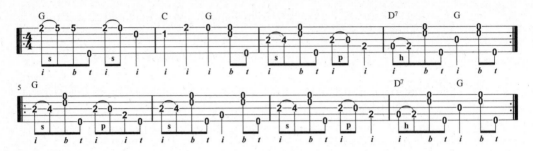

Tab 7-7: Clawhammer arrangement of "Cripple Creek" (Audio Track 65).

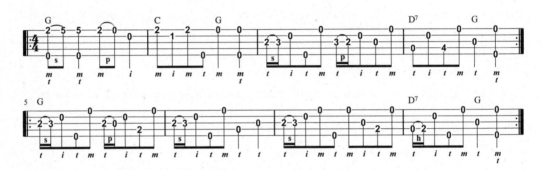

Tab 7-8: Bluegrass arrangement of "Cripple Creek" (Audio Track 66).

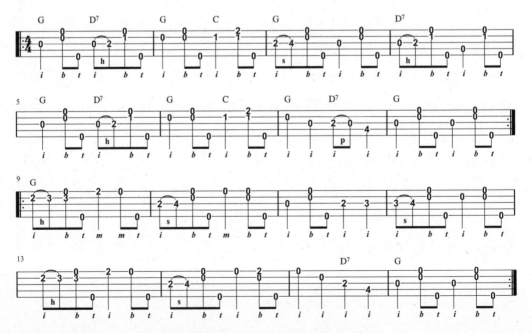

Tab 7-9: Clawhammer arrangement of "Goodbye Liza Jane" (Audio Track 67).

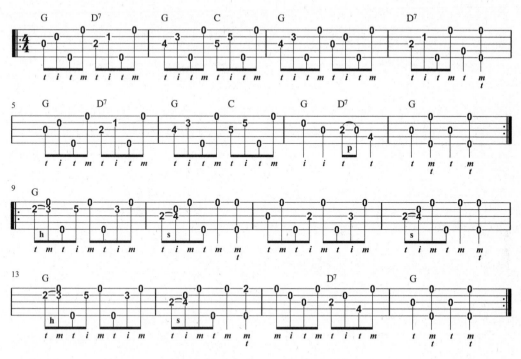

Tab 7-10: Bluegrass arrangement of "Goodbye Liza Jane" (Audio Track 68).

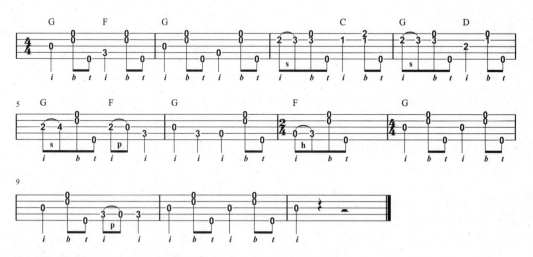

Tab 7-11: Clawhammer arrangement of "Ground Hog" (Audio Track 69).

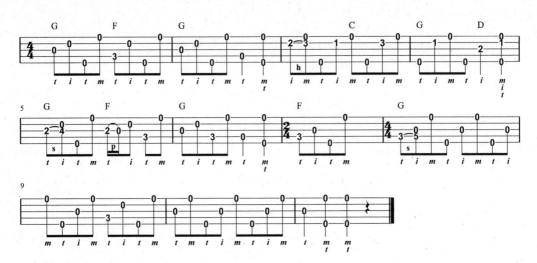

Tab 7-12: Bluegrass arrangement of "Ground Hog" (Audio Track 70).

Part III
Playing Styles Past, Present, and Future

Check out a crash course on the essentials of Scruggs, melodic, and single-string blue-grass styles at www.dummies.com/extras/banjo.

In this part...

- Dig deeper into clawhammer and bluegrass styles with more advanced playing techniques and 18 classic songs.

- Discover the most popular old-time banjo tunings and try them out on classic tunes.

- Venture deep into bluegrass territory with Scruggs rolls, licks, and tunes.

- Explore the world of contemporary bluegrass banjo with melodic and single-string styles and songs.

- Go back in time to try your hand at 19th and early 20th century minstrel and classic banjo songs.

- Explore accompaniment techniques you can use in jam sessions.

Chapter 8

Playing the Old-Time Way: Clawhammer and Traditional Styles

. . . .

In This Chapter

▶ Exploring advanced clawhammer techniques

▶ Adding some classic jamming tunes to your repertoire

▶ Getting acquainted with Pete Seeger's banjo style

▶ Playing two finger-picking classics

▶ Access the audio tracks and video clips at www.dummies.com/go/banjo

. . . .

*W*hen you put the words *old-time* and *banjo* together, the first thing that may come to mind is a picturesque log cabin tucked in a Southern mountain landscape with an old man in overalls playing banjo on the front porch, a milk cow just outside the front door, and a jug of moonshine close at hand. These days, however, you're just as likely to hear the sounds of old-time banjo ringing from a concert stage in the hands of Steve Martin or the Carolina Chocolate Drops; or find it at the center of a young, hipster acoustic jam in Brooklyn, San Francisco, or London; or hear it at one of the many old-time music gatherings that occur each year all over the world.

Old-time banjo is the fastest growing banjo style on the planet for lots of good reasons. The basic techniques are easy and fun to learn, and it's a great way to play the banjo while singing. In old-time music, which usually combines the sound of the banjo with the fiddle, guitar, and mandolin, everyone often plays melodies at the same time, and this allows players of different experience levels to sound great together. Once you master a few old-time moves, you'll soon be able to experience a profound, life-altering experience: the outrageous joy of playing music with others. It's better than moonshine!

Old-time banjo refers to several different ways of playing; this chapter acquaints you with three of the most important old-time approaches. You move beyond the clawhammer basics presented in Part II to play four jam session favorites that add new right- and left-hand techniques to your banjo picking toolbox. You also explore Pete Seeger's unique approach and try your hands at two old-time fingerpicking classics. Along the way, you mix and match in new ways many familiar techniques and discover the most widely used old-time banjo tunings. It's a good idea to review the songs and techniques presented in Chapters 5, 6, and 7 before starting down this chapter's old-time banjo road.

Digging Deeper into Clawhammer Banjo

Some banjo players call it *clawhammer* while others call it *frailing*. Out in the country, this banjo style has also been called rapping, beating, thumping, whomping, and my own personal favorite, knockdown banjo. With names like these, it's no wonder that hordes of rock and punk musicians are taking up the instrument! Whatever you like to call it, these colorful labels draw attention to the most important characteristic of clawhammer banjo: the right-hand fingers moving down across the strings. It's this driving, percussive sound that is the essence of the clawhammer style. From the moment you hear it, you want to get up and dance!

If you're brand new to clawhammer playing, I recommend heading back to Chapters 5, 6, and 7 to get acquainted with the essential elements of this style. These chapters help you find a comfortable right-hand playing position, and they present the basic playing techniques that come in handy for the more challenging tunes you tackle in this section.

It's time to work on two new techniques that are unique to clawhammer playing that you'll put to good use in many of the tunes presented in this chapter. The first concept focuses on left-hand pull-offs and the second introduces an essential right-hand picking pattern called *double thumbing*.

Fretting 1st-string clawhammer pull-offs

In Chapter 6, you master the left-hand open-string pull-off. Now you use that same skill in a way that's unique to clawhammer banjo. In this new technique, the left hand is the same as what you play for an open-string pull-off, but you don't pick the string with the right hand at all. It's only the motion of your left-hand finger that creates the note.

This kind of pull-off is played almost always on just the 1st string. Luckily, this technique is more difficult to describe than it is to play! Here's a step-by-step guide on how to execute this exclusively clawhammer-style pull-off:

1. **Touch the 1st string with your left-hand middle finger just below the 2nd fret.**

   You don't have to exert as much left-hand pressure as you need when you're fretting the string, but you do need to have enough contact with the string to create the sideways motion that you'll need for the pull-off.

2. **Without striking the string with the right hand, pull off the 1st string with the middle finger of your left hand, moving down with the finger away from the banjo neck.**

You hear just the sound of the open string. Because a note isn't actually fretted, many players simply grab the string with their left-hand finger (without actually bringing their finger all the way down to the fingerboard) and pull down from the 1st string away from the neck.

Tab 8-1 shows you an exercise to get the right hand flowing with these pull-offs. To begin, establish a steady rhythm by repeating the basic clawhammer stroke as many times as you need to until you can play it almost without thinking about it. Then add the 1st-string pull-off without changing your right-hand sequence or rhythm. You can hear this technique in Audio Track 71.

Tab 8-1: Playing 1st-string clawhammer pull-offs (Audio Track 71).

Stretching out with double thumbing

Double thumbing is an elaboration of the basic right-hand clawhammer technique that enables you to play on the inside strings with your thumb. The ability to do this probably doesn't mean very much to you right now, but double thumbing is a commonly used technique that expands your clawhammer possibilities and comes in handy for all kinds of songs. Like most other elements of clawhammer banjo, it's pretty easy to play after you practice. (Yes, future double thumbers, you have to practice! See Tab 8-2 to get started.)

When you double-thumb in clawhammer style, you're doubling the number of times you play notes with your right-hand thumb. You play not only the 5th string as you would in basic clawhammer style but also the 2nd and sometimes even the 3rd string with your thumb — hence the name *double* thumbing. Here's a step-by-step guide:

1. **Play the 1st string open with your right-hand index finger, moving down across the string.**

2. **Move your right-hand thumb down from its anchor spot against the 5th string and play the 2nd string, moving down across the string.**

3. **Repeat Step 1.**

4. **Play the 5th string with your right-hand thumb, moving down across the string.**

After you've mastered this basic double-thumbing move, try this same technique on the 3rd and 4th strings. When playing a real song, the thumb plays one string or another depending upon which string contains the note you want to hear. Check out double thumbing on Audio Track 72 and in Video Clip 26.

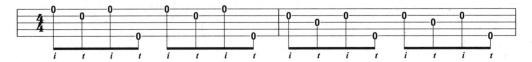

Tab 8-2: Playing double-thumbing patterns (Audio Track 72).

Discovering Four Clawhammer Classics

It's now time to use these new techniques to enhance your clawhammer banjo sound! In this section, you coax your fingers to attempt some favorite melodies that everyone will want to play with you at your next old-time jam session. You get moving with a double-thumbing workout with "Old Joe Clark" before retuning your banjo to C tuning to play the Scotch-Irish classic "Soldier's Joy." You retune once again to capture the high, lonesome sounds of "Cluck Old Hen" and finish up with the mysterious, deep, mountain tune "Last Chance."

Old-time banjo players pride themselves on coming up with their own versions of their favorite songs, using their ear to guide their fingers to the notes they want to play. Don't expect this kind of virtuosity right off the bat in your own playing. Musicians discover their own style by listening to many different players and blending the best of the sounds and techniques that they enjoy in others' playing. Memorizing my versions of these songs is fine, but feel free to discover your own ways of playing all old-time songs. It's the old-time way!

Check out video clips at www.dummies.com/go/banjo to observe me playing each song slowly. You can also download sound files online to take with you wherever you and your banjo may roam.

Playing "Old Joe Clark"

You can apply both the 1st-string pull-off and double-thumbing techniques to a tune that gets played just about every time old-time musicians get together. As you can see in Tab 8-3, "Old Joe Clark" begins with an ascending 1st-string melody line that gives way to a growly, low second section that features everyone's favorite — an F chord! If you're unfamiliar with the basic clawhammer technique that's used in this second section of the tune, head back to Chapter 5 for a tutorial in right-hand basics. Chapter 6 brings you up to speed on how to execute left-hand slides (marked with an *s* in tablature) and pull-offs (marked with a *p*); check out the F chord in Appendix A.

The double-thumbing technique is the perfect way to capture the climbing melody of the first section of "Old Joe Clark." Be sure you're comfortable playing the double-thumbing right-hand exercise (see the earlier section "Stretching out with double thumbing") before adding the 1st-string fretted notes you find in the first part of this arrangement.

The second part of "Old Joe Clark" adds 1st-string pull-offs to the basic clawhammer pattern. When you put together these new techniques for the first time in a song, always begin by playing each new phrase slowly, concentrating on the rhythm in the right hand. Don't worry about playing faster until you're completely comfortable with these new combinations at a slow tempo, and don't forget to listen to Audio Track 73 and take a look at Video Clip 27.

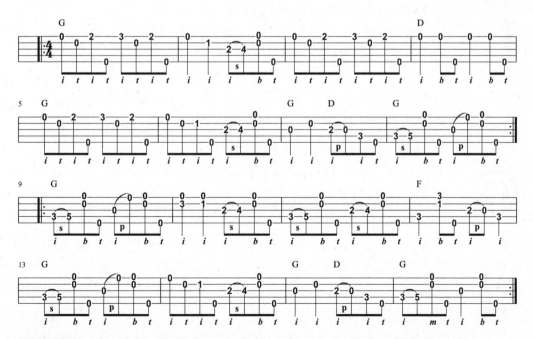

Tab 8-3: "Old Joe Clark," using double thumbing and 1st-string pull-off techniques (Audio Track 73).

Turning on to double C tuning

Old-time banjo players love to employ a variety of different banjo tunings to play songs in different keys. With each new tuning, unique combinations of open and fretted strings emerge, resulting in new sounds and playing possibilities. It's amazing how these tunings can create different emotions and moods in both players and listeners. The two most popular clawhammer banjo tunings are the G tuning used for "Old Joe Clark" and the double C tuning, where both the 2nd and 4th strings are tuned to a C note. You use this tuning for the old-time favorite "Soldier's Joy."

Using G tuning as a starting point, you put the banjo in C tuning by lowering the pitch of your 4th string the equivalent of two frets from D to C and raising the pitch of your 2nd string from B to C. Your 1st, 3rd, and 5th strings are the same in C and G tuning (see Chapter 2 if you need help getting your banjo into G tuning).

If your banjo is already in G tuning, lowering the 4th string from a D to a C is easy. Here's a step-by-step guide:

1. **Attach your electronic tuner to the banjo headstock.**

2. **Turn the peg on the 4th string in a counterclockwise direction until your electronic tuner indicates that you've lowered the pitch the equivalent of two frets from a D to a C.**

3. **Double-check your 4th string tuning.**

   Fret the 4th string at the 7th fret and compare the sound of this string with the open 3rd string. If both strings are in tune, your electronic tuner should indicate a G note.

Next, follow these simple steps to raise the 2nd string from a B to a C:

1. **Tighten the 2nd string peg by moving it in a counterclockwise motion until your tuner indicates that the string is sounding a C note, a change in pitch of one fret.**

2. **Double-check your 2nd string tuning.**

   Fret the 2nd string at the 2nd fret to compare the sound of this string with the open 1st string. If both strings are in tune, your tuner should indicate a D note.

As you turn each peg to retune, try striking the string with any right-hand finger to hear whether the pitch is going in the desired direction. By using your ear in addition to your electronic tuner, you refine your tuning ability, which is a very important skill in old-time banjo.

When you change the tension of one string by raising or lowering its pitch, don't be surprised to find that the adjacent strings on your banjo have now unfortunately gone out of tune. No worries. If that's the case, simply touch up the other strings so that your 3rd and 5th strings are tuned to G and the 1st string to D. Then double-check the 4th and 2nd strings to make sure that they're still holding the desired pitch.

From the 5th string to the 1st string, here's a summary of the pitches that you need for double C tuning:

5th string: G (highest-pitched string)

4th string: C (lowest-pitched string)

3rd string: G

2nd string: C

1st string: D

For double C tuning, as well as the other tunings featured in this section, you can hear me demonstrate the tuning before I play the song. As a companion to your own ear and your electronic tuner, listening to this demo is a great way to get your banjo into the different tunings you need for this section. ***Note:*** You're not cheating if you use an electronic tuner to help you retune the banjo. At an old-time jam session, almost all musicians use tuners as aids to their ears, so you can too!

Playing "Soldier's Joy"

Now that you're in double C tuning, you're ready to play "Soldier's Joy," one of the oldest tunes in all old-time music — and maybe the most frequently played. As shown in Tab 8-4, this is a straightforward arrangement that focuses on a clear presentation of the melody using the basic clawhammer techniques presented in Chapter 5. In addition to Audio Track 74, check out Video Clip 28.

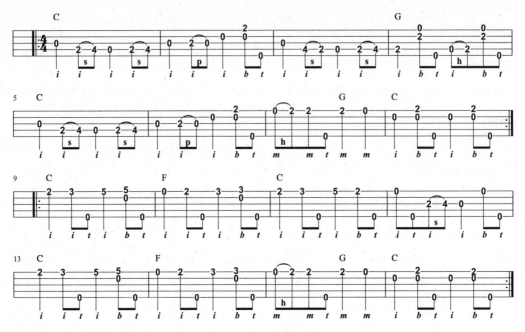

Tab 8-4: "Soldier's Joy," using double C tuning (Audio Track 74).

Moving into modal tuning

Banjo players just love to play haunting, lonesome tunes that sound like something that's just emerged from some deep Appalachian mountain holler. Old-time musicians often call these kinds of pieces *modal* tunes and banjo players have come up with a tuning that's perfect for capturing the special quality of these songs. In preparation for playing the clawhammer classic "Cluck Old Hen," you need to get your banjo into modal tuning.

If your banjo is already in G tuning, you only have to retune the 2nd string, raising the pitch one fret from a B to a C, to put your banjo into modal tuning. If your banjo happens to be in double C tuning, your 2nd string is already tuned to a C pitch. In this case, simply raise your 4th string two frets from a C to a D. Your other strings are already in tune and ready to go!

To review, here are the pitches you need for modal tuning:

  5th string: G (highest-pitched string)

  4th string: D (lowest-pitched string)

  3rd string: G

  2nd string: C

  1st string: D

Playing "Cluck Old Hen"

"Cluck Old Hen," shown in Tab 8-5, begins with something new: a downward right-hand index finger brush across the top three strings of your banjo, immediately followed by the thumb playing the 5th string. This technique is often called "The Galax Lick," after the small southwest Virginia town that hosts one of the oldest old-time music conventions in the world.

The key to playing the Galax lick is to move across the 3rd, 2nd, and 1st strings in an even rhythm as you play the right-hand-index brush stroke. Check out my Audio Track 75 and Video Clip 29 to hear how this technique should sound. After you get the hang of this technique, you'll find uses for it in many other tunes.

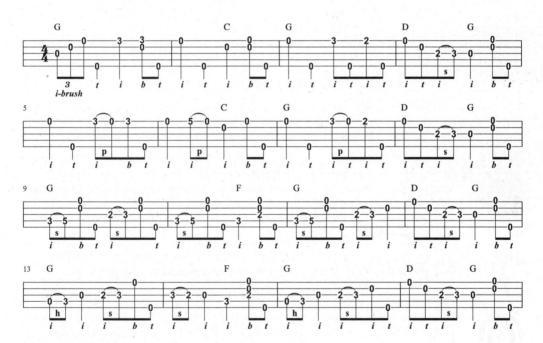

Tab 8-5: "Cluck Old Hen," using modal tuning (Audio Track 75).

Playing "Last Chance"

It's now time to head to the outer edge of lonesome with "Last Chance," a tune associated with the Saltville, Virginia, musician Hobart Smith (1897–1965). "Last Chance" has all the eccentric qualities that old-time banjo players love: its own *very* unusual tuning (called "Last Chance" tuning, oddly enough), a super mournful melody, and a quirky, irregular structure that qualifies it as a *crooked tune,* which is defined as a song that has an uneven number of beats. Heck, it's even got a lonesome title!

Looking into "Last Chance" tuning

You want to have your electronic tuner close at hand for this tuning, because you have to adjust four of the five strings of your banjo. Here's a step-by-step guide, starting from standard G tuning with the five strings tuned to G-D-G-B-D:

1. **Tune your 3rd string down two frets from G to F.**

2. **Tune your 5th string down two frets from G to F.**

   Note that your 5th string should sound the same note as the 3rd string but one octave higher.

3. **Tune your 2nd string up one fret from B to C.**

4. **Tune your 4th string down two frets from D to C.**

Here are the pitches you need for "Last Chance" tuning:

   5th string: F (two frets down from G)

   4th string: C

   3rd string: F (two frets down from G)

   2nd string: C (one fret up from B)

   1st string: D

Although an electronic tuner is a great help, it's always best to use your ear. Tuning by ear takes practice, just like any other playing technique, but you'll be amazed at how much better you'll be able to hear once you start listening (my wife tells me this all the time, by the way)!

Catching a crooked tune

Try tapping your foot along to "Last Chance" in Video Clip 30 or Audio Track 76. If you're like most folks, you'll feel an uneven number of beats in the rhythm at the very end, just before the tune repeats. It sounds as if the tune starts over again too soon, doesn't it? A crooked tune gives you the feeling that a couple of beats have either been added or taken out, and that's the case with "Last Chance."

Now take a look at the tab for "Last Chance" (see Tab 8-6). Note that the time signature at the beginning of the written music indicates 4/4, but at the very last measure, the time signature changes to 2/4. (If you're having trouble remembering about time signatures, head back to Chapter 4 for a quick review.) It's as if two beats have been taken away from that last measure! However, this feature is a central attraction of "Last Chance," and it's an important element of how the tune is supposed to be played.

Many thanks to Mac Benford, who I heard play this tune many years ago at the American Banjo Camp in Washington. Mac came up with his version after listening to Hobart Smith's version, and my version shown here is based on Mac's — such is the old-time way! You listen to someone's playing you admire and come up with a version that you can play that sounds good to you.

Tab 8-6: "Last Chance," a crooked tune using "Last Chance" tuning (Audio Track 76).

Discovering Pete Seeger–Style Banjo

Pete Seeger has been getting people excited about playing the banjo for over 70 years now. He's one of the most eclectic banjo players on the planet, playing a wide variety of music from all over the world on the instrument. In 1948, he authored the first-ever banjo instructional book, *How to Play the 5-String Banjo,* and this amazing book (published by Pete himself) is still in print today. The style that bears his name is just one of many ways that Pete plays the banjo, and although he's the musician most responsible for popularizing this playing technique, he didn't invent it. Seeger style is a widely played variation on clawhammer technique that he likely first heard North Carolina old-time musician Samantha Bumgarner play back in 1935. Pete probably liked what he heard, learned to play Samantha's way, and soon after popularized this technique among players all over the world.

Syncing with the Seeger stroke

Sometimes, just a slight variation in playing technique leads musicians to view a particular way of playing as a distinct style. Pete's right-hand approach is very similar to standard clawhammer banjo but with one crucial difference: The right-hand-index melody note is picked up instead of played in a downward motion across the melody note string as in clawhammer banjo. (Head back to Chapter 5 for a refresher course on up- and down-picking and the basic clawhammer stroke.)

More than a few old-time players prefer this way of playing to the all-down stroke method of conventional clawhammer banjo, and there's no question that it's possible for experienced players to play really, really *fast* using this technique (and what's not to love about that?). My advice is to give Pete's variation a try and see whether it works for you, keeping in mind that most players today are completely happy using the more conventional clawhammer technique that's fully explained in Chapter 5.

Here's a step-by-step guide to the Seeger stroke:

1. **Pick up (not down!) with the right-hand index finger, either on the 1st, 2nd, 3rd, or 4th string, as indicated in the tablature.**

   The index finger in this case is moving up toward the 5th string.

2. **Brush down with the right-hand middle finger across the top three strings, as in conventional clawhammer technique.**

   You can brush all three strings, just the top two strings, or even just the 1st string by itself. Play what sounds good to you!

3. **Strike the 5th string with your right-hand thumb, moving across the string as in conventional clawhammer playing.**

Check out Tab 8-7 as well as Audio Track 77 and Video Clip 31 to get familiar with Pete's unique old-time banjo style. It takes some getting used to but once you get the hang of it, you'll likely find it to be a fun-to-play variation on basic clawhammer technique.

Tab 8-7: Seeger's basic strum, picking up with the right-hand index finger (Audio Track 77).

Playing "Swing Low" and "Little Birdie" with the Seeger stroke

When you're comfortable with the basic Seeger stroke, you can apply it to two tunes, "Swing Low, Sweet Chariot" and "Little Birdie," shown in Tabs 8-8 and 8-9 and recorded on Audio Tracks 78 and 79, respectively. A great way to familiarize yourself with a new technique is to use it on a melody that you already know, which I'm hoping is the case with "Swing Low, Sweet Chariot." "Little Birdie" is an old-time vocal favorite, often played in the key of C. The chorus lyrics are "Little birdie, little birdie/Come and sing to me your song/I've a short time to stay here/And a long time to be gone." Ralph Stanley has recorded several great versions of this classic.

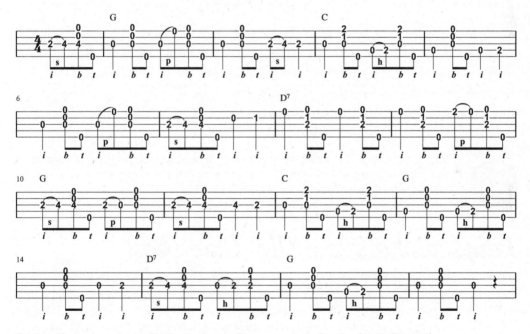

Tab 8-8: "Swing Low, Sweet Chariot," using the Seeger stroke in G tuning (Audio Track 78).

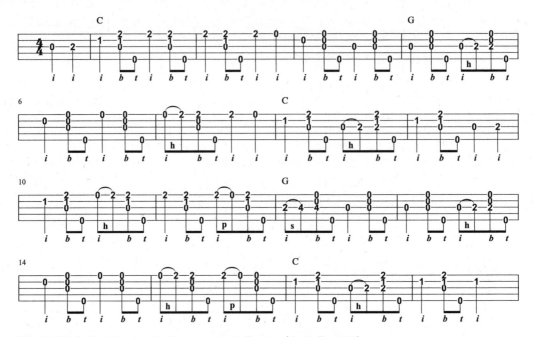

Tab 8-9: "Little Birdie," using the Seeger stroke in G tuning (Audio Track 79).

TIP

Note that both of these tunes can also be played using conventional clawhammer technique by just moving downward across the melody note string with the right-hand index finger, instead of picking up.

Fingerpicking the Old-Time Way

Old-time banjo isn't just clawhammer style. It also includes a wide variety of fingerpicking techniques that were played by old-time musicians before Earl Scruggs developed his bluegrass style in the mid-1940s. Today, most old-time musicians prefer to use their bare fingers when fingerpicking rather than using the metal fingerpicks and plastic thumbpick that bluegrass players almost always use. Whether you use picks or not, head back to Chapter 5 and brush up on bluegrass right-hand basics, because you use these same hand positions and basic techniques for playing old-time fingerpicking styles.

Exploring Dock Boggs's style with "Pretty Polly"

Southwest Virginia musician and coal miner Dock Boggs (1898–1971) is one of the most revered banjo players in old-time music, with a unique style that reflects the influence of both Southern Anglo-American and African-American blues styles. His 1927 version of the old English ballad "Pretty Polly" (featuring Polly and the always-nefarious Willie, who seems to be the perpetrator of many of the ill deeds documented in English balladry) is relatively easy to play, once you figure out Dock's unique tuning for this song! Here's a step-by-step guide, starting from standard G tuning:

1. **Lower the 2nd string two frets from B to A.**

   To double-check your tuning, fret the 2nd string at the 5th fret. The 2nd and 1st string should now sound the same, and the reading on your electronic tuner should be a D note, the pitch of your open 1st string.

2. **Lower the 5th string one fret from G to F♯.**

   To double-check your tuning, fret and pick the 1st string at the 4th fret. The sound of your open 5th string should now be the same as your 1st string at the 4th fret.

The remaining three strings are the same as in G tuning. Here's the complete tuning for Dock Boggs's "Pretty Polly":

5th string: F♯ (one fret down from G)

4th string: D

3rd string: G

2nd string: A (two frets down from B)

1st string: D

PLAY THIS!

Take a look at the tab to "Pretty Polly" in Tab 8-10. The second full measure is Dock's basic right-hand stroke. Try practicing this over and over again until it's flowing before tackling the entire tune. You can hear it played on Audio Track 80.

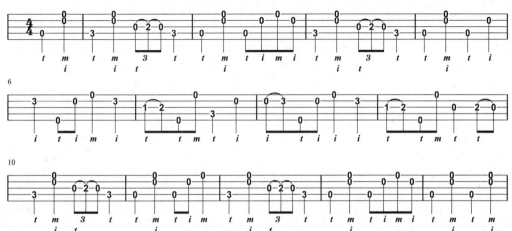

Tab 8-10: "Pretty Polly," using old-time fingerpicking techniques (Audio Track 80).

Picking "Coal Creek March"

Like Dock Boggs, Kentucky and Ohio banjo player Pete Steele worked in the coal mines. His classic "Coal Creek March" was recorded in 1938 by folklorist Alan Lomax and has been an old-time fingerpicking standard ever since. It should come as no surprise by now that you need to put your banjo in yet another new tuning. "Coal Creek March" is usually played in D tuning, where the banjo is tuned to the pitches of a D major chord. This tuning is also used by bluegrass players, so it's definitely worth checking out. Here's a step-by-step guide with your banjo already in G tuning:

1. **Tune the 2nd string down two frets from B to A.**

2. **Tune the 3rd string down one fret from G to F♯.**

3. **Tune the 5th string down one fret from G to F♯.**

The 1st and 4th strings are the same as in G tuning. Here's how all of your strings should be tuned for D tuning:

5th string: F♯ (one fret down from G)

4th string: D

3rd string: F♯ (one fret down from G)

2nd string: A (two frets down from B)

1st string: D

As recorded by Pete Steele, "Coal Creek March" has an unusual pattern of repetition. Taking a look at the tab in Tab 8-11, you see that I labeled the tune's three sections with the letters A, B, and C. To play the tune once through completely in the way that Pete usually performs it, you want to play the piece in this order: A–B–C–B. Don't forget to check out Audio Track 81 and Video Clip 32 to watch me play this great piece!

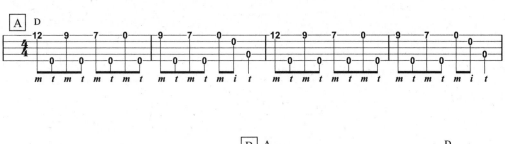

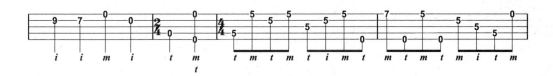

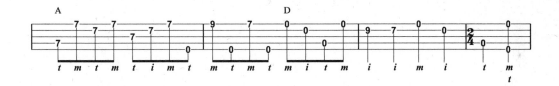

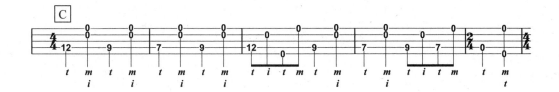

Tab 8-11: "Coal Creek March," from Pete Steele, using old-time fingerpicking techniques (Audio Track 81).

Chapter 9

Playing Three-Finger Styles: Scruggs, Melodic, and Single String

. . . .

In This Chapter

▶ Getting deeper into Scruggs-style banjo

▶ Branching out with melodic style

▶ Discovering single-string style banjo

▶ Using three-finger techniques together

▶ Access the audio tracks and video clips at www.dummies.com/go/banjo

. . . .

*F*rom bluegrass to jazz, country, classical, folk, and rock, the banjo is right at home in all kinds of music today (okay, maybe not Wagnerian opera or the latest Psy video . . . not yet, anyway!). Three-finger style (where you use the thumb, index, and middle fingers of the right hand to strike the strings) is the playing technique that's being used to blaze many new banjo trails these days.

Three-finger banjo is usually associated with the bluegrass banjo style that was first developed by North Carolina banjo player Earl Scruggs. Earl Scruggs's banjo style is based around capturing the melody using right-hand roll patterns that create a bold, fast flurry of notes. Scruggs ushered in a banjo revolution in the mid-1940s when he introduced this technique to bluegrass and country music. Scruggs style is one of the most emulated playing styles in the world — on any instrument — and has truly become a universal way of playing music on the banjo (yes, if aliens were to take up the banjo, they would probably try Scruggs style — it's that good!).

Succeeding generations of players have built on Earl's contributions to come up with new three-finger possibilities that continue to expand the musical potential of the banjo. Melodic and single-string styles are the most important of these innovations. Both approaches enable you to more easily use scales in your playing (*scales* are the collections of notes you use to play melodies). In *melodic style,* you play scales and melodies by using roll patterns that are similar to those used in Scruggs style. With *single-string* playing, you use a right-hand technique that enables you to play notes on the same string consecutively when needed, much like guitar and mandolin players do when playing with their flatpicks.

To play the Scruggs, melodic, and single-string styles I describe in this chapter, you use a thumbpick and two fingerpicks on your fingers as well as the right-hand position favored by bluegrass players. If you're new to the banjo, you may want to visit Chapter 5 to get a feel for these topics before jumping into the great music that awaits you here.

Playing Scruggs-Style Banjo

Overestimating the contribution of Earl Scruggs to the world of the banjo is impossible. Although other players used three-finger techniques before him, Scruggs took this way of playing the banjo and perfected it, literally creating an entirely new musical vocabulary for the banjo that enabled him to both play blazing-fast solos and accompany others in a bluegrass band. (To read more about Earl Scruggs's life and music, check out Chapter 17.)

Scruggs style is practically synonymous with bluegrass-banjo style. If your goal is to someday play banjo in a bluegrass band, you need to soak in as much of Earl's playing as you can. Scruggs-style banjo is also an essential foundation for playing melodic and single-string styles, and Earl's techniques are also great to use when accompanying others. If you want to play any three-finger style that uses fingerpicks, you just about have to get into Earl!

Some great fun lies ahead! In the following sections, you discover the right-hand patterns used in Scruggs-style banjo and use these patterns to play short, interchangeable phrases called *licks* by using left-hand slides, hammer-ons, and pull-offs. You then combine these phrases to play full-length banjo solos and songs in Scruggs style.

Flowing with the rolls

Much of Scruggs-style playing is based around *roll patterns* — right-hand sequences of notes that crop up again and again when playing in this style. Roll patterns are made up of eight notes played by the right-hand thumb, index, and middle fingers. As a general rule, you use a different right-hand finger to strike a different string for each consecutive note when playing a roll pattern (in other words, you don't want to use the same right-hand finger or hit the same string twice in a row). This way of playing creates a smooth and constant flow of notes and is a big part of what make Scruggs-style banjo sound so great.

I include the most important roll patterns used in Scruggs-style playing in the following list, which you can see in Tab 9-1. Players often categorize rolls by the sequence of right-hand notes played (using *T* for thumb, *I* for index, and *M* for middle), along with the string sequence used (with numbers standing for each of the five strings on your banjo), which is what I do here:

- ✔ **Alternating thumb roll:** The right-hand sequence of this roll is T-I-T-M-T-I-T-M. Use this sequence with the following string order: 3-2-5-1-4-2-5-1.

- ✔ **Forward-reverse roll:** This roll's right-hand sequence is T-I-M-T-M-I-T-M and uses a string order of 3-2-1-5-1-2-3-1. Note that this roll begins like the alternating thumb roll but moves in a new direction with the third note you play.

- ✔ **Forward roll:** This roll is very exciting to play in bluegrass banjo. You can play with more power if you kick off the roll by using your right-hand thumb, as indicated in the tab's right-hand sequence: T-M-T-I-M-T-I-M. This example uses the following order of strings: 2-1-5-2-1-5-2-1.

- ✔ **The "lick" roll:** This is the roll you use for the most frequently played *fill-in lick* phrase in bluegrass banjo (see the next section for a full explanation). This roll starts with the same sequence of right-hand notes that you use in the forward roll but then shifts to the sequence used in the last four notes of the forward-reverse roll: T-M-T-I-M-I-T-M. The string order for this example is 3-1-5-3-1-3-5-1.

- ✔ **Foggy Mountain roll:** Yes, this is the roll used to play the first measures of "Foggy Mountain Breakdown"! Be careful to play the first four notes of this roll correctly: Begin with the right-hand index finger striking the 2nd string and the middle finger playing the 1st string but then be sure to use the thumb to strike the next 2nd string. This approach provides you with more speed and power as you get comfortable playing this roll. The right-hand sequence is I-M-T-M-T-I-M-T, playing these strings: 2-1-2-1-5-2-1-5.

- ✔ **Backward roll:** This roll begins with the middle finger and moves backward towards the 5th string. Note the right-hand sequence for this roll: M-I-T-M-I-T-M-I. The strings indicated in the tab example are 1-2-5-1-2-5-2-1. You often use this roll when the melody note is on the 1st string of your banjo.

- ✔ **Middle-leading roll:** As you may have guessed, you use the middle finger a lot in this roll pattern as revealed in the right-hand sequence: M-I-M-T-M-I-M-T. The strings you play in this example are 1-2-1-5-1-2-1-5. This roll is also called the Osborne roll after banjo great Sonny Osborne.

- ✔ **Index-leading roll:** This roll begins with the right-hand index finger playing the 2nd string. The right-hand sequence for this roll is I-T-I-M-I-T-I-M. The strings played in this example are 2-3-2-1-2-3-2-1.

Listen to Audio Track 82 to hear the sound of each roll and to double-check your playing against these tab examples.

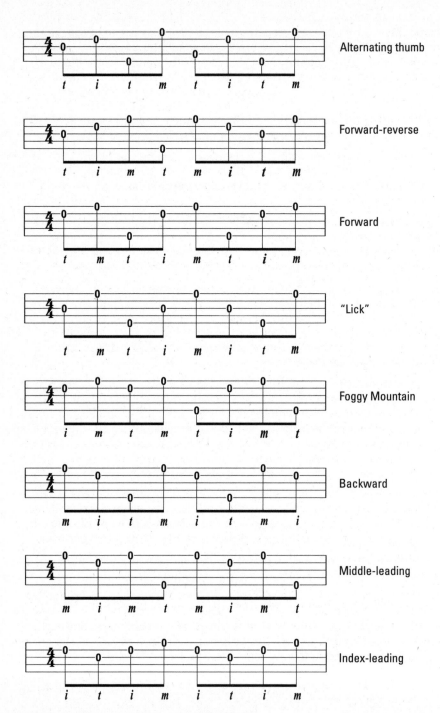

Tab 9-1: Scruggs-style roll patterns (Audio Track 82).

Practice these rolls until they become second nature. You can then cover ground much faster when you encounter these roll patterns in actual tunes. A great way to internalize these patterns quickly is to use them as an accompaniment to your favorite songs. After you're comfortable with the chord progression of any song, you can play any of these rolls to accompany a guitarist or singer. Each roll pattern takes up one measure in a chord progression. Try as many as you can, settling on what sounds best to you (and feel free to return to Chapter 3 for a review of chord progressions).

Making your music hot with some licks

In Chapter 6, I show you how to add left-hand slides, hammer-ons, and pull-offs to the right-hand roll patterns to begin making some real banjo music. Scruggs-style playing is based around creating music that uniquely combines these elements. As you listen to and play pieces in this style, you may begin to notice short phrases that appear in more than one tune. These phrases, called *licks*, are the building blocks of Scruggs-style banjo. In the following sections, you can figure out what licks are and how to play them Scruggs-style.

Figuring out the basics about licks

A short phrase that can be lifted out of one tune and played in another is called a *lick* (a *hot lick* is a particularly great-sounding phrase that is perfectly acceptable to play in public or even in front of your parents). Licks are used in melodic and single-string playing as well, but are especially at home in Scruggs style. Licks make your playing sound more interesting and varied and are essential elements to improvising on the banjo.

You can sometimes use licks as part of a melody, but often licks stand by themselves as good things to play on the banjo even when they aren't necessarily related to the melody of the song that's being played. Becoming comfortable integrating licks into melodies and knowing which licks can be used at what points in a song takes a lot of hours of hands-on playing experience and a lot of listening to other good banjo players.

To get started on your journey to becoming a great bluegrass player, all you need to do is play as much as possible, have an open mind, keep it fun, and try as many different things as your practice time allows. Really, the only mistake you can make is to *stop* playing! The more time you devote to playing, the more everything falls into place.

Using licks in your playing

Licks are almost always associated with chords. For example, you play G licks at that part of the song where the accompaniment is a G chord; you use C licks when everyone else is playing a C chord, and so on.

Each lick is a bit different, depending on which chord goes along with it and the specific roll patterns and left-hand techniques you use. When you encounter a new lick in tablature, do the following:

1. **Figure out the right-hand pattern indicated in the tab and practice this by itself until it sounds steady and solid.**

   If you can memorize the right-hand sequence as you play, all the better!

2. **Add whatever left-hand techniques the tab shows (slides, hammer-ons, or pull-offs) while maintaining a solid rhythm in your right hand.**

The best way to figure out whether a lick works in a particular place in a song is to try it and see what happens. You usually know pretty quickly whether you've played something that works by the expressions on the faces of the other musicians around you! And for the songs in this book, don't forget to listen to the corresponding audio tracks, check out the video clips, and aim to match your sound to what you hear and see me play.

By listening to Audio Tracks 83, 84, and 85 (and using Tabs 9-2, 9-3, and 9-4), play a group of essential licks for the G, C, and D chords — the three most frequently played chords in bluegrass banjo music. These phrases pop up time and again in the playing of Earl Scruggs, Sonny Osborne, and other bluegrass masters.

The process of adding licks to your musical vocabulary is a lot like adding new words and phrases when mastering a foreign language. In both cases, you expand the range of your expression as you internalize new things to say and new ways of saying them. After a lot of practice, you can combine licks into original phrases and come up with your own unique musical thoughts.

Tab 9-2: G licks (Audio Track 83).

Tab 9-3: C licks (Audio Track 84).

Tab 9-4: D licks (Audio Track 85).

Incorporating fill-in licks

A special kind of lick that's frequently played at the end of a banjo solo or used in accompaniment when a singer takes a breath or pauses between the lines of a song is called a *fill-in lick*. This lick is especially useful to have in your grab bag of banjo tricks.

To play fill-in licks, you utilize the same techniques and roll patterns that you use for regular licks (see the preceding sections). However, fill-in licks tend to pack more left-hand techniques into the same amount of musical space as a regular lick and, for this reason, can be more challenging to play.

By playing Tab 9-5 (and listening to Audio Track 86), you can get a feel for the four common fill-in licks that you use when you return to the G chord at the end of a tune's chord progression. You use at least one of these fill-in licks just about every time you play a song in the key of G.

Tab 9-5: Four common G fill-in licks (Audio Track 86).

Combining licks to play a solo

You can build entire solos by stringing licks together. Although you probably won't be able to capture much of the melody of a song this way, following one lick with another is a great survival strategy to use in a jam session as you fake your way through a song that you don't really know. Don't forget to make sure that your lick matches the chord that everyone else is playing!

You can see how this strategy works by creating a solo from the licks I present in the previous two sections. You can see (and play) it for yourself in Tab 9-6 (Audio Track 87). The chord progression is an eight-measure cycle made up of two measures of G, followed by two measures of C, and then two measures of D, ending with two measures of G.

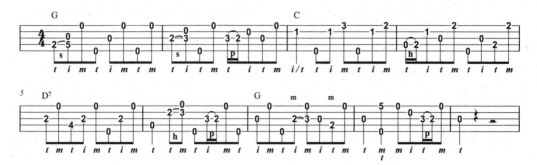

Tab 9-6: Creating a solo by combining licks (Audio Track 87).

Progressing to Scruggs-style songs

As you gain confidence playing licks and combining them to create longer phrases, you eventually want to use the licks you know to create and enhance the melodies of songs. The following two tunes show you just how you can do this.

"Everyday Breakdown"

Because this song is made up of a number of essential two-measure phrases commonly used for the G, C, and D chords, "Everyday Breakdown" can get you started in your quest to create longer phrases and play entire songs by combining licks.

Many bluegrass banjo solos begin with a short, characteristic phrase that propels you into the main melody. These phrases are called *kickoffs.* "Everyday Breakdown," which you can see in Tab 9-7 (Audio Track 88 and Video Clip 33), uses a three-note kickoff that also works with "Foggy Mountain Breakdown."

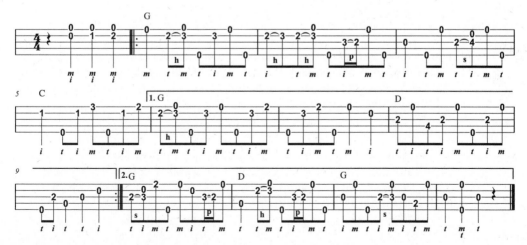

Tab 9-7: Playing "Everyday Breakdown," composed by me (Audio Track 88).

"Shortening Bread"

Take a look at my arrangement of a melody that Earl Scruggs played often on radio and television broadcasts in the 1950s and '60s. "Shortening Bread" is the familiar melody you may have first heard as a child ("Mama's little baby loves shortening, shortening/Mama's little baby loves shortening bread").

Sometimes trying to capture the melody of a song in the simplest and most elegant way possible is best — something that Earl Scruggs seemed to do with ease just about all the time. I've tried to continue in Scruggs's footsteps with my arrangement of "Shortening Bread" in Tab 9-8 (Audio Track 89).

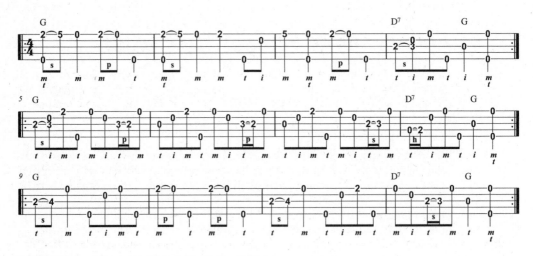

Tab 9-8: Playing "Shortening Bread" (Audio Track 89).

Making Music with Melodic Banjo

Although Scruggs style (see the preceding section) is just about the most logical and ingenious technique ever created to play music on the banjo, you unfortunately can't play *everything* in this way. Because you strike a different string with each roll note in Scruggs style, playing note-for-note versions of a melody that happens to contain lots of consecutive notes adjacent to one another is the one thing that's next to impossible using Scruggs style.

In the early 1960s, bluegrass banjo players Bill Keith and Bobby Thompson were independently working on solving this problem as they tried to find a way to play fiddle tunes more easily in a three-finger style on the banjo. These musicians came up with a new way of playing scales on the banjo called *melodic banjo*, where a different string is picked with each successive note, as in roll pattern–based styles of playing.

Melodic banjo is great to use as an addition to Scruggs style within bluegrass. This way of playing, which I describe in the following sections, gives you a new set of three-finger tools that you can apply to all kinds of music and also use in improvising. In addition to playing complex melodies with this approach, you can create virtuosic improvisations that rival the best work of any jazz improviser!

Melodic-style banjo is a real attention getter and is great for playing melodies that can't easily be played using Scruggs style and for improvising. However, when it comes time to play with others, you should rely on the roll patterns and techniques used in Scruggs style to provide the most appropriate accompaniment (check out Chapter 10 for great Scruggs-style accompaniment ideas).

Discovering how to play melodic scales

Although Scruggs style uses right-hand roll patterns as the basic building blocks of banjo technique, *melodic banjo* is based on finding and playing scales up and down the neck.

In Chapter 4, I locate all the notes for the G-major scale on the first five frets of the banjo (so if you want some additional scale info, you may want to turn to that chapter). In this section, instead of labeling the notes with the syllables "do-re-mi" as the Von Trapp Family Singers might do, I'm more scientific and assign numbers to each step of the scale, with the number 1 indicating your starting point on the G note, as shown in Tab 9-9.

Tab 9-9: Assigning numbers to the notes in the G-major scale.

Note in Tab 9-9 how many consecutive scale notes are located on the same string (for instance, scale notes three and four are both on the 2nd string while scale notes five, six, seven, and eight are all on the 1st string). With the melodic banjo approach, you play the same pitches, but you locate each consecutive note on a different string, using a different right-hand picking finger to play each string, as you can see in the following sections.

Beginning with the melodic banjo G-major scale

The secret to playing a melodic banjo G-major scale is to relocate the fretted notes in Tab 9-9 to a lower string on your banjo (these are notes two, four, six, and seven of the G-major scale). You can then play different strings consecutively as you climb up the scale, using right-hand roll patterns that are related to Scruggs's rolls.

For example, the second note of the G scale (called an A note) is not only found on the 2nd fret of the 3rd string, but also at the 7th fret of the 4th string. The fourth note of the G scale, the C note, is at the 1st fret of the 2nd string, but you can also find it at the 5th fret of the 3rd string. Playing these fretted notes on a lower string allows you to play a different string and can make your playing sound smoother and more flowing.

To play a G-major scale using melodic banjo technique, do the following:

1. **Pick the 3rd string open with the right-hand index finger.**

   You're playing the G note: the first note of the G-major scale.

2. **Fret the 4th string at the 7th fret with the left-hand ring finger and pick this string with your right-hand thumb.**

   This note is an A note, the second note of the G-major scale.

3. **Pick the 2nd string open with the right-hand index finger.**

   In this step, you play the third note of the G-major scale, the B note.

4. **Fret the 3rd string at the 5th fret with the left-hand index finger and pick this string with the right-hand thumb.**

   You're playing the fourth note of the G-major scale, which is the C note.

5. **Pick the 1st string open with the right-hand middle finger.**

   You play the D note, the fifth note of the G-major scale, in this step.

6. **Fret the 2nd string at the 5th fret with the left-hand middle finger and pick this string with the right-hand index finger.**

   Here you play an E note, and if you've been counting, you know that this is the sixth note of the G-major scale.

7. **Fret the 1st string at the 4th fret with the left-hand index finger and pick this string with the right-hand middle finger.**

   This note is an F♯ note — the seventh note of the G-major scale.

8. **Play the 5th string open with the right-hand thumb.**

   You're playing a G note that is one octave higher than the G note found on your open 3rd string.

The right-hand index finger does a lot of work in melodic banjo, so make sure you're playing these notes with good volume and power. In the left hand, you can add speed to your fingering if you release each fretting finger soon after striking the note with the right hand. This allows the left hand to get ready for the next fretted position.

Tab 9-10 shows you how you can play the G-major scale using melodic banjo technique. You can follow the left-hand fingering indications by looking at the lowercase letters above the tab staff (*i* stands for index, *m* for middle, *r* for ring, and *p* for the pinky finger).

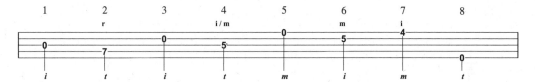

Tab 9-10: Playing the G-major scale using melodic banjo techniques.

The trickiest aspect of melodic technique on this part of the banjo fingerboard is getting used to the idea of playing a higher-sounding fretted note on a lower-pitched string. Practicing a good bit to work melodic scales into your motor memory can really come in handy. After you've internalized the fingerboard "route," you won't think about how unusual playing a scale this way really is!

Getting acquainted with more scales

Although getting comfortable with the G-major scale first is best (see the preceding section), sooner or later you need to play scales that start on other notes. If you keep in mind that the principle behind melodic banjo is to find an adjacent scale note on a different string, you can figure out and play many different scales using the melodic approach.

For example, to play a melodic banjo C-major scale, you start on the 5th fret, 3rd string. The next note (D) is the open 1st string. Although you can play the following scale note (E) on the 2nd fret of the 1st string, playing this note on the 5th fret of the 2nd string is better in melodic banjo. The next note of the C-major scale is an F note, and you can find it on the 3rd fret, 1st string. The open 5th string is the next note (G) in the C-major scale.

The last three notes of the C-major scale are A, B, and C and require you to fret notes above the 5th fret. Because you just played the open 5th string, the best choice for the A note is the 2nd string, 10th fret; followed by a 9th fret, 1st string for the B note; and a 10th fret, 5th string for the G, as shown in Tab 9-11.

Tab 9-11: Playing the C-major scale using melodic banjo techniques.

Melodic banjo playing up the neck often uses left-hand positions where you're not only fretting the 5th string, but also fretting two or three other strings with the left hand at the same time — not easy! Some players prefer to use their thumb to fret the 5th string in these situations, while others rely on their middle, ring, or pinky fingers, as needed. The finger (or thumb) you use then determines which left-hand fingers you use to fret the other strings in a melodic position. In the example in Tab 9-11, I've indicated two options above the tab staff. See which way works best for you!

Getting a feel for melodic banjo songs

Practicing scales familiarizes you with the basic moves you use in melodic style, but this isn't nearly as much fun as playing tunes that utilize this approach. As you branch out and apply melodic banjo techniques to your own arrangements, the following tips can help guide your choices of what to play:

- ✔ **Melodic style works best when you play melodies that have a lot of quick notes that are adjacent to one another in a scale.** Many fiddle tunes fit this description exactly, making this a great time to go melodic. Most vocal songs have melodies with longer notes and usually sound better with Scruggs-based playing.

- ✔ **The key of the song is directly related to the scales and licks you use.** For songs in the key of G, you can use the G-major scale to create melodic licks that also work for C and D chords. However, songs with more complex chord progressions sound better by using other scales that match the chords being played.

✔ **You can expand the possibilities of melodic banjo beyond just playing scales by applying roll-pattern ideas to the left-hand-fretted melodic positions to create impressive-sounding descending and ascending runs.** If you simply race up and down a major scale for any extended length of time, your music can become boring pretty quickly (for your listeners at least — I can personally do this all day and be as happy as a clam!). For more info on roll patterns, check out the section "Flowing with the rolls" earlier in this chapter. You can use roll patterns with melodic banjo in the song "Banjo Cascade" later in this section.

✔ **Melodic style is great for improvising too!** You have different melodic licks for different chords, just as in Scruggs style. Don't be afraid to play your favorite C (or G or D) melodic lick each time that chord comes around in whatever song you're playing (it may not always work, but you'll never know until you actually try it).

✔ **Try different left-hand fingerings, especially when using melodic techniques up the neck.** You usually have more than one way to play the same note sequence in melodic style. You can determine how to play a note largely by what your left hand needs to be fretting at that moment.

Coming up, you can try three tunes using the melodic approach. The first, "Banjo Cascade," is really more of an exercise to get you used to playing descending and ascending scale patterns. The second is the perennial favorite "Turkey in the Straw," and you finish off with the melodic banjo classic "Blackberry Blossom." Don't forget that the tabs indicate left-hand fingering above the staff, using lowercase letters, and right-hand fingering below the staff, using italics.

Enhancing melodic techniques with roll patterns: "Banjo Cascade"

Try your hand (or fingers) at "Banjo Cascade," a short song that explores some of these possibilities with a chord progression that moves from G to C to D by using forward and backward rolls (see Tab 9-12, which is Audio Track 90). These kinds of sounds are what three-finger players draw on when improvising over chord progressions in the melodic style. Note how the left hand shifts from one fretted position to another as you move down and then up the scale. Every now and then, it's great to pull in a note that's not in the major scale to suggest a transition to the next chords. That's what you'll find with the F note in measures 3, 11, and 12, which sounds great leading from the G to the C chord in this tune.

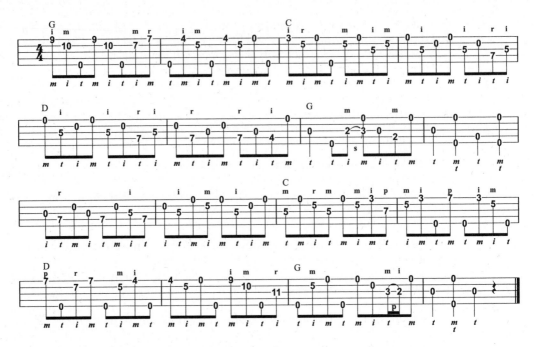

Tab 9-12: "Banjo Cascade" by yours truly (Audio Track 90).

Getting fancy with fiddle tunes: "Turkey in the Straw" and "Blackberry Blossom"

Fiddle tunes are a staple of any bluegrass jam session (especially if a fiddle is present!). Bluegrass and old-time musicians use the label *fiddle tune* to refer to a large body of instrumental pieces that may or may not have their actual origin as fiddle music. Regardless of the instrument you play, everyone loves to play fiddle tunes, and encountering many of them in jam sessions isn't unusual (you don't even have to have a fiddle in your jam session to play a fiddle tune, by the way).

Most fiddle tunes are made up of two sections with different melodies. Musicians usually repeat each section once before moving on to the next section (players sometimes describe this tune structure as an *AABB form*). Using melodic banjo technique for the first section and a more Scruggs-oriented approach for the tune's second half (see the section "Playing Scruggs-Style Banjo" for more info), try to work out the familiar fiddle tune "Turkey in the Straw."

In this version of "Turkey in the Straw," you use a lot of the fretted positions you encountered in "Banjo Cascade," and you also put in some laps running up and down the G-major scale (see Tab 9-13, which is Audio Track 91). When in doubt about the left-hand fingering, don't forget to look up for answers (not to the heavens, but above the tab staff).

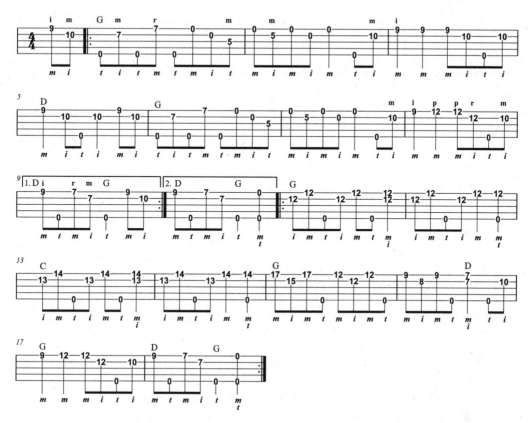

Tab 9-13: "Turkey in the Straw," arranged by me (Audio Track 91).

"Blackberry Blossom" gets played at just about every good bluegrass jam session. All instrumentalists love to play this one — fiddlers, mandolin players, and guitarists will jump at the chance to join you on this tune, so don't hesitate to give it a try. As you wrap your left-hand fingers around this melody (see Tab 9-14 and check out Audio Track 92 and Video Clip 34), take notice that that you're once again fretting many of the same positions you encountered in the previous two tunes. This is to be expected because all three of these tunes are in the key of G. Two of the most striking characteristics of "Blackberry" are the fast-moving chord progression in the tune's first section and the lonesome-sounding E minor chords played in the tune's second part (check out Appendix A for a cornucopia of banjo chords, including the ever-popular E minor!).

In a jam session or band, musicians take turn playing solos. While you're waiting until it's your time to shine (which you get to do up to two or three times per song, usually), you need to be a worthy support player, helping the other musicians to sound good as they take their solos. Every great-sounding accompaniment begins with playing the right chords, so don't cut corners when it comes to chord progressions!

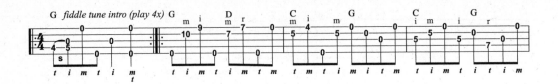

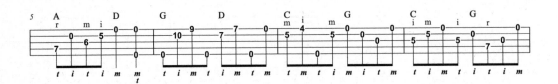

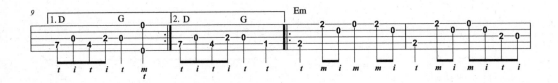

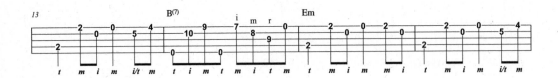

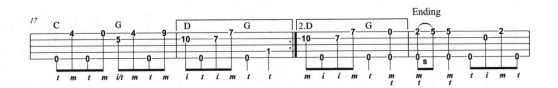

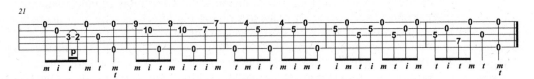

Tab 9-14: "Blackberry Blossom," a melodic banjo favorite (Audio Track 92).

Playing Single-String Banjo

In the hands of such skilled innovators as Béla Fleck, Noam Pikelny, Wes Corbett, and Chris Pandolfi, among many others, the musical possibilities of three-finger banjo are expanding ever outward from bluegrass to jazz, classical, and other musical styles. Incredibly virtuosic and complex music is being made on the banjo today in significant measure because of new developments in single-string banjo technique.

Single-string banjo provides another solution to the dilemma of finding a way to play scales and scale-based melodies on the banjo. Instead of playing consecutive scale notes on different strings as in melodic banjo (see the preceding section), *single-string* banjo utilizes a right-hand technique that's based around finding ways to play notes on the same string. The left-hand fretting moves are also different with single-string banjo, because you're finding the notes in different places on the fingerboard with this way of playing.

Short, single-string passages abound in the classic banjo music of the late-19th and early-20th centuries (for more on classic banjo, check out Chapter 11 on historical styles). Bluegrass pioneers Don Reno and Eddie Adcock introduced this way of playing to bluegrass banjo style in the late 1950s and early 1960s. Over the next several decades, younger players incorporated ideas from rock and jazz guitar technique to expand the range of single-string technique.

In the following sections, you become familiar with the right-hand picking patterns used in single-string banjo before moving on to experiment with different ways to play a single-string G scale. After playing the following exercises, you'll have a much better picture of what single-string banjo is all about and grasp the many exciting musical possibilities that are possible with this approach.

Using the right hand

Single-string banjo technique is similar in many ways to playing lead guitar with a flatpick. In lieu of the flatpick moving up and down to play notes on the same string, in single-string banjo you use your thumb and index fingers in alternation or use roll-pattern combinations of your thumb, index, and middle fingers to play melodies on individual (or *single*) strings.

Your choice of which right-hand pattern to use is determined by the specific song or lick you're playing, so feel free to experiment to see what works best for your playing and that particular song.

And keep in mind that creating a smooth and flowing sound using single-string techniques can be a real challenge. So as you play the following right-hand exercises, keep the rhythm as steady and even as possible and play each note with the same volume. In Video Clip 35, you can see the different ways of executing single-string style with the right hand.

Single string with thumb and index finger

Currently, banjo players are in a moment of transition regarding how they choose to play single-string techniques with the right hand. The more established way is to use a steady alternation of right-hand thumb and index fingers, as in the following exercise (you can follow along with Tab 9-15, which is the first part of Audio Track 93):

1. **Pick the 1st string with the right-hand thumb and then strike it again using the right-hand index finger.**

2. **Repeat Step 1, alternating the thumb and index to play the 1st string a total of four times in a row.**

   Each of these notes should be equal in length and in volume.

3. **Play the same pattern from Steps 1 and 2 on the 2nd, 3rd, and 4th strings, keeping a steady rhythm throughout and striking each string four times.**

4. **Move up from the 4th string, playing the four-note pattern on the 3rd, 2nd, and 1st strings before ending on the 3rd string.**

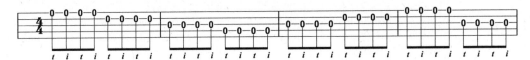

Tab 9-15: Single-string exercise using the right-hand thumb and index finger (Audio Track 93).

Single string with thumb, index, and middle fingers

Another way of playing single-string patterns is to bring the middle finger into the picture to play roll patterns on individual strings. For example, try playing the same string sequence as in Tab 9-15, but this time use an alternating thumb roll on just *one* string, as shown in Tab 9-16, which is the second part of Audio Track 93. (For more info on roll patterns and the alternating thumb roll, check out the section "Flowing with the rolls" earlier in this chapter.)

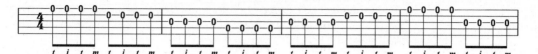

Tab 9-16: Single-string exercise using the alternating thumb roll (Audio Track 93).

If you have six notes per measure (as you do in an Irish-inspired jig in 6/8 time later in this chapter), you can try a three-note forward roll on each string. To do this, you strike each string first with the right-hand thumb, followed by the index and middle fingers, as you move from the 1st string to the 2nd, 3rd, and 4th strings, as shown in Tab 9-17, which is the third part of Audio Track 93.

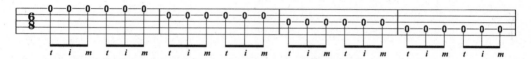

Tab 9-17: Single-string exercise in 6/8 time using the forward roll (Audio Track 93).

Taking a crack at single-string scales

Much of the left-hand work in single-string banjo is in mapping out the fretted positions that provide an easy reach to the notes you use to play a particular lick or melody fragment. You almost always have more than one way to play just about anything in single-string style. But don't let this discourage you — when you begin to play licks and songs by using these techniques, you'll appreciate having choices!

When you play scales using single-string techniques down the neck (on the first five frets of the banjo), you play a combination of both open (or unfretted) and fretted strings, using what banjo players call *open* positions for your left-hand fretting. However, when you begin to play single-string patterns up the neck (above the 5th fret), you use left-hand fingerings in which most, if not all, of the notes are fretted. These left-hand positions are called *closed* positions.

And borrowing a bit of terminology from guitar players, you may notice that in this section I refer to the various positions you use to play a scale across strings as *boxes.* Where you're coming from and where you're going on the banjo fingerboard in a particular passage of a song determines which box you use for a particular phrase. As you gain more experience playing single-string banjo, you gain more confidence shifting from one box to another.

To get a taste of the technique that's at the heart of great single-string playing, take a look at four different ways to play the G-major scale as well as D-major single-string scales. In the tablature examples, I ask you to alternate the thumb and index finger in the right hand. However, if you feel like using your right-hand middle finger to catch a note here and there, go for it and see whether it works for you. I demonstrate all of these different ways of using fret-box positions for a G major scale in Video Clip 36.

Unfortunately, this section doesn't have enough room to cover every scale you'll ever need. However, after you can handle the closed-position G-scale formations (later in this section), you can play other major scales by playing the same exercise but starting on a different fret (musicians call this process of playing licks and songs in different keys *transposing;* check out Appendix A to locate all the notes on the banjo neck). To find out more about scales of all kinds, check out *Music Theory For Dummies,* 2nd Edition, by Michael Pilhofer and Holly Day (Wiley).

Single-string, open, G-major scale

Get out your banjo and try a G-major scale in an open position, playing as many unfretted strings as possible:

1. **Begin by striking the open 3rd string with your right-hand thumb.**

2. **Pick the 3rd string, 2nd fret with your right-hand index finger.**

   Playing the same string twice in a row using different right-hand fingers is the heart of the single-string technique.

3. **Play the open 2nd string, followed by the 2nd string fretted at the 1st fret, using your thumb and index fingers to play these strings.**

4. **Play the last four notes of this G-major scale on the 1st string, once again alternating between the thumb and index in the right hand.**

   Take a moment to check out the left-hand fingering, which is indicated above the tab staff with lowercase letters in Tab 9-18 and corresponds to the first part of Audio Track 94.

5. **After playing the open 1st string, climb up this string, using your left-hand index, ring, and pinky fingers, to play the 1st string at the 2nd, 4th, and 5th frets.**

6. **Finish up the exercise by moving back down the G-major scale to the open 3rd-string G where you originally started.**

Tab 9-18: Playing an open-position, single-string, G-major scale (Audio Track 94).

Single-string, closed, G-major scales

You can also play the same notes from Tab 9-18 by using a 5th-fret closed box. This way of playing takes a little more left-hand firepower, but a big advantage is that you can move closed box patterns anywhere on the neck to match other chords and scales.

Here's one way to play a closed G-major scale (you can also check out Tab 9-19, which is the second part of Audio Track 94); remember that this particular exercise travels up the G-major scale all the way to an A note located on the 1st string, 7th fret:

1. **Begin by playing the open 4th string.**

2. **Climb up to the G note at the 5th fret of the 4th string by playing the 4th string at the 2nd fret (an E note) and the 4th string at the 4th fret (an F♯ note).**

3. **Use the fretted positions from Step 2 to play all the subsequent notes of the G-major scale out of this box.**

Tab 9-19: Playing a 2nd- to 5th-fret-box position, single-string, G-major scale (Audio Track 94).

Box positions help you to remember left-hand fingering patterns. Many players take advantage of what I call the *one-finger-per-fret rule* when using box positions. After you're in a box position, your left hand covers a fretting range of four (and sometimes five) frets — with one left-hand finger responsible for each fret in the box. Your first choice in left-hand fingering on any string is to use the finger in the box that's designated for this fret.

For example, in this exercise (and in Tab 9-19), the pinky finger is used to fret the 5th fret on any string, the ring on the 4th fret, the middle on the 3rd fret, and the index on the 2nd fret. You don't want to remain in just one region of the fretboard for very long, however, so players often shift the box up or down one or more frets as needed to reach the notes that they want to play. This is exactly what happens in Tab 9-19 at the last note of measure one as the left-hand index finger shifts from a 2nd- to a 3rd-fret position, moving the entire box up one fret. This movement allows the left hand to catch the A note on the 1st string by extending the box (and the reach of the pinky finger) up to the 1st string, 7th fret, as shown in Tab 9-19.

After you have these basic steps down pat, try the same G-major scale but this time use the middle finger to play the G note on the 5th fret of the 4th string instead of the pinky finger. Note that four fingers of your left hand have now created a box that's two frets higher than the box you used for Tab 9-19. Another left-hand finger shift occurs in this scale exercise at the beginning of measure two as the index finger moves up one fret to fret the 1st string, 5th fret.

As you shift either up or down the fretboard, you can play higher or lower notes as needed. Check out Tab 9-20 for all the details and listen to the third part of Audio Track 94.

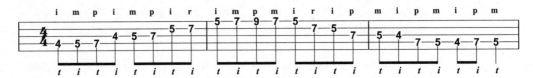

Tab 9-20: Using 4th- to 7th- and 5th- to 9th-fret-box positions (Audio Track 94).

Now try moving the box up one more fret and play a G scale in which the left-hand index finger frets the G note located at the 5th fret of the 4th string (see Tab 9-21 and listen to the last part of Audio Track 94). Note that your box now covers five frets, enabling you to play three scale notes on each string. Also, you have a left-hand shift at the next-to-last note of the first measure (where the left-hand index moves up two frets to the 7th fret, 2nd string) and again at the second note of the second measure (where the index moves up two frets again to play the 9th fret, 1st string). These shifts are common in single-string playing, allowing greater fretting range in the left hand.

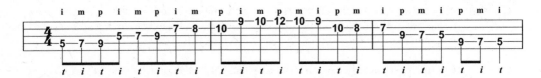

Tab 9-21: Using 5th- to 9th-, 7th- to 10th-, and 9th- to 12th-fret-box positions (Audio Track 94).

Single-string, D-major scale

After you're comfortable using single-string ideas in the key of G (see the preceding sections), branching out to new keys, using single-string techniques, is fairly easy.

Try an open-position, D-major scale beginning on the open 4th string (you can follow along in Tab 9-22, which is Audio Track 95). You can find the second and third notes of the D-major scale (E and F♯) on the 2nd and 4th frets of the 4th string. Next, play an open 3rd-string G followed by a 3rd-string, 2nd-fret A note. You can find the B note by playing an open 2nd string. Follow this with a C♯ on the 2nd string, 2nd fret, and an open 1st-string D.

You can extend the D-major scale a few more notes by playing the 1st-string, 2nd-fret E; the 1st-string, 4th-fret F♯; and the 1st-string, 5th-fret G.

Tab 9-22: Playing an open-position, single-string, D-major scale (Audio Track 95).

Exercising single-string techniques in songs

Single-string banjo provides another way to broaden your range of musical expression. Depending on what each musical situation needs, you can use single-string techniques to play an entire solo or song, or you can just play a few fancy single-string licks to add variety to a tune played in Scruggs or melodic style. However you decide to incorporate these ideas into your playing, the following tips can help you master using single-string techniques in a tune faster and make them more fun to play:

- ✔ **Make your single-string playing sound as smooth and as flowing as you possibly can.** You can do this by keeping a very steady rhythm in your right-hand picking as well as holding one fretted note down for as long as possible before moving to the next fretted note with your left hand.

- ✔ **Know your scales and your box positions.** You'll quickly appreciate how much easier it is to figure out a new tune if you've already spent time working on scales and the different box positions you can use to play single-string passages (see previous sections on these topics). Do your homework (jazz musicians call this *woodshedding*)!

- ✔ **Work up speed slowly.** Playing single-string style fast isn't easy! Don't be discouraged if it takes months, or even years, to sound like your progressive banjo heroes. Begin by playing as slowly as you need to in order to sound good, and increase speed very gradually over time.

Now you're ready to tackle a few tunes in single-string style!

"Red Haired Boy"

Many fiddle tunes come from the British Isles or Ireland, and that's the case with this first melody that you work out in single-string style. Almost all of this song is played down the neck using open positions, with just one leap up to a higher left-hand position at the end of the A and B sections. The melody of "Red Haired Boy" (see Tab 9-23 and check out Audio Track 96 and Video Clip 37) is closely related to the chord progression, so don't forget to internalize those chords as you practice. As you fret each chord, you'll automatically be ready to play many of the corresponding melody notes. If you get tied up with your left-hand fingering, take a look above the staff for my fingering suggestions.

Musicians usually play "Red Haired Boy" in the key of A. For many tunes played in this key, banjo players work out arrangements in the key of G and then place their capo behind the 2nd fret to play in the key of A with others. Don't forget you also have to tune your 5th string up two frets to an A pitch to have all five strings ready to go!

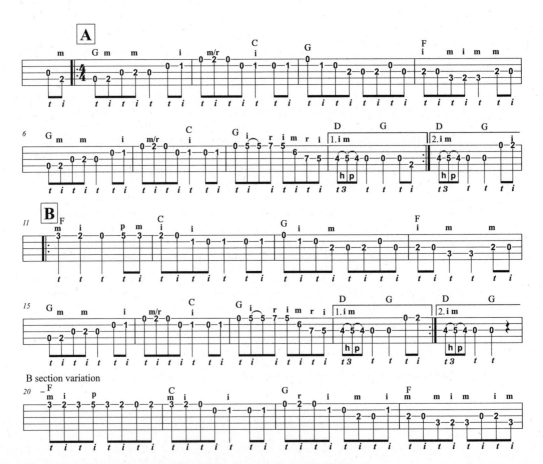

Tab 9-23: "Red Haired Boy" played in single-string style (Audio Track 96).

"Arkansas Traveler"

Try another fiddle-tune favorite in the key of D, "Arkansas Traveler." Before you dig into the tab, it's a good idea to first map out a D-major scale to get accustomed to the left-hand fretted positions you use in this key (see the section "Single-string, D-major scale" earlier in this chapter). For this song, the version of the D-major scale you need begins on the open 4th string and climbs all the way up to the G note on the 5th fret of the 1st string.

Now you're ready to play "Arkansas Traveler" using single-string techniques. It appears in Tab 9-24 and Audio Track 97. Note that the second half of the tune shifts to a higher box as it climbs up to the A note found at the 7th fret of the 1st string. You play a lot of consecutive 1st-string notes in the right hand in this section, so be sure to pay close attention to the left-hand fingering indicated above the tab staff. If you do that, you'll be just fine!

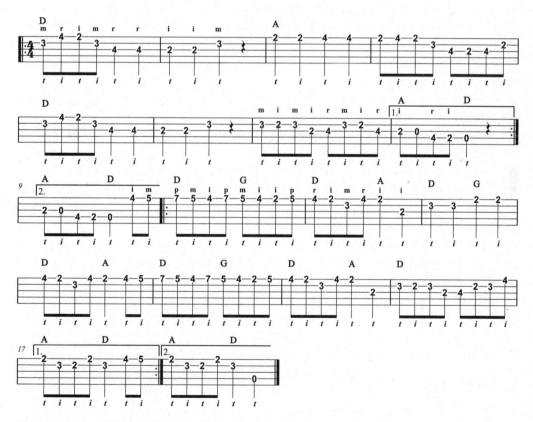

Tab 9-24: "Arkansas Traveler," arranged by me (Audio Track 97).

"Reno's Rag"

One of the advantages of single-string banjo is that you have easy access to many different notes within a single box position. You can figure out much of the left-hand fingering for the chord-based licks in "Reno's Rag" by using the one-finger-per-fret rule (which I describe in the section "Single-string, closed, G-major scales," earlier in this chapter). This tune appears in Tab 9-25 and Audio Track 98.

With the G chord that begins this piece, you want to use your left-hand index finger to fret across the 7th fret on all strings. You then use your middle finger to fret any note that falls on the 8th fret and your ring finger to fret all 9th-fret notes. You then shift this box down two frets for the A chord, using one finger per fret once again.

Single-string innovator Don Reno created some great-sounding single-string licks based around the F and D chord positions way back in the 1950s, and these rock 'n' roll–influenced licks still sound great on the banjo today. Several of these licks are incorporated into the melody of my tune "Reno's Rag."

Tab 9-25: "Reno's Rag," composed by me (Audio Track 98).

"Winston's Jig"

You can try a bit of Irish-inspired music by using single-string techniques on the song "Winston's Jig" (Tab 9-26). Jigs have a different rhythm than other kinds of fiddle tunes, with six beats in each cycle and six right-hand notes per measure. When playing jigs, you have a prime opportunity to bring the right-hand middle finger into your playing technique to use forward rolls that match this rhythm (you can read more about using the forward roll in single-string playing in the section "Using the right hand" earlier in this chapter). Be sure to pay attention to this unique feature of jigs as you work your way through this tune — and don't forget to listen to Audio Track 99 to hear my version.

Tab 9-26: "Winston's Jig," composed by me (Audio Track 99).

Combining Three-Finger Techniques

Modern banjo players combine Scruggs, melodic, and single-string techniques to create a wide variety of three-finger soundscapes. Although you can't find any rules written in stone, Scruggs style is generally used for hard-driving bluegrass songs and for accompanying other musicians, while melodic and single-string banjo techniques launch the instrument into musical fusions blending bluegrass with jazz, classical, and international music styles.

You shift from one technique to another in order to best capture what you want to play at any particular moment. The greater your technical facility on the instrument — something that comes with years of hard work — the more you can express on the banjo. This lifelong journey provides great personal rewards when you reach the point where you can instantly connect mind and fingers to play the music you hear in your head and feel in your heart.

Until you've gained a lot of experience in each style on its own, you can't really put them all together. So if you need a refresher or more experience on these three-finger techniques before tackling this section, I suggest you take a look at the previous sections of this chapter.

To close out this chapter's survey of modern three-finger styles, I present my tune "The Distance Between Two Points" from the CD *In Good Company,* which appears in Tab 9-27 and Audio Track 100. (You can find out more about this recording by visiting my homepage at www.billevansbanjo.com.) Playing along with me are some of the best musicians in bluegrass music today: Mike Marshall, mandolin; Todd Phillips, bass; David Grier, guitar; and Darol Anger, Tristan Clarridge, and Tashina Clarridge on fiddles. I hope you enjoy this tune!

This advanced-level tune demonstrates how many of the techniques I discuss in this chapter can be blended together and used as inspiration for original music that moves beyond the boundaries of bluegrass. "The Distance Between Two Points" features three sections: a slow introduction (at letter A), an accelerating B section featuring phrases played in melodic style, and a C section that's the main body of the tune.

Key of D, tune 5th string to A: a DGBD

(continued)

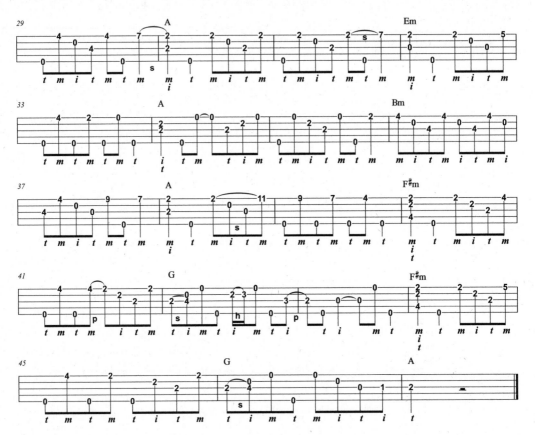

Tab 9-27: "The Distance Between Two Points," composed by Bill Evans and Corey Evans (Audio Track 100).

Chapter 10

Playing Up-the-Neck Backup: Chords and Vamping

In This Chapter

▶ Fretting movable major and minor chords

▶ Using vamping techniques to accompany tunes

▶ Determining when vamping is appropriate

▶ Access the audio tracks and video clips at `www.dummies.com/go/banjo`

Making music with other musicians is one of the greatest joys of playing the banjo. In this chapter, you start down the road to becoming a good team player by mastering the basic skills you need to play confidently with others in jam sessions and in bands. You gain a new understanding of the fretboard and of how to make your playing support and enhance that of the other musicians around you.

Whether you're playing in a bluegrass or old-time jam with guitar, fiddle, mandolin, bass, and dobro or exploring the outer reaches of the banjo universe with drums, piano, and horns, you can use these accompaniment techniques every time you take your instrument out of the case to play with others.

Playing Movable Major Chords

Although it's fun to play blazing fast solos and be the center of attention with the banjo, when you're playing in a jam session or band, you spend a lot of time doing your best to support the other instrumentalists and singers. Banjo players use the term *backup* to refer to the fine art of playing the banjo in a way that makes everyone else in the band sound good. Mastering tasteful backup can be a lifelong process, but even new players can quickly grasp many of the most important aspects of being a good accompanist.

Backup frequently involves playing chords *up the neck* on your banjo. *Up the neck* refers to the frets that are closer to the pot of the banjo, while *down the neck* refers to the frets closer to the tuners. In banjo tablature, up-the-neck fretted positions have larger numbers than down-the-neck positions. Although no exact location on the fretboard indicates where "down the neck" ends and "up the neck" begins, when you're fretting a chord around the 8th fret or higher, you're up the neck.

A *movable chord* is a chord that can be played at any fret on the banjo. Here, I use the term *shape* to refer to the way the left-hand fingers are arranged in a fretted position for each type of movable chord. The advantage of knowing movable chords is that you can play many different chords by using the same fretted shape up and down the neck of your banjo. You fret the 4th, 3rd, 2nd, and 1st strings (but not the 5th string) with these kinds of chords. Three different shapes are used to play movable major chords: the barre shape, the F shape, and the D shape.

The barre shape

If you're in G tuning, you get a pleasant-sounding G major chord when you strum across the open, unfretted strings of your banjo. (This is where banjo players have a distinct advantage over guitar and mandolin players — try strumming across *their* open strings sometime — it doesn't sound so good.)

The *barre* (pronounced "bar" in polite banjo circles — never "bar-*ray*" or anything else with two syllables) *shape* enables you to use this open major chord idea to play every major chord possible simply by moving the shape up and down the banjo neck. The good news is that it's an easy chord shape to remember because you use just one finger to fret straight across all four strings.

Try this shape by stretching the left-hand index finger from the 1st string across to the 4th string, fretting just behind the 2nd fret, using your left-hand thumb on the back of the neck for support. Now strum across these strings with the right hand to hear the sound of the chord. Experiment with slight adjustments in positioning to make all four strings ring as clearly as possible. At this location on your fretboard, you're playing an A major chord using the barre shape (see Figure 10-1).

To have more left-hand control, don't extend the tip of your index finger too far past the 4th string to fret the barre shape. Also, try moving the thumb up and down the back of the neck to find the best position to support the fretting index finger.

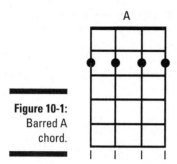

Figure 10-1:
Barred A
chord.

Naming barre-shape chords

The letter name you use for the barre-shape major chord is determined by the name of the note you're playing on the 3rd string. The 3rd string at the 2nd fret is an A note, so the barre-shape chord at the 2nd fret is an A major chord. (By the way, when you're playing a major chord, which is the bright, happy-sounding kind of chord, you don't actually have to use the word *major* to describe it — just say *A chord,* and you'll sound like you know what you're talking about.) A quick look at Appendix A shows you the names of the notes on the other frets of the open 3rd string G. You can use this information to find the names of all the other barre-shape chords up and down the neck.

Playing the G-C-D progression with barre shapes

As you get used to the different movable shapes in this chapter, you can try them out with G, C, and D chords, the three most essential chords in banjo music. Using the barre shape, you find the C chord at the 5th fret and the D chord at the 7th fret. Using the open position for the G chord, try the short exercise shown in Tab 10-1 and listen to Audio Track 101.

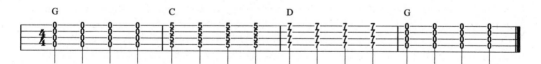

Tab 10-1: G-C-D with barre shape (Audio Track 101).

Play four strums per measure making even, downward strokes across all five strings with your right-hand thumb or index finger. Try to maintain a steady rhythm in the right hand as you move from one chord position to the next.

The left hand can get worn out pretty quickly fretting these movable chord shapes. To conserve left-hand *qi* (sorry, but I just had to be the first author to use this word in a banjo instructional book!), try easing the fretting pressure as you move from one chord to the next with all movable chord shapes. If you keep your left-hand finger (or fingers) lightly touching the strings as you move, you'll be amazed at how quickly you can transport your left hand to virtually anywhere on the banjo neck to be ready to fret the next chord.

The F shape

Although the barre shape is nice to fret and easy to remember, banjo players don't go for nice and easy very much of the time. The *F-shape* movable chord position is used much more frequently for backup. It's called the F shape because it uses the same left-hand position that you use for the F major chord at the 3rd fret (see Figure 10-2).

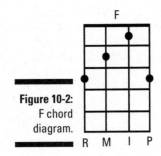

F

Figure 10-2:
F chord
diagram.

R M I P

Note that the F chord uses the same fretted positions on the 3rd and 2nd strings as the open D7 chord, with the ring and middle fingers added to fret the 4th and 1st strings at the 3rd fret. Don't forget to use as little left-hand pressure as possible for a clear sound from each fretted string — you'll find that it really doesn't take much!

You're now fretting four strings with four fingers. Congratulations! If you move all the fretting fingers up one fret, keeping the fingers fretting the same positions relative to one another, you'll be playing an F♯ chord. If you move up another fret (with the ring and little fingers now fretting the 5th fret), you'll be playing a G chord. Move up five more frets and you have a C chord at the 10th fret; move up two more frets to the 12th fret, and you're fretting a D chord using the F shape.

Naming F-shape chords

The letter name for the F-shape chord matches the note you're fretting on the open 4th string D, fretted at the 3rd fret. Consult the oracle of Appendix A to find the names of the notes on the other frets of the 4th string and use this information to locate and name the other major chords in this shape.

Playing the G-C-D progression with F shapes

Try strumming as described in the section "Playing the G-C-D progression with barre shapes," but this time play the G, C, and D chords using the F shape. Don't forget to release the left-hand pressure between chords as you slide up the neck from one chord to the next. See Tab 10-2 and listen to Audio Track 102.

Tab 10-2: G-C-D chords with F position (Audio Track 102).

The D shape

You need to know one more movable major chord progression before you put shapes to use in banjo backup. The *D shape* takes its name from the fretted positions used for the D major chord that's found at the 4th fret (see Figure 10-3).

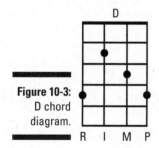

Figure 10-3: D chord diagram.

Naming D-shape chords

Just as with the barre and F shapes, you can play all the major chords by simply moving the D shape up and down the banjo neck. The note you're fretting on the open 2nd string B determines the name of the chord with the D shape. Using the D shape, you find the G chord at the 9th fret (in other words, the ring and little fingers are fretting the 4th and 1st strings at the 9th fret), the C chord at the 14th fret, and the D chord at either the 4th or the 16th fret.

Playing the G-C-D progression with D shapes

Are you up for some more strumming? Try playing the G, C, and D chords with the D shape; see Tab 10-3 and listen to Audio Track 103.

Tab 10-3: G-C-D with D shape (Audio Track 103).

Moving from the F shape to the D shape

Take a moment and compare the fretted positions used for the F and D shapes. If you keep the ring and little fingers in the same fretted positions, observe how you can change from one shape to the next by simply moving the index and middle fingers back and forth across strings.

Banjo players frequently shift from one shape to another in backup in order to play the same letter-name chord in different ways or to reach a new chord with a minimum amount of movement up or down the banjo neck. If you start with the G chord that uses the F shape at the 5th fret, you'll find that the G chord that uses the D shape is at the 9th fret, four frets higher. This "four-fret" rule applies to all other major chords as well.

Try the following exercise, shifting between the F and D shapes for the G, C, and D chords. This time you play each chord for two measures (see Tab 10-4 and listen to Audio Track 104).

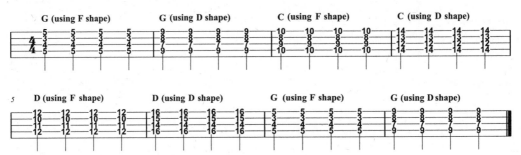

Tab 10-4: G-C-D moving from F to D shapes (Audio Track 104).

Playing Movable Minor Chords

Just as you can use movable major chords everywhere on the banjo fretboard, you can also use movable shapes to fret all the different minor chords. One way to remember how the movable minor shapes are fretted is to relate these fretted positions to the major chord with the same letter name. This section explains how this works for the F-shape, D-shape, and barre-shape major chord positions.

Converting F-shape major chords

Try the following steps to convert an F-shape major chord into a minor chord, as shown in Figure 10-4:

1. **Play a G major chord (F shape) at the 5th fret.**

2. **Replace the middle finger at the 3rd string, 4th fret, with the index finger at the 3rd fret; use the side of your index finger to cover both the 3rd and 2nd strings.**

   You're now fretting a G minor chord.

Figure 10-4: Charts for G major and G minor chords (Audio Track 105).

Listen to Audio Track 105 and take a moment to try moving back and forth between the G major and G minor chords, strumming each chord to experience its sound quality and mood. The name of this minor shape chord is determined by the note you're fretting on the 4th string, just like the corresponding major chord shape.

If you move the minor chord shape up two frets to the 7th fret, you'll be playing an A minor chord. You run across the G major to A minor progression in several popular banjo pieces, including "Devil's Dream." Try practicing this progression as shown in Tab 10-5 and listen to Audio Track 106.

Tab 10-5: Playing a G major chord and moving to an A minor chord (Audio Track 106).

Converting D-shape major chords

Try converting a D-shape major chord into its corresponding minor chord. Your fretted fingers have to shuffle around a lot more with this conversion, so follow the instructions carefully and check out Figure 10-5 and Audio Track 107:

1. **Play an E major chord (D shape) at the 6th fret.**

2. **Lift off all the fretted notes except for the index finger on the 3rd string, 4th fret.**

3. **Move the middle finger to the 4th string, 5th fret.**

4. **Move the ring finger to the 2nd string, 5th fret.**

5. **Move the little finger to the 1st string, 5th fret.**

   You're now fretting an E minor chord.

Figure 10-5:
Charts for
an E major
and an E
minor chord
(Audio
Track 107).

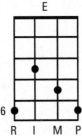 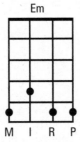

A common chord progression that's found in tunes like "Blackberry Blossom" and "Foggy Mountain Breakdown" involves moving from a G major chord to an E minor chord. If you fret the G major chord at the 5th fret using the F shape, you'll find that the E minor that's derived from the D shape is also at the 5th fret. As you move from the G major chord to the E minor chord (refer to Tab 10-6 and Audio Track 108), keep the little finger fretting the 1st string at the 5th fret as you move the other fingers into the minor chord position. This transition isn't easy, but with some practice, you'll get it — I promise!

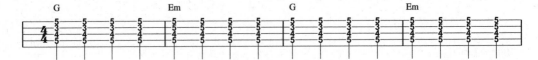

Tab 10-6: Playing a G major and an E minor chord (Audio Track 108).

The letter name of this minor chord shape is set by where you're fretting the chord on the neck and the name of the note on the 2nd string, just as with the major chord shape.

Converting barre-shape major chords

The barre shape is the easiest major chord to fret, because all you have to do is lay the side of your index finger across the strings. Not so, however, for the minor chord that's derived from this shape — you need to shift all four fingers this time to change into the minor chord position. Follow these steps and consult Figure 10-6 and Audio Track 109:

1. **Play a D major chord (barre shape) at the 7th fret.**

2. **Lift off all the fretted notes and move your index finger to the 2nd string, 6th fret.**

3. **Move the middle finger to the 4th string, 7th fret.**

4. **Move the ring finger to the 3rd string, 7th fret.**

5. **Move the little finger to the 1st string, 7th fret.**

   You're now fretting a D minor chord.

Figure 10-6:
Shifting
from a
D major
chord to a D
minor chord
(Audio
Track 109).

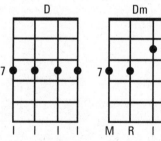

As you use this minor chord shape up and down the neck, remember that you name the chord by the note that's being fretted on the 3rd string, just as you do in the corresponding major chord shape for the barre position.

Whew! That was definitely a lot of work, wasn't it? If your brain is reeling from all this information, consider it confirmation that you're a totally normal banjo player (well, as much as one can be totally normal and want to *play* the banjo!). Don't expect to master all these transitions in one sitting, or even in a couple weeks. My advice is to start working on these shapes and transitions

Up-the-neck fretting made easier

Cleanly fretting up-the-neck chords can be a bit more difficult than fretting chords down the neck. One reason for this is because the string action (the distance between the strings and the fretboard) is higher the closer you are to the banjo pot, forcing you to be a bit more precise with your left hand. Also, as the frets get closer together the higher up the neck you go, you may feel that there isn't enough room for all your left-hand fingers to fret all the strings cleanly.

The remedy for these fearful feelings of fretful vertigo is to adopt a good left-hand position for up-the-neck fretting, especially in regard to the angle of your hand and the location of your left-hand thumb. Here's one way to do it, using the 12th-fret D chord, F shape, as an example:

1. **Place your left-hand thumb perpendicular to the neck behind the 11th fret with the thumb resting on the neck's upper curve.**

   Check out the following figure.

2. **While maintaining the position of your left-hand thumb, fret a D chord using the F-chord shape.**

   The left-hand ring and little fingers should be fretting just behind the 12th fret.

3. **Check to ensure that your thumb is more or less perpendicular to the neck as you fret.**

   This positioning causes the fingers to approach their fretting positions from behind. This is good! In this way, the left-hand fingers stay out of each other's way and have more room to maneuver as you move up the neck (see the figure that follows).

4. **Try shifting this position one fret at a time all the way up the neck to see whether you can maintain a good fretting position as you move higher.**

   At about the 19th fret, the banjo neck expands outward and you aren't able to keep your thumb directly behind your left-hand fretting fingers.

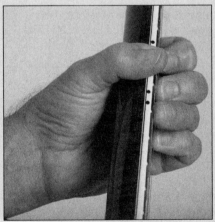

Photographs by Anne Hamersky

only when you start working on tunes that have minor chords in their progressions. When that time comes, come back to this section and put your left-hand fingers to work!

Using Vamping in Backup Playing

If you're a real newcomer to the banjo, this section is probably one of the most mystifying — or scariest — things you've run across in this book! However banjo vamping has nothing to do with vampires or wearing provocative clothing (well, unless cowboy hats strike your fancy) or anything else exotic or out of the ordinary. *Vamping* is one of the most practical and useful techniques you'll ever use to play banjo with others. After you're comfortable with movable chords (see the previous sections), you can put those chords to use with vamping — banjo-style!

Working out the mechanics of vamping

Vamping is a percussive-sounding backup technique that banjo players use to help keep the entire band or jam playing together in good rhythm and is sometimes called *chopping, chunking,* or *chucking* (my least favorite label, especially when used up the neck). It's also a great way to play when you want to contribute your share to the ongoing energy of a jam session while allowing other musicians to take the main spotlight. Most important, you can also use vamping as a way to fake your way through the chord progression of a tune until you feel you know the song well enough to use other ways of playing. For this reason alone, vamping is a *very* worthwhile skill to master!

The right hand in vamping

The right hand in vamping plays something that sounds similar to the basic "boom-chick" rhythm pattern used by many country guitar players (sometimes called the *Carter lick* after country guitar visionary Maybelle Carter). If you're counting four beats in a cycle, you want to play the 4th string on the 1st and 3rd beats (that's your "boom") followed by the top three strings on the 2nd and 4th beats (you guessed it, that's the "chick" part). Although adding complexity to this pattern with additional right-hand notes is possible, the basic way of doing things is just fine for most group situations and is actually desirable in many cases (when it comes to accompaniment, simpler is usually better!).

The left hand in vamping

With vamping, you fret movable chord positions, but it's the additional left-hand muting techniques that attract the most attention. On the 2nd and 4th beats of each cycle, you want to mute the ringing sound by lifting up on the fretting pressure. Depending upon the mood you want to create, you can let the chord ring for a moment and then cut off its sound, or you can get an even more percussive effect by muting the chord very quickly after striking the strings.

The G-C-D progression with vamping

Try vamping along using the F shape for the G, C, and D chords (see Tab 10-7 and listen to Audio Track 110). Remember, you find the G chord at the 5th fret, the C chord at the 10th fret, and the D chord at the 12th fret with this shape. On the 1st and 3rd beats, you want the 4th string to ring — don't mute it as you do the other three strings.

Tab 10-7: G-C-D progression with F-shape vamping (Audio Track 110).

Using F and D shapes with vamping

Although using just the F-shape chords to vamp your way through any chord progression is fine, you can bring more variety to your sound by switching between the F and D shapes for the same letter-name chord as you vamp. Remember that the D shape is located four frets higher than the F shape for the same letter-name of any major or minor chord. For instance, you find a G chord using the F shape at the 5th fret and another G chord that's fretted with the D shape at the 9th fret.

As you move up the neck from the F-shape chord to the D-shape chord, try to keep both your left-hand ring and little fingers just barely in contact with the 4th and 1st strings. You're much less likely to lose your place on the neck, and you can literally feel your way four frets higher to your D-shape destination!

Vamping to "Red River Valley"

Use the idea of switching between chord shapes as you vamp to "Red River Valley" (see Tab 10-8 and listen to Audio Track 111), first using the F-shape version of each major chord and then moving to the D shape in the following measure. Follow this pattern all the way through to the end of the tune, where you use just the D shape for the D chord at Measure 15.

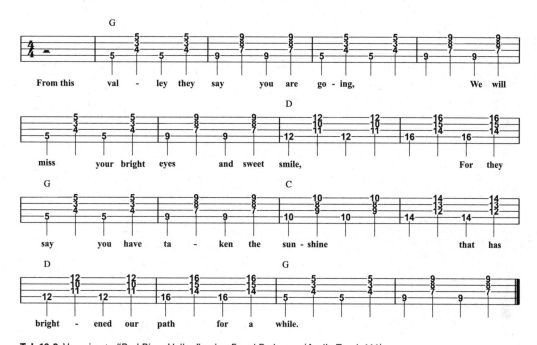

Tab 10-8: Vamping to "Red River Valley" using F and D shapes (Audio Track 111).

Vamping to "Blackberry Blossom"

Banjo players frequently mix F and D shapes to minimize left-hand movement up and down the neck and to create a more flowing sound in their playing. The fiddle tune "Blackberry Blossom" (check out Tab 10-9 and Audio Track 112) is a jam-session favorite with a lot of quick chord changes. It's a perfect vehicle for exploring the fingerboard to find different chords to use in vamping. Note that the second section of this tune moves to an E minor chord.

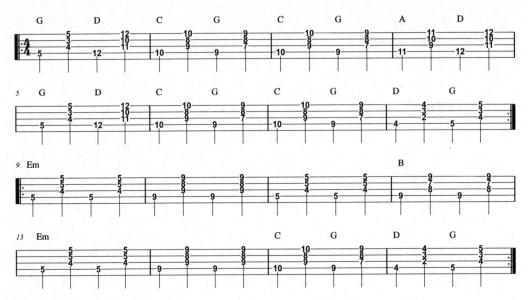

Tab 10-9: Vamping to "Blackberry Blossom" using F and D shapes (Audio Track 112).

Knowing When to Use Vamping

Vamping is a great way to accompany other musicians in a band or jam session. It lays out the chord progression with a simple and steady rhythm that provides plenty of support to the other musicians in your jam session so they can play their best.

Vamping is an especially good technique to use when jamming with other banjo players. When another banjo player takes a solo, that's the time for you to stop playing the basic clawhammer stroke or bluegrass roll patterns and begin the vamping technique. It's also a great time to keep the chord changes simple and, above all, maintain a good rhythm.

Sometimes, vamping is also good when a guitar or mandolin is taking a solo. However, always be careful not to play with so much volume that you overpower the musician you're attempting to support. It's easy for all banjo players to get carried away with the excitement of a tune and suddenly find themselves playing too loud or too fast in comparison to everyone else. If you have a banjo, this is a key element in knowing how to use it!

If you can't hear what the other musicians are playing or what the singer is singing, play more quietly until you can. Also, keep an ear open not only to what you're playing but to what everyone else is playing as well, so that you can stay in good rhythm with everyone else in your jam.

Chapter 11

Playing Historical Styles: African, Minstrel, and Classic Banjo

In This Chapter

▶ Discovering the banjo's African heritage

▶ Getting acquainted with 19th-century minstrel banjo style

▶ Playing in the late 19th- and early 20th-century classic banjo style

▶ Access the audio tracks and video clips at www.dummies.com/go/banjo

Banjo players have a thing about history. They play old songs and sing a lot about the "old days"; they like old instruments and playing music the old-time way. When you pick up your banjo to play "Cripple Creek" or "Soldier's Joy" or sing the old ballad "Pretty Polly," you become part of a deep and enduring current of music history. Clawhammer and bluegrass banjo, the two most popular ways of playing banjo today, have historical roots that go back over 150 years to late 19th- and early 20th-century classic banjo styles, to mid 19th-century minstrel banjo styles, and to even earlier African musical influences. These historical banjo styles are the subject of this chapter.

Get ready to travel back in time to trace the African ancestry of the banjo and explore the fascinating world of 19th- and early 20th-century banjo music. I show you an African piece from the late 1700s along with some tunes in minstrel style from the pre–Civil War years that are historical predecessors to clawhammer banjo music. I also help you test your fingerpicking skills with some pre-bluegrass, classic banjo ragtime from the early 20th century. Whatever style of banjo you like to play, you can discover a whole new world of musical possibilities in these *really* old, historical sounds.

Exploring African-American Banjo Roots

The idea of stretching a skin tightly across a resonating chamber, attaching a neck, adding one or more drone strings, and playing the resulting instrument in a rhythmical and percussive manner originated with the West Africans who were forcibly imported as slaves to the New World. The first banjo-type instruments were documented in the Caribbean as early as 1689, and the first mention of the banjo in the American colonies occurred in 1754 (where it was called a "banjer" in a Maryland newspaper).

What music historians know about early African and African-American banjo music comes from what observers at the time had to say about banjo playing and from artists' drawings and illustrations of banjos and banjo players (check out *Sinful Tunes and Spirituals: Black Folk Music to the Civil War* by Dena Epstein [University of Illinois Press] for an excellent overview of this documentation). Researchers also look to how Africans play banjo-type instruments today for clues about historical African-American playing styles.

African and early African-American banjos are assembled from a gourd or a carved wood body with a stretched skin head and usually little more than a stick for a neck.

From early on, observers have commented on the complex and percussive playing style Africans and African-Americans have used to play the banjo, and you can easily hear elements of this approach in modern clawhammer banjo playing. Clawhammer players strike the strings by moving their right-hand index or middle fingers down across the strings, in a way that's very similar to how many West Africans make music on their own native banjo-type instruments today. Historians agree that this aspect of the American clawhammer approach is the result of African influence.

Although you can't know exactly what early African and African-American music sounded like 200 or more years ago, you can play my arrangement of an African tune that ended up in a 1782 collection of British Isles fiddle tunes. Called "Pompey Ran Away," this tune makes for a wonderful clawhammer banjo piece (see Tab 11-1 and listen to Audio Track 113).

This piece has many of the characteristics commonly heard in traditional West African music. Each musical idea (or *phrase*) is made up of just a few notes (each phrase occupies one measure of tab in this particular tune). The second phrases of each line (which are the second and fourth measures of each line) answer the first phrases (which are the first and third measures of each line) in a call-and-response (or question-and-answer) relationship. Each phrase also offers a slight variation on the phrase heard just before it as this simple tune organically unfolds.

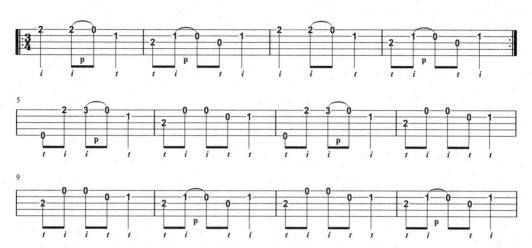

Tab 11-1: Playing "Pompey Ran Away," a clawhammer version of an 18th-century African tune (Audio Track 113).

To play this tune using traditional clawhammer techniques, use the right-hand index finger to strike the 1st and 2nd strings with a downward motion and let the right-hand thumb strike the 2nd, 3rd, and 5th strings in a downward direction. (For more on the world of clawhammer banjo, check out Chapters 7 and 8.)

Converging Cultures: The World of Minstrel Banjo

When Africans and Europeans came together in North America, they had enough similarity in their ideas and attitudes about music for a new musical synthesis to occur, despite the dramatically unequal status of black and white populations. In large part, the history of American music, from minstrelsy to jazz and from rock 'n' roll to rap music, is the story of this continuing convergence of musical sensibilities.

Uncovering the historical background

The mid 19th-century minstrel banjo is one of the first manifestations of the meeting of these musical worlds. Along with the fiddle, the banjo was the most popular instrument in African-American music in the United States through the 18th and into the 19th century. In the early 1800s, white musicians began to take up the banjo in imitation of southern African-American players. By the mid-1800s, white professional stage performers had popularized the banjo all across the United States and in England and had begun their own banjo traditions as they popularized new songs. Because these musicians usually performed with blackened faces, they came to be known as *blackface minstrels.*

In 19th-century minstrel banjo, African elements — the instrument itself, the right-hand playing technique, and the use of varied and complex rhythms — combined with the musical influence of the British Isles as exhibited in song form, repertoire, and the use of harmony to create a uniquely American musical phenomenon.

Because the minstrel stage depicted slaves and southern life in inaccurate and degrading ways, the legacy of blackface minstrelsy has many negative aspects. Nevertheless, as part of America's first nationally popular music, minstrelsy served to popularize the banjo and make it an instrument shared by both white and black populations. With this popularity came the publication of the first instruction manuals for the instrument and the first factory-made banjos in the 1840s. Soon after, five strings became the accepted norm for banjos.

Getting into minstrel banjo

As you play tunes using techniques that date from the 1840s, the sound of minstrel banjo opens a door to the instrument's past where you can hear and feel the echoes of the banjo's shared African and European heritage. If you're a clawhammer player, transitioning to minstrel style should be easy because most of the playing techniques are similar for both approaches.

Although you can purchase a replica of a fretless 19th-century banjo, you can play the minstrel repertoire on any five-string instrument, fretted or not. Minstrel banjos are also usually strung with gut or nylon strings and are tuned several steps lower than the conventional tunings used by banjo players today. However, you can play these pieces with any kind of strings on your banjo, and in the next section, I show you how to play in the minstrel style by staying as close to conventional G tuning as possible.

Discovering drop-C tuning

Minstrel banjo uses a tuning that's close to the familiar G tuning, but the 4th string is lowered in pitch the equivalent of two frets from a D to a C (see Chapter 2 if you need help with getting your banjo into G tuning and Chapter 8 for some of the most common tunings used today in clawhammer banjo). Usually called *drop-C tuning,* this technique is used in other popular banjo tunes such as "Home Sweet Home" and "Farewell Blues." You also use drop-C tuning in classic banjo, so it's good to know this tuning even if your plans aren't to become a great minstrel player!

If your banjo is already in G tuning, lowering the 4th string from a D to a C is easy. Simply loosen the tension on the 4th string so that the pitch is lowered from a D to a C♯, and then keep going until your electronic tuner indicates that you've reached a C note. If you're trying this by ear, congratulations! That's *definitely* the old-time way, and in this case, you want to lower the 4th string so that it matches the 3rd string in pitch when you fret the 4th string at the 7th fret.

Unfortunately, after you've lowered that 4th string to C, the chance is very good that the rest of your banjo will be out of tune. If that's the case, touch up the other strings by making sure that your 3rd string is tuned to G, the 2nd string to B, the 1st string to D, and the 5th string to G.

Mastering minstrel technique

Minstrel banjo uses many of the same techniques used by clawhammer banjo players, so it's a good idea to know basic clawhammer technique well before venturing into minstrel-banjo territory. As with clawhammer, in minstrel banjo, you move downward across the strings with your index or middle fingers to strike most melody notes, and you use your thumb for the 5th string.

Minstrel banjo also frequently uses *double-thumbing* patterns, a right-hand technique that is also used in advanced clawhammer banjo. In double-thumbing, the thumb not only plays the 5th string but also catches melody notes on the inside strings (for a review of basic clawhammer and double-thumbing right-hand techniques, visit Chapters 5 and 8).

You also encounter these new challenges with minstrel banjo:

- ✔ **Triplets:** Minstrel banjo frequently juxtaposes different kinds of rhythms — sometimes in the same measure. A *triplet* is a rhythm where you play three notes within a musical space normally occupied by two notes. Say "trip-o-let" while tapping your foot on the syllable "trip" to get the idea of a triplet.

- ✔ **Dotted notes:** A dot after a note indicates that the note's durational value is to be increased by half. If you increase the value of one note, you usually have to make the next note shorter by an equal amount. Dotted notes result in a more abrupt and syncopated rhythm, as heard in ragtime music.

For example, if you're playing two eighth notes, these notes are counted as "1 +" (or "1 and") with each note having the same duration. However, if you increase the rhythmic value of the first note by one half (and give that note a dot in the tab notation), this new note is *three* times as long as the second note (which is then given another flag in tab notation, changing its value from an eighth note to a sixteenth note). These two notes are now counted as "1 e + uh" (or "1 e and uh") with the first note played on the "1" and the second note played on the "uh."

Trying some minstrel tunes

Are you ready to do some banjo time travel by attempting a few tunes in the minstrel style? Both tunes in this section utilize the double-thumbing techniques discussed in the preceding section in addition to employing more conventional right-hand clawhammer patterns and left-hand pull-offs (for more info on pull-offs, see Chapter 6).

"Juba"

"Juba" is from *Frank B. Converse's New and Complete Method for the Banjo*, an instruction manual first published in 1865. The name *Juba* was given to a popular minstrel dance as well as to this tune. This piece, a simple theme and variation, was often used in the instructional manuals to teach the basic minstrel technique, and it's a great way to practice your double-thumbing (see Tab 11-2 and listen to Audio Track 114).

Note the use of the right-hand thumb on the 2nd string throughout "Juba." Measures 5 and 6 alternate 5th-string and 2nd-string notes, all played by the thumb, providing a real 19th-century workout!

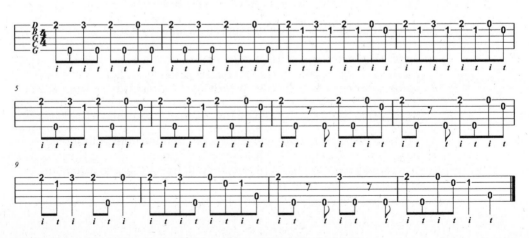

Tab 11-2: Playing "Juba," a minstrel banjo piece from 1865 (Audio Track 114).

"Hard Times"

"Hard Times" is a piece from *Briggs' Banjo Instructor* published in 1855 (see Tab 11-3). Note that the time signature of this piece is 6/8, which means this tune has six main beats per measure with an eighth note equaling one beat (or one count). Use a bit more right-hand punch to play the notes that fall on the "one" and "four" (as in ONE-two-three-FOUR-five-six) to really make this tune come alive. Don't forget to listen to Audio Track 115 and Video Clip 38 to get the right feel for this tune.

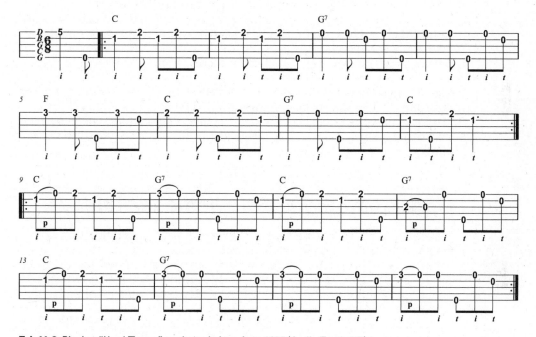

Tab 11-3: Playing "Hard Times," a minstrel piece from 1855 (Audio Track 115).

Branching Out with Classic Banjo

In 1865, Frank B. Converse introduced the *guitar style* to the minstrel banjo world, adapting the right-hand fingerpicking techniques used by 19th-century guitarists to the banjo and presenting a new way to play music on the banjo. In the guitar style, the right-hand fingers pick up on the strings as in bluegrass banjo (see Chapter 5 for an introduction to right-hand technique in blue-grass), rather than downward on the strings as in minstrel and clawhammer banjo (see the section "Mastering minstrel technique" earlier in this chapter).

The guitar style soon eclipsed the minstrel banjo in popularity with those mid to late 19th-century players who preferred to learn their banjo music from sheet music. By the early 1900s, a vast repertoire of banjo pieces were written and arranged in what is now called *classic banjo* style.

Classic banjo offers everything from Sousa marches to arrangements of classical works to ragtime pieces. Of special interest to banjo players are compositions written specifically for the instrument by American and English banjo composers such as Joe Morley, Alfred Cammeyer, and Parke Hunter in the late 19th and early 20th centuries. A great deal of technical expertise is required to play many of these pieces, which were often performed with piano accompaniment or perhaps played by a banjo duo or trio. In those days, there were even entire banjo orchestras made up of — you guessed it — many, many different-sized banjos playing orchestral scores. Amazing, isn't it?

Classic banjo refers not only to a specific repertoire (those pieces written or arranged between approximately 1880 and 1920) but also to a specific way of playing these pieces on the banjo. In the following sections, you're introduced to the ways of classic banjo and get the chance to try your hand at a few beginner-level classic pieces.

Understanding classic banjo technique

Bona fide classic players use their bare fingers to play (no fingerpicks!) and employ open-back instruments strung with nylon or gut strings. However, it's fine to use whatever kind of banjo you have handy to get started. Most classic pieces (including the two examples to follow) are in drop-C tuning, as in minstrel banjo (see the section "Discovering drop-C tuning" earlier in this chapter).

Although all five fingers of the right hand are sometimes required to play some passages in classic banjo music, the thumb, index finger, and middle fingers are the ones you most often use to play this style (similar to bluegrass banjo). Like the ragtime piano compositions of Scott Joplin (such as "Maple Leaf Rag" or "The Entertainer"), classic banjo pieces often consist of several contrasting sections in different keys and use many up-the-neck chords. For these reasons, the best classic banjo players are very familiar with the location and left-hand fingering of notes and chords on the banjo neck. The best way for you to follow in these footsteps is to play as many pieces as possible, internalizing new fretted positions as you tackle new pieces.

To really get into classic-style playing, you should become comfortable with reading conventional music notation, because the great majority of pieces use regular music rather than banjo tablature. Check out *Music Theory For Dummies* by Michael Pilhofer and Holly Day (Wiley) for more information on reading conventional music notation as well as a lot of other useful information that comes in handy for whatever banjo style you choose to play.

Introducing yourself to the classics

If you're a bluegrass player, you can be right at home with many of the right-hand fingerpicking techniques used in classic banjo. However, don't be surprised if you find that these pieces are challenging. Classic banjo pieces are typically longer than bluegrass pieces, with a lot of material to memorize (you don't usually improvise on classic pieces — you play them as they appear on the printed page, adding your own expression and feeling).

Also, prepare your left hand for a good workout as you travel up and down the neck in the following pieces. Listen to the audio tracks as you carefully work through the tabs, but above all, have fun with these sounds from a century ago!

Don't forget to tune your 4th string down to C for both of the following classic pieces. Your playing will sound a lot better that way!

"Colorado Buck Dance"

A. H. Nassau-Kennedy's "Colorado Buck Dance" is taken from *Turner's Banjo Budget* series from around 1898. This piece is a great introduction to classic banjo, as you can hear on Audio Track 116. In Tab 11-4, I give you the tune's first two sections. You may find some of the right-hand work a challenge, especially as you use your right-hand index and middle fingers to play consecutive notes on the 1st string in the second section (as in measures 10, 12, and 16).

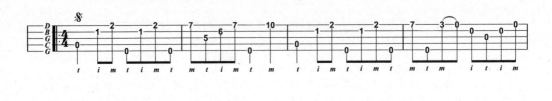

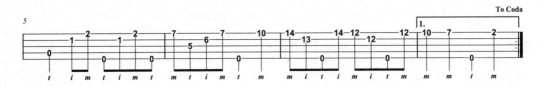

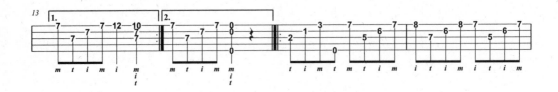

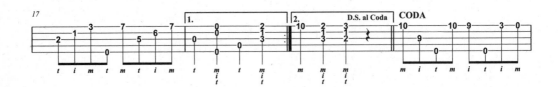

Tab 11-4: Playing "Colorado Buck Dance," a classic banjo piece from 1898 (Audio Track 116).

The American Banjo Fraternity

If you're serious about playing classic banjo, you should consider joining the American Banjo Fraternity, the group that's dedicated to the preservation of this banjo style. I guarantee that there are no hazing rituals or beer runs with this fraternity; however, you get access to boatloads of sheet music, and you're welcomed by other classic players who are glad to share their expertise. The ABF hosts two get-togethers each year, usually in either New York state or Pennsylvania, and these gatherings bring together the best classic-style players in the United States. The organization also publishes two newsletters annually (containing music!) for its members (you can find this organization on the web at www.banjofraternity. org). In addition, check out the website Classic Banjo (www.classic-banjo.ning.com) for free downloadable music, videos, a message board, and much more.

"Banjoisticus"

Tab 11-5 presents two sections of a piece from 1909, "Banjoisticus," written by Philadelphia banjo orchestra leader and composer Paul Eno, one of the best composers of classic banjo music. This tune has strong ragtime leanings and is typical of the kinds of banjo pieces enjoyed in the United States at the turn of the century by listening to cylinder recordings (these were the first "records" and were played on a phonograph with a needle, but they were cylindrically shaped rather than flat as their latter-day predecessors, the 45 rpm and LP record — remember *those?*). Anyway, give it a listen on Audio Track 117 and Video Clip 39.

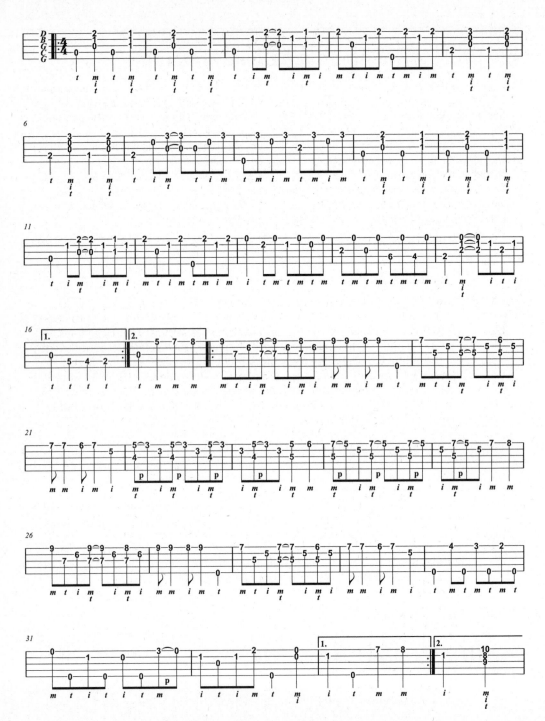

Tab 11-5: Playing "Banjoisticus," a classic banjo piece from 1909 (Audio Track 117).

Chapter 12

Networking into Banjo Culture

. . . .

. . . .

*P*laying the banjo isn't intended to be a solitary experience. Although you may feel that you're the only person in town who has been bitten by the banjo bug, I can assure you that hundreds of thousands of other people share your passion for the instrument. I know this may be hard to believe, but these folks are just as nuts as you are about everything that has to do with the banjo.

This worldwide community is just waiting for you to find them, and in this chapter, you can figure out how to connect with other players who can help you on your banjo journey. I discuss how to find a good teacher, how to locate other musicians in your area who play your kind of music, and what to expect at your first jam session. You also discover how workshops, camps, and festivals can heighten your banjo-playing experience.

Most people become interested in the banjo because they love the sound of the instrument. Most players *stay* interested because of the new friendships and experiences that come from their involvement with the banjo and with bluegrass, old-time, and related styles of music. Whatever your ability level, becoming a part of banjo culture is one of the most important things you can do to become a better player and increase your knowledge of the instrument as well as have more fun.

Taking Private Lessons

One-on-one lessons or a group class from a skilled teacher are the best ways to learn how to play the banjo. However, if you've never studied with a teacher before, recognizing a good instructor from a not-so-good one and gathering up enough nerve to go in for a lesson can be intimidating. This section unlocks the process of finding a teacher and getting comfortable with lessons by using a little psychology and a little detective work.

Overcoming lesson anxiety

The thought of music lessons may dredge up negative experiences you've had with music teachers in the past or other not-so-successful attempts at learning an instrument (I still remember my childhood piano teacher and her ruler — ouch!). Or you may feel that you're too old (or too young) to start serious study with a teacher. The bottom line is that everyone experiences fear of failure in his life. Try your best not to let these kinds of thoughts limit you from doing everything within your power to find a banjo teacher in your area and start taking lessons.

Another reason that many folks don't take lessons is that they think they aren't yet good enough to get together with a teacher. They convince themselves that they'll contact a teacher after they've taught themselves the next section in that book or DVD that came with the banjo or after they've finally figured out how to get the banjo in tune!

Stop a minute and examine this way of thinking. Seems illogical, doesn't it? However, I've met many folks who have talked themselves out of lessons because they don't want to waste the teacher's time. I've talked myself out of everything from tennis lessons to subjecting my dog to obedience training with this kind of thinking. (Okay, it really *would* be a waste of the dog trainer's time, but that's a story for another time.)

Most professional teachers love working with students who have no playing experience. Brand-new players don't have bad habits to unlearn and are often more fun (and less work) to teach than someone who already plays banjo. You won't be wasting a teacher's time if you don't know the first thing about playing. That's the reason you're starting lessons! Teachers want to help you and welcome you just as you are. Also, don't worry if you're starting as an adult. Many new banjo players are middle-aged or older. I've known quite a few people who began to play banjo in their 70s!

Finding the right teacher

After you make up your mind to take lessons, you have to go about the process of locating a good teacher. Sound like a headache waiting to happen? Don't stress about it. With the advice in this section, you can be well on your way to finding an A+ teacher.

If you're new to the banjo, my best advice for finding a teacher is to start close to home. However, if you've already played for a few years, you may have to cast a wider net to find a teacher who can take you to the next level.

Using local and online resources

Your regional acoustic specialty store is the best place to find out about banjo teachers in your area. This store may even have an instructor who teaches in-house. If the store is some distance away, you should still place a phone call to inquire about teachers closer to home. This kind of store has contacts over a wide area and can probably connect you with teachers in your immediate area who the folks at your local, all-purpose, rock 'n' roll music store may not know.

The Internet has also made finding a good teacher easier. Type the key words *banjo teacher (your city and state)* or *banjo teacher directory* into an Internet search engine and see where it leads you. You may also be able to find a state or regional old-time or bluegrass club or association that sponsors events in your area, and its members should have the scoop on area instructors. Try conducting a search using *old-time* or *bluegrass association (your state)* as key words and see what comes up.

You can also post to one of several Internet banjo community websites to inquire about teachers in your area. You can get a response within hours! A few sites with good teacher directories include www.banjohangout.org and www.angiesbanjo.com.

Choosing the right teacher

After you uncover a couple names of teachers (see the preceding section), you need to decide which one to visit first. Try taking a lesson with each instructor who seems qualified and sounds interesting. Here are some of the most important questions to ask your prospective teacher:

✔ **Does the teacher actually play banjo?** The answer to this question may seem like a no-brainer, but many "banjo" teachers play something else — usually the guitar — as their primary instrument. Although the person who offers lessons in guitar, mandolin, autoharp, violin, bass, piano, drums, glockenspiel, hurdy gurdy, theremin, *and* banjo may actually be a fantastic banjo teacher, approach this kind of lesson situation with caution. A few pointed questions should quickly reveal your prospective teacher's depth of knowledge.

If you're a total beginner and can't find anyone else, this kind of teacher can at least help you to fret chords and get you started with right-hand technique, which is better than nothing! However, you soon want to move on to an instructor who really does play banjo.

✔ **Does the teacher play clawhammer or bluegrass?** Be sure to ask up front about this important aspect of teaching. Most teachers feel more comfortable giving lessons in one approach or the other, but if you find an instructor who is capable of teaching you both clawhammer and bluegrass, all the better (if you want to learn both ways of playing)!

✔ **Does the teacher welcome all levels of students?** Most dedicated, professional-level banjo teachers accept all levels of students. If a teacher accepts only beginning students, this may indicate that she's not a very skilled player. If you're looking for lessons for a child, be sure to ask about the teacher's experience and comfort level with kids. Also feel free to ask how many banjo students the teacher is currently teaching. This number gives you a good idea of how serious this person is about teaching banjo.

✔ **How are lessons put together?** Does the teacher instruct everyone in the same way or are lessons tailored to fit the individual needs of students? Does the teacher use tablature, or will you be learning by ear? (Either is fine — the quality of teaching in either area is what counts.) Is the teacher willing to instruct you on accompaniment skills? Does he have a lesson plan? You want to be sure your prospective teacher is flexible enough to match your learning style, and the answers to these kinds of questions give you an idea of the instructor's willingness to shape lessons to what's best for you.

✔ **How often, and how much?** Weekly lessons, with travel time to and from your teacher's studio, can be difficult to work into an adult's busy schedule. However, if your lessons are too far apart in time, staying focused in your practice is difficult. In my experience of teaching hundreds of students over the last 30 years, most adults can make good progress on the banjo with a one-hour lesson every two to three weeks. Kids (teenagers and younger) need more structure, and a weekly half-hour lesson is just about perfect for them. Discuss scheduling with your teacher upfront to see what's going to work out best for both of you.

Lesson prices can range from $25 to $80 or more per hour, depending on where you live and your individual teacher's scale. Better teachers cost more — this truth is the way of the world! However, even if you're a beginning-level player, I recommend splurging on at least one or two lessons from the very best teacher that you can find in your area, regardless of price. You can avoid months of frustration if you use this opportunity for an expert player and teacher to fine-tune your overall technique and help you with your sound at the initial stages of your banjo journey.

Trying out group classes

Group classes are a great way to benefit from a teacher's knowledge while connecting with other banjo players in your area. These classes should be considerably cheaper than one-on-one lessons, and they provide an excellent way for beginners to get started on the banjo. Another big advantage of group classes is that you'll rarely, if ever, have to play by yourself (and I realize for many of you shy banjo players, this alone could be worth the price of admission!).

Classes are grouped by topic and experience level, usually focusing on either old-time or bluegrass styles. If ensemble classes are available in your area, you should definitely check these out as well because this kind of group class gives you hands-on experience playing in a band. As in so many banjo-related things, your local acoustic music store is the best place to inquire about group classes in your area.

Heading online for lessons

There's a good chance that you've already checked out banjo lessons online via YouTube, Vimeo, or another web destination. Although you certainly can't beat the price, you've probably also discovered that this format is a hit-or-miss proposition, even if it does allow you to take a lesson in your pajamas.

The quality of teaching varies widely on these sites, and the format makes it impossible to learn much more than a single tune or technique at one time. Even more importantly, you can't get feedback from a YouTube banjo teacher or have confidence that you're following a course of study that will help you achieve your goals as a player.

However, the Internet can play a positive role in your banjo experience in a number of ways. Many teachers, including a few internationally known players, such as bluegrass picker extraordinaire Tom Adams or melodic clawhammer innovator Ken Perlman, offer online lessons via Skype. If you haven't been able to find a good local teacher or if you want to study with one of your musical heros, then Skype lessons are worth checking out.

Bluegrass great Tony Trischka (visit `artistworks.com` and Chapter 17 for more on this great player) and old-time master Cathy Fink (visit `truefire.com`) offer online courses of study that combine lessons with personalized evaluation by the teacher and the support of a community of players. Be sure to explore these options to maximize the time you spend with your banjo in front of a computer.

Playing Music with Others

One of the greatest pleasures you experience playing banjo is making music with others. These days, connecting with other acoustic musicians is easier than ever before. Whether you're a beginner or a more experienced player, you make faster progress on the banjo if you take the opportunity to make music with other musicians as often as you can.

The primary way that amateur bluegrass and old-time musicians get together to make music is via a jam session. At a *jam session,* musicians at a variety of different skill levels come together to share tunes. Each musician gets an equal chance to be featured, but you aren't expected to know every tune that's played. One of the best things about jams is getting to hear and try your hand at new songs. Most jam sessions provide a welcoming environment for just about all levels of players (I note some exceptions in the following sections).

Jam sessions are common in other styles of music such as jazz, folk, blues, and even rock, but they play an especially important role with the kinds of music you play on the banjo. Bluegrass and old-time music are participatory art forms, and if you're a serious fan, you're more than likely a musician as well. Jamming is a primary way to become a better banjo player as well as get connected to your local music scene.

In the following sections, you unlock the secrets of how musicians are able to miraculously play together in a jam session. You also figure out how to match a jam session to your ability level and become familiar with how musicians interact with one another to make the music flow more smoothly. By observing good jam etiquette, you can be a welcome participant at any musical gathering that needs a banjo!

Finding a good jam

In most urban areas, the amateur acoustic music scene is based around free weekly jam sessions in music stores, cafes, coffeehouses, churches, private homes, and festivals. Your acoustic specialty store, banjo teacher, local music association, or the Internet should be able to point you in the direction of the most appropriate local sessions for your ability level.

Be sure to investigate *slow jams* or *jam classes* in your area. Both are relatively new phenomena on the acoustic music scene and are ideal ways for newer players to start making music in a group context. The following describes what these kinds of jams are all about:

- ✔ **Slow jams** are led by one or two professional teachers and are designed for brand-new or beginning-level players to get accustomed to playing with other musicians by following along on bluegrass and old-time standards played *slowly.* The instructors lead you in playing simple tunes to give you a chance to use the capo, play in different time signatures, and become familiar with many different bluegrass and old-time standards. Slow jams usually have no limit in size, and they provide an easy and painless way to begin developing the techniques you need to play music with others in real jam sessions.

✔ **Jam classes** bring together one or two people on each ensemble instrument (banjo, guitar, fiddle, mandolin, dobro, and bass) to make music in a way that's a lot like playing in a real band. With the help of one or two professional teachers who are at the ready to provide comfort and aid to the jam afflicted, you work with other players to arrange tunes, work out vocal harmonies, and divide up the instrumental solos. You have the first-hand opportunity to experience what works (and what doesn't) when playing banjo with others. Jam classes are usually designed for musicians who have played six months to a year or more and already have many of the skills they need to get out and play with others.

As a complement to private lessons, both slow jams and jam classes are great ways to expand your playing horizons and help you get ready for a real jam. Banjo player Pete Wernick has created a complete course of study for beginning-level bluegrass jammers and facilitates courses all over the United States, taught by certified local teachers (check out drbanjo.com to find a class near you).

Getting ready for a jam session

The egalitarian attitude shared by most bluegrass and old-time musicians is one of the most remarkable aspects about the communal experience of playing music with others. At a bluegrass festival, you may see professional players showing a song or lick to a young novice or see people from all walks of life (and all musical ability levels) joining together in an impromptu jam session around a festival campfire. The accessibility of the music's most skilled performers and the willingness of practically all players to share knowledge are unique to bluegrass and old-time music.

However, you don't want to just walk up to any jam session, take out your instrument, and start to play. Before you consider joining a real jam, you need to have mastered the following skills on the banjo:

✔ **Keeping your banjo in tune.** All participants in a jam session must be in tune with one another for the music to sound pleasing — nothing is less welcome than an out-of-tune banjo! You need to be able to tune your banjo by using either an electronic tuner or by getting a reference pitch from a guitar player. If you're a beginner, ask for tuning help from others instead of continuing to play out of tune. (For more on tuning, see Chapter 2.)

✔ **Fretting the G, C, and D or D7 chords and playing along to a simple chord progression by using basic right-hand techniques.** Hundreds of songs use just these chords. If you're comfortable fretting these chords and moving from one to another, you're well on your way to being able to play along with many tunes.

✔ **Maintaining good rhythm as you play.** Rhythm is the most important organizing factor in making music with others, because all the musicians participating in a jam session need to play a song at the same tempo. If they didn't do this, everyone would quickly be at a different place in the same song and *that* would really sound interesting!

Banjo players have the unfortunate reputation for wanting to play faster than everyone else. The secret to playing in good rhythm with others is to calm down, take a deep breath, and listen to what other musicians are playing. Then you can adjust your own playing to match what you hear other musicians doing. If you stop playing, everyone else is going to keep going! Figuring out how to play in good rhythm is a lifelong process, but finding and staying in the groove with others is one of the most fun parts of making music. (For more on rhythm, see Chapters 3 and 4.)

In reality, this list is just the bare minimum set of skills you need to keep your head above water in a real jam session. You should also know a wide variety of chords both in first position and up the neck and be comfortable with accompaniment techniques such as *vamping* (a bluegrass banjo rhythm technique that uses up-the-neck chords and allows you to play on faster songs; see Chapter 10 for more). In addition, you should know how to use the capo and be able to play songs in the keys of C and D.

Keep in mind that a jam session isn't a private banjo lesson. Although other players or the jam leader are usually willing to help you with some aspects of a song, such as showing you a new chord or assisting you with the capo, you're essentially on your own after a tune begins. Unless the jam is specifically advertised as a slow jam (see the preceding section), musicians play tunes up to speed and won't slow down or stop for you.

Joining in a jam

Whether you're wandering around the campground at a bluegrass festival or heading to an evening session at the local acoustic music store, deciding whether, when, or how to join a jam session can be difficult and awkward. Each jam session is a bit different from any other one, and many factors can affect your decision regarding whether to join in. You may see that a banjo player (or two) is already part of the group, or maybe they're playing faster than what you're used to. So how do you know whether you should take out your banjo and join in? And how do you best start to play with others in a session?

Although the group dynamics of a jam session can be subtle, you need to consider two important things before joining in:

✔ **What is the general ability level of the jam session?** If the skill level of the other players seems to be significantly above your capabilities, the better decision is probably to leave the banjo in the case and spend some time watching and listening. However, if you've found a session where the other players are just slightly better than you are, you may have found an ideal jam to take part in.

If you join in a jam session where the players have less experience than you do, keep your playing at their level. The other players will appreciate your generosity and may even say good things about you behind your back after the session is over. (And who wouldn't like that?)

✔ **How many other banjo players are already playing?** In a more advanced-level bluegrass jam, many musicians prefer to take part in a session where just one player, or two at most, is on each instrument — just like you see in a band playing on stage. By adding your banjo to the mix, you could disrupt the musical dynamic that's already been established. On the other hand, if the jam is large and everyone seems to be having a good time just playing along (and making a racket!), that's a good indication to join right in!

Look for signs from the other musicians to gauge how welcome you may be to their session. Players often sit or stand in a circle and if that circle opens up right where you're standing, that's an unspoken invitation to join in. If one of the other banjo players, or the person who seems to be leading the jam, invites you to play, you've also just been given the green light.

Even when one of these signals occurs, you still need to figure out whether you can hold your own on the banjo with these folks. But at least you now know you're welcome to play along if you choose to do so. By the way, turning down an invitation to join in is fine if you'd rather listen.

Closed jams: A time to listen

Although you never see a sign indicating a jam session is closed, you may find some jam sessions where you aren't welcome, regardless of your playing level. *Closed jams* take place for a variety of reasons that have absolutely nothing to do with you: Perhaps the jam is an annual reunion of old friends who travel long distances to a festival just to play music with one another, or a band is showing off its stuff for fans in an informal setting or rehearsing for their next on-stage set. Exercise great caution and a lot of common sense before joining in on what sounds like a very high-level jam session around a private RV, featuring just one other banjo player. This session is likely private!

Observing good jamming etiquette

After you've been accepted into a jam circle, it's time to play! These first moments can be stressful as you figure out your role (as well as remember your rolls) in the session. Here are a few tips to remain a welcome guest after you start playing:

- **Play conservatively to get comfortable.** If you've been asked to be a part of a jam that's already started, begin by playing quietly and simply, taking cues from the other musicians as to when to take a solo. You want to give room to the other banjo players in the session, especially with backup.

- **Strive to make the group sound good.** The best jams happen when all the participants try their best to make the entire group sound good. Showing off can be considered bad form, especially if you're the newcomer in a session. Don't use an introduction to a new group of players as an opportunity to display everything you know, played at excessive speed.

- **Keep good rhythm.** Nothing spoils a jam session for other musicians more than someone who rushes the tempo, slows down, or starts and stops while playing. Although missing a chord change or even blowing your solo is alright, bad timing truly disrupts everyone in the session. If you can't keep up, you're better off not playing.

- **Use good dynamics.** For banjo players, good dynamics translates into not playing too loudly. Tone it down when playing behind another instrumental solo or a singer who sings quietly. 'Nuff said!

- **Be ready to contribute a song.** In most jams, everyone gets the opportunity to play one or more songs he chooses. Have several songs worked up well enough so you can lead others through the song by telling them the chords and directing the order of solos.

- **Make sure that your song choice is appropriate and everyone knows it.** Don't suggest "Stairway to Heaven," "Take Five," or "Smoke on the Water." Fit your song choices to the kinds of tunes that have already been played in the session. If everyone is having fun playing traditional songs with three chords, suggest another tune of this type. If more than one or two folks are hesitant about playing with you on your tune, choose something else that the other players can quickly catch on to as the song is being played.

Sitting out a particularly challenging song in a jam is perfectly fine, but if you find you're sitting out on almost every song, you may want to put the banjo back in the case. One strategy that works in many sessions is to stay outside the primary circle of pickers and follow along quietly by mirroring what other banjo players are doing, but being careful not to disturb the inner circle of players as you play.

Attending Workshops and Camps

A fantastic way to jump-start your banjo playing is to attend a workshop or camp. Both events allow you to leave the rest of the world behind for a while and focus on nothing else but playing banjo. You also get the chance to hang out with legendary players and teachers as well as connect with other musicians from not only your own part of the country but also all over the world. If you're interested in this type of experience, keep reading the following sections.

The most common excuse I hear from folks who don't attend workshops and camps is that they feel that they aren't "good enough" to benefit from these kinds of experiences or that their own playing skills are so marginal that they will drag the other players down. Don't be a needless victim of workshop anxiety syndrome! These events are designed to help each and every banjo player move to the next level in their playing.

Workshops: Fine-tuning your techniques

A *workshop* is usually a one-day event, lasting from a couple hours to a full day. Often, your area acoustic music store sponsors a weekday evening or a weekend afternoon workshop when a well-known player passes through town or when the local teacher wants to present a session on a particular topic, such as working up solos, banjo setup, or playing backup.

Workshops present a great opportunity to network with other local players as well as provide an opportunity to experience different teachers' perspectives on playing. Plus, hanging out with a famous player for a couple of hours and hearing this musician demonstrate techniques and play tunes in an intimate setting is a whole lot of fun.

Many workshops are geared towards intermediate- to advanced-level players. However, don't let that dissuade you from attending a workshop if you're a beginning player — especially if the featured teacher is one of your banjo heroes. Audio and video recording is usually encouraged at workshops, so if you don't understand everything that's covered right then and there, you can come back to this material later on when you're ready for it.

Workshops are group instruction sessions, so don't expect to receive much individual attention from the instructor in this kind of learning environment. On the other hand, you also won't be asked to play for the teacher or the rest of the class, so you don't need to worry about trying to impress everyone with your playing.

Catching the workshop bug

Although workshops on topics related to the banjo are naturally of greatest interest, don't pass up sessions that cover subjects such as harmony singing, music theory, the history of old-time and bluegrass music, arranging songs, or developing good listening skills. The more general music knowledge you can absorb, the stronger a banjo player you'll be in the long run. General workshop sessions also provide a chance to meet local folks who play other instruments, and these new friendships can result in new jamming opportunities or even the formation of a new band — featuring you on the banjo!

You can expect to spend from $25 to $80 on a workshop, depending on the number of hours of instruction and the notoriety of the teacher. Don't forget to bring extra money to buy some of the instructor's CDs, books, and DVDs!

To find workshops in your area, check with your local acoustic music store as well as your regional folk or bluegrass music association. Don't forget to also take a look at your favorite performers' or teachers' touring schedules, which can quickly be accessed via their websites. In addition, many festivals sponsor workshops as part of their programming at no extra charge. Be sure to take advantage of these opportunities.

Banjo, bluegrass, and old-time camps: Rubbing elbows with the pros

Camps are more intense experiences than workshops (see the preceding section), because they involve living from two to five days or more with 50 to 280 other music enthusiasts of all ages from all over the world who share your passion for the banjo, bluegrass, and old-time music. Imagine spending time with and getting to know such banjo legends as Tony Trischka, Cathy Fink, Bill Keith, Pete Wernick, Riley Bagus, Ken Perlman, and Alan Munde — and even getting the chance to play music with them and share a meal (or a game of hoops). As the television commercial says, that's priceless!

Well, not exactly. Camps are big investments, and after you factor in transportation costs, you can easily spend $600 to $1,500 or more for this kind of experience. Choosing a camp that matches your ability level, your musical interests, and your personality is important. Camps are experiments in communal living, so you want to make sure you select an event that fits your tastes in food and accommodations as well as your overall comfort level.

The biggest decision to make in choosing a camp is whether to attend a *banjo camp* that's designed just for banjo players or a *bluegrass* or *old-time camp* in which the banjo class is part of a larger event that provides instruction on all of the different instruments in the bluegrass and old-time ensemble (such as guitar, mandolin, fiddle, bass, and dobro). Each type of camp has its own strengths and advantages, so consider the points in the following sections as you shop for a camp that's a good match for you.

Banjo camp

The great thing about banjo camps is — you guessed it — they're all about banjos! You get small-group instruction in old-time and bluegrass styles in an all-banjo, all-the-time environment where you play banjos, talk about banjos, eat and sleep banjos, and maybe even take a few of them apart and put them back together. Plus, you'll never run across a more interesting bunch of folks in your life than those you meet at a banjo camp — you'll love it.

The main advantage of a banjo camp is that you soak in more banjo at this event than you can at an all-purpose bluegrass or old-time music camp. The larger banjo camps have teaching staffs of up to 20 professional players with class offerings that encompass a wider variety of styles than what you may encounter at a bluegrass or old-time camp with fewer banjo teachers.

Most banjo camps offer instructional tracks designed for beginning-level players, with some camps even offering classes for those who are picking up a banjo for the very first time. Even if you're an advanced-level player, plenty of great class topics are available for you to choose from. Read up on the types of classes offered by each camp and the level of student that typically attends.

A few banjo camps I recommend include the Midwest Banjo Camp near Lansing, Michigan (www.midwestbanjocamp.com); Banjo Camp North in the Boston, Massachusetts, area (www.mugwumps.com/bcn.html); the American Banjo Camp near Seattle, Washington (www.langston.com/ABC); Pete Wernick's Winter Banjo Camps in Boulder, Colorado (www.drbanjo.com); the Suwannee Banjo Camp in northern Florida (www.suwanneebanjocamp.com); and my own NashCamp Fall Banjo Retreat near Nashville, Tennessee (www.nashcamp.com).

Bluegrass and old-time camps

Bluegrass camps offer instruction in bluegrass banjo style while *old-time camps* focus on clawhammer and old-time fingerpicking techniques. Some camps, such as the California Bluegrass Association's Music Camp in Grass Valley (www.cbaontheweb.org), offer instruction in both styles at the same time. Other sponsors, such as the Augusta Heritage Center's camps in Elkins,

West Virginia (`http://augustaheritagecenter.org`), hold separate bluegrass and old-time events at different times.

The advantage of a bluegrass or old-time camp that offers instruction in all the instruments is that your jamming possibilities are much broader with an event of this type. Many bluegrass camps put you together with other musicians at your ability level to form a real (if temporary) band. The music you make in this context can be the most rewarding and memorable experience of your week at camp.

In addition to several hours per day of small-group instruction on banjo, you spend the afternoons during the week practicing with your bandmates and getting help from professional instructors as you work up a song or two to play on stage for the other campers at the end of the week. You come away from this kind of camp being more comfortable playing with other musicians and having a greater understanding of the role of the banjo in a band.

In addition to the bluegrass and old-time camps I mention previously, other great camps to check out include

- Camp Bluegrass in Levelland, Texas (`www.campbluegrass.com`)
- NashCamp's Bluegrass Week near Nashville, Tennessee (`www.nashcamp.com`)
- NimbleFingers in Sorrento, British Columbia, Canada (`www.nimblefingers.ca`)
- The Folk Alliance Winter Music Camp in Kansas City, Missouri (`www.folkalliance.org`)
- The Walker Creek Music Camp in northern California (`www.walkercreekmusiccamp.org`)
- Sore Fingers Summer Schools in England (`www.sorefingers.co.uk`)
- The Swannanoa Gathering near Asheville, North Carolina (`www.swangathering.org`)
- RockyGrass music camp in Lyons, Colorado (`www.bluegrass.com/rga`)

Room and board

Food and accommodations are usually included in the price of a music camp. I bet you thought your days of sharing a bathroom with several other hallmates in a college dorm and eating at the cafeteria were behind you, right? Not so — at least not at a banjo camp! Many camps utilize college campuses or actual summer camp venues to host their events to keep tuition prices as reasonable as possible. Don't be surprised to share a room with one or two other people at most camps.

Living in such close quarters to other aspiring musicians is usually a high-light of the camp experience for most students. You aren't at camp long enough for this living arrangement to be a hassle. However, if dormitory life and shared bathrooms prove to be a bit too much for you, you can arrange for private lodging at a local hotel during your camp stay.

A few camps, such as my own event, the NashCamp Fall Banjo Retreat held each fall near Nashville, Tennessee (www.nashcamp.com), offer bed-and-breakfast-style accommodations with gourmet meals. You pay a higher tuition for such extravagances, but if your creature comforts are a primary concern, be sure to check out the fine print regarding food and lodging for your camp as you make your decision on which camp to attend.

Heading to a Bluegrass Festival

The most popular way to experience bluegrass and old-time music and find others to play music with is to attend one of the several thousand annual outdoor bluegrass festivals that are held all over the United States each year as well as in Japan, the United Kingdom, and Europe. At a festival, you hear renowned performers on stage as well as participate in jam sessions that take place at all hours in campsites throughout the festival grounds. People flock from all over to be a part of the fun, and you can too! In the following sections, I break down what's so great about bluegrass and old-time festivals and help you find one near you.

Discovering what festivals are all about

A bluegrass festival can be one of the highlights not only of your banjo-playing experience, but also your year. These festivals are designed for musicians and their families to temporarily be part of a community who enjoys and plays bluegrass and old-time music. The outdoor setting provides a perfect context for down-home music making.

You can find festivals of all shapes and sizes. Some bluegrass festivals, such as Hardly Strictly Bluegrass in San Francisco, California (www.hardly strictlybluegrass.com); MerleFest in Wilkesboro, North Carolina (www.merlefest.org); the Telluride Bluegrass Festival in Colorado (www.blue grass.com/telluride); or the Grey Fox Bluegrass Festival in upstate New York (www.greyfoxbluegrass.com) attract large, international audiences numbering 100,000 or more that travel to hear the most well-known per-formers in American roots music today. Contrast this kind of event to a local bluegrass or old-time festival held at a nearby county fairground with around

300 to 400 people in attendance or a regional contest held out in the country that attracts the best amateur musicians from a wide region.

Most festivals last from two to five days and are held outside, but a few cold-weather events, like Wintergrass in Tacoma, Washington (`www.acoustic sound.org`), and Bluegrass First Class in Asheville, North Carolina (`www. bluegrassfirstclass.com`), are held indoors at a hotel or convention site. Very few festivals are free of charge, and most events charge up to $100 or more for a full weekend adult ticket (which really isn't bad for a full weekend of music). Children's admission prices are frequently much less than an adult ticket price, which allows the entire family to attend.

A bluegrass festival is different in several ways from a rock, jazz, or classical music festival, and you can have more fun if you keep the following guidelines in mind:

- **Bring the whole family.** Bluegrass festivals offer a secure and safe environment for the entire family to have a good time. Your kids are soon playing with new friends, and you're playing music with the folks you've just met at the campsite next door. And although you should bring the spouse and the kids, remember that most festivals don't allow pets.

- **Pack your camping gear.** You enjoy a bluegrass festival more if you camp out at the festival site for the weekend. Bring all the equipment that you would normally bring with you to a drive-in campground (or bring your RV if you have one). You can buy a variety of food from festival vendors or bring your own. Don't forget sunscreen, insect repellant, rain gear, and a flashlight (which you use to walk from one midnight jam session to another without falling over a tent stake).

- **Take your instruments.** Don't forget your banjo! At a larger festival, you have many opportunities to play with others in campground jam sessions at virtually all hours of the day (and night). Also, don't forget extra strings and picks, and bring your smartphone to preserve a hot jam session or a new tune in either an audio or video format.

  A festival is also a great opportunity to get other members of your family interested in playing, so be sure to pack extra instruments and bring these with you. Don't be surprised if someone in your family starts playing a new instrument by the end of the weekend.

- **Remember your earplugs . . . and aspirin.** Your adrenaline keeps you going until about Saturday afternoon at a three- or four-day festival. Sooner or later, you need to catch up on your sleep and recover a bit from whatever overindulgences you may have committed the night before.

Finding a festival that's right for you

Although seeing legendary performers at a large mega-festival is thrilling, you may have just as much fun and get the chance to play more music by attending a smaller event closer to home. Many of my favorite bluegrass festivals, like the California Bluegrass Association's Father's Day Bluegrass Festival in Grass Valley (www.cbaontheweb.org), FreshGrass at the Massachusetts Museum of Modern Art in North Adams (www.freshgrass.com), and the Gettysburg Bluegrass Festival in Pennsylvania (www.gettysburgbluegrass.com), lie somewhere between the two extremes. Make sure you choose a festival that's large enough to attract the best musicians in your region, but small enough to still easily allow lots of opportunities to make music with others in a safe environment.

So how do you find just the right bluegrass festival? The Internet once again is a great resource in finding the right music festivals for you in your area and beyond. Visit www.bluegrassfestivalguide.com for a national database of bluegrass and old-time festivals. You may also want to check out *Bluegrass Unlimited* (www.bluegrassmusic.com) and *The Old-Time Herald* (www.oldtimeherald.org) magazines, because each publishes an annual festival guide in their spring issues.

The website of your regional music association, the bulletin board of your local acoustic music store, and the calendar listings provided by your local bluegrass radio DJ can also point you in the right direction toward the best area festivals. And don't be afraid to ask other musicians what festivals they like to attend — word of mouth is important too!

A wide variety of festivals around the country these days use the name *bluegrass* to describe their programming. Some of these events hire bands popular with younger audiences, while others attract many retired folks. Other festivals include a wide variety of music in their programming. The kinds of bands hired to play at different festivals are a good indication of what kind of audience will be in attendance. Make your decisions based on which festival looks like the most fun for you and your family.

Part IV
Buying a Banjo and Keeping It in Good Shape

Head

Tension hoop

Side of head

Tone ring

Bracket

Resonator screw

Resonator

Photograph by Anne Hamersky

Swapping out parts is an economical way to dramatically improve the sound of your banjo. Discover the different kinds of bridges and heads that you can try out on your banjo at www.dummies.com/extras/banjo.

In this part...

- Find a great first banjo by knowing what to look for and what to avoid.

- Step up to a professional instrument that matches your playing goals and your budget.

- Change strings fearlessly using a step-by-step guide.

- Choose the right accessories: cases, straps, capos, metronomes, and more.

- Keep your banjo in top shape with simple maintenance tips.

Chapter 13

Finding Your Banjo Bliss: A Buyer's Guide

In This Chapter

▶ Deciding between a resonator banjo and an open-back banjo

▶ Knowing what to look for in your first banjo

▶ Upgrading to a higher-quality banjo

▶ Locating a great acoustic music store

I'm going to let you in on a secret: Buying a banjo can be really fun *if* you know how to do it. You can find more choices and more ways to buy a banjo today than ever before — and an instrument is out there for just about every budget. Your banjo *is* waiting for you, and this chapter helps you to find it.

Whether you have your eye on a beginner's model or a professional instrument, you need to know some fundamental differences in banjos before you lay down your hard-earned cash. If (or when) you've been playing for a few years, you may be ready to step up to a better instrument, or you may someday want to buy a collectable vintage banjo. This chapter guides you through each step of the process and helps you avoid some of the common pitfalls that you may encounter on your banjo acquisition quest.

Establishing Your Banjo Boundaries

Before you step into a music store or venture onto the Internet to begin your banjo search, you need to set some guidelines to make your search more fun and effective:

✔ **Determining your level of dedication:** Do you have a track record of getting excited about various hobbies but then moving on quickly to something else that strikes your fancy? Or do you have a gut feeling that the banjo is just the thing that you've been waiting for all your life? (If you want to be sure you're being honest with yourself, consider asking for your significant other's opinion.)

✔ **Deciding what's important:** Do you want an instrument with flash or something simple? Do you want something just to play around the house, or do you expect to travel with your banjo? Do you see yourself playing by yourself or with others? Are you also budgeting for banjo lessons or instructional materials? The answers to these kinds of questions help you sharpen your focus.

Here's another important thing to consider: As a rule, banjos tend to be heavier than guitars or mandolins. If you have back problems, you want to find an instrument that's on the lighter side.

✔ **Determining your budget:** I realize that thinking about the financial part is a drag, but you have to do it. After you've taken some time to think about what will make you happy (and what you can live with!), you need to determine both how much you can afford and the quality of banjo you're seeking. The minimum amount you need to spend for a playable new beginner's banjo and a few essential accessories is about $400 to $500. A banjo with "all the right stuff" sets you back anywhere from $600 to $4,500 or more, depending on just how many of the extra goodies you really need! My advice is to get the kind of banjo that's best for the style you think you want to play, even if it costs more.

If you're discovering a fretted instrument for the first time and have a busy life full of work and family commitments, count on 9 to 24 months of dedicated practice before you can move past the beginners' level. If you purchase the right beginner's banjo, two years or more may go by before you want or need to buy up. However, if you already play, a better-sounding instrument can jump-start your enthusiasm and push you onward and upward. In this case, I suggest you head to the section "Stepping Up to a Better Banjo" later in this chapter.

Making the Leap: Resonator or Open-Back?

You have a choice of two different kinds of five-string banjos:

✔ **A resonator banjo** has a wooden back that's attached to the back of the instrument (see Figures 13-1c and 13-1d).

✔ **An open-back banjo** doesn't have anything attached to the back. You can easily look into the inside of the banjo's sound-producing chamber (see Figures 13-1a and 13-1b).

Figure 13-1:
An open-back banjo (a, b) and a resonator banjo (c, d).

Photographs by Anne Hamersky

Your decision as to which kind of banjo is best for you should be based primarily on the style of music that you think you want to play. The differences between these two types of banjos can be hard to understand at first, but they're mainly about the sounds that players prefer from each kind of instrument. After you try out both kinds of banjos at a music store by holding them in your hands, strumming a few chords, or playing a song or two, you can immediately begin to understand some of these differences, even if you've never played banjo before. The following sections discuss the advantages of each type of banjo.

Pumping up the volume: Resonator banjos

Over the last 150 years, banjo builders have continually tried to make banjos louder. I know what you're asking yourself: Aren't banjos loud enough *already?* Well, maybe they are now, but it wasn't always that way. Around 1860, someone came up with the idea of attaching a wooden chamber, or *resonator,* to the back of the banjo body in order to increase the volume of the instrument. The resonator reflects the sound off of its inside surface and projects the sound out of the front of the instrument and away from the player. The result is more volume and a brighter banjo sound. The resonator is usually attached to the banjo with thumbscrews.

In bluegrass music, you need to be able to play with enough volume so that the other band members and your audience can hear your virtuosic solos (for more on bluegrass banjo, see Chapters 5, 6, 7, and 9). Therefore, practically all bluegrass-based banjo players prefer a resonator banjo strung with metal strings. Musicians also use resonator banjos whenever they desire additional volume and a brighter tone for other styles, from folk and old-time to progressive three-finger approaches that are elaborations of bluegrass technique.

Entry-level resonator banjos are more expensive than comparable open-back instruments. You can expect to pay from $50 to $150 more for a beginner's resonator banjo than for the same instrument in an open-back configuration. However, if you're interested in playing bluegrass, you should spend the extra money and get a resonator banjo.

If you ever need less volume or the tone of an open-back banjo, you can always loosen the thumbscrews and remove the resonator to create an instant open-back instrument. (For an overview of the parts of the banjo, see Chapter 1.)

Going the old-time way: Open-back banjos

Open-back banjos generally have a mellower tone, are lighter in weight, and can be less expensive than resonator banjos. They also usually have a different setup than resonator banjos, often with a higher string action that's preferred by clawhammer players (*string action* refers to how high the strings are positioned above the fingerboard of the instrument). Open-back players use metal, nylon, or gut strings, depending upon the specific style of music they're playing, how their instrument is set up, and the sound they want to get from their banjo.

Beginners can find new entry-level open-back banjos starting at around $400. You can find differences in price, look, and construction between open-back models, depending upon whether they're made for old-time (including clawhammer) playing, or for classic or minstrel styles.

Several manufacturers have entry-level open-back banjos with the same sound chamber (or *pot*) and overall design and construction as a matching resonator model available. However, more expensive open-back banjos likely have a different configuration of metal and wood than you find on a resonator banjo.

Banjos were around for 100 years or more before someone thought it would be a good idea to put resonators on them. The minstrel style of the mid-19th century, the classic style of the late 19th and early 20th centuries, and many of the old-time styles of the early years of country music in the 1920s and '30s were all played at the time on open-back banjos. Folk music patriarch Pete Seeger prefers an open-back instrument, and most clawhammer players find the sound of an open-back banjo just right for playing old-time string-band music. (For more on clawhammer banjo, see Chapters 5, 6, 7, and 8; for minstrel and classic banjo, visit Chapter 11.)

Finding a Great Beginner's Banjo

When I was learning to play banjo in the 1970s, I had virtually *no* good choices in a beginner's instrument. Luckily, that's not the story today. You can purchase a good startup banjo for a little more than $400 (or even less if you can find a used model). However, you can also purchase an instrument that's perfectly awful. The following sections help you separate the good from the bad.

Although the appearance of an instrument may provide an initial attraction, the banjo that sounds the best to you is the one that you will be happiest owning in the long run. You need to determine which instrument within your price range speaks to you most powerfully. If your gut choice matches your stylistic aspirations, you're definitely on the right track to making a good decision.

When you're in a music store that has several different kinds of banjos in stock, don't be afraid to ask a salesperson to demonstrate each type. Better yet, if the store has a banjo teacher, introduce yourself and arrange a time when you can meet and be treated to a mini-concert. Another option is to take a banjo-playing friend with you to play each instrument and offer advice. Sit directly across from the person who's playing so that you can absorb the sound of each instrument as deeply as possible.

Knowing what's in the pot

The body of the banjo — the round part plus the resonator if it has one — is called the *banjo pot.* Good banjo pots are built around laminated pieces of wood called a *rim,* usually made of maple, that's pressed into a circular ring shape. More expensive instruments also have a circular piece of metal called the *tone ring* or an unseen metal hoop resting on top of the wooden rim. The banjo *head* is stretched across either the top surface of the wooden rim or of the tone ring.

The pots on some inexpensive banjos are made of a single piece of aluminum. These banjos not only don't sound as good as a banjo pot built from a wooden rim, but their round shape may become distorted over time. Regardless of your budget, go for wood in your pot!

Getting good string action

How high the strings are from the fingerboard of the banjo refers to the *string action.* You want a string action that's high enough so that you don't hear buzzing against the frets when you play, but low enough so that the banjo is easy to fret and stays in tune. Remember, players generally prefer higher action for some styles (like clawhammer) than for others (like bluegrass). One exactly correct string action doesn't exist. You will naturally develop your own preferences as you play.

For now, make sure that the string action is around 1/8 inch around the 12th fret for a bluegrass banjo, measuring from the top of the fret to the 1st string (see Figure 13-2a). For clawhammer playing, it's fine for the action to be 1/4 inch where the neck meets the banjo pot. Some clawhammer banjos, like the instrument in Figure 13-2b, have a scoop in the fingerboard at the top of the neck that's designed to provide extra room for the right hand. If the string action is 1/16 inch more or less than these ideal measurements, that's okay. You have several ways to precisely adjust the string action, and at this point, you just want to make sure that it's in the ballpark. If the string action is wildly higher or lower, move on to another banjo — or to another music store!

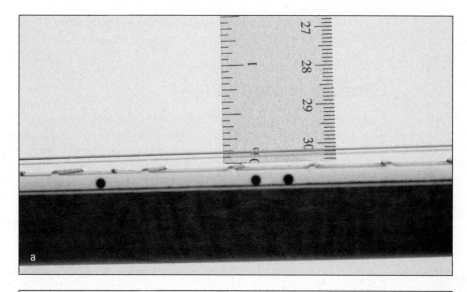

Figure 13-2: Measuring string action: 1/8 inch for a bluegrass banjo (a) and 1/4 inch for a claw-hammer banjo (b).

Photographs by Anne Hamersky

The string action over the banjo fingerboard should be the lowest where the strings meet the nut and highest where the banjo neck meets the body (the *nut* is the notched white bar at the end of the fretboard at the opposite end of the banjo from the bridge and guides the strings to the tuners). The banjo should have a gradual and consistent increase in the string action as you look from the lowest to the highest fret. If you see a big jump in the string action occurring at one point on the neck, avoid this banjo because the neck of the instrument may have problems.

Finding bridge height

A proper bridge height is essential if you want to enjoy playing your banjo. Some inexpensive imported banjos come with bridges that are so short that getting a good right-hand position for any playing style is difficult. You want a banjo bridge that measures around 5/8 inch or more from bottom to top. You can take this measurement on either the 1st- or 5th-string side of the bridge (see Figure 13-3).

Stay away from any instrument with a bridge that's less than 5/8-inch tall and has string action at the 12th fret that's above 3/16 inch. This combination of ingredients results in a banjo that is difficult to play and keep in tune.

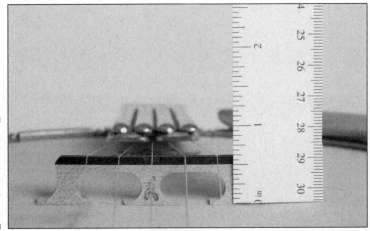

Figure 13-3:
Measuring bridge height: 5/8 inch or more is best.

Photograph by Anne Hamersky

Unlike a guitar, banjo bridges are easily removable from the instrument (after you know how to do it, that is). Professional players often try many different kinds of bridges on their banjos to find one that makes the banjo sound great and is just the right height.

TIP

If the bridge on your banjo is just a bit too short or tall, but the other aspects of your prospective banjo purchase look good, you can always replace the bridge later. If your string action is too high and the bridge is over 5/8 inch, you can replace the bridge with a shorter one and also adjust your string action at the same time.

Measuring string spacing

The distance between the strings is called the *string spacing* and is usually measured at the nut. If the strings are too close together, you'll have trouble fretting cleanly, or you may find yourself muting adjacent open strings. You need more space between the strings if your hands are large or if your fingers are stubby. On the other hand, if the strings are too far apart for the size of your hand, reaching across the fingerboard to accurately fret chords will be a chore, and your left hand will tire quickly.

To measure the string spacing, measure across the top of the nut from the 4th-string notch across to the 1st string (see Figure 13-4). For most folks, the string spacing at the nut should be around 7/8 inch, give or take 1/16 inch. These days, encountering a banjo that doesn't have adequate string spacing is unusual. However, you can still find a few new imported banjos that don't have enough room between the strings to ever allow the left hand to feel comfortable. Avoid these banjos unless your hands are really small!

Figure 13-4: Measuring string spacing: Around 7/8 inch between the 1st and 4th strings is good.

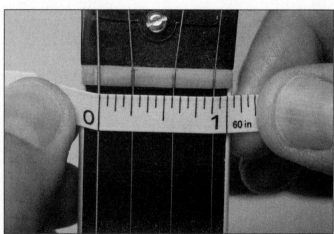

Photograph by Anne Hamersky

Checking the tuners

It probably goes without saying that the job of the tuners on a banjo is to keep the instrument in tune (although knowing *when* the banjo's in tune is up to you — check out Chapter 2 to find out how). These days, most banjos have geared tuners, with gears attached to the tuning shaft that make tuning easier and more precise. The tuners on an entry-level instrument likely have external gears that you can easily locate by looking at the back of the peghead. More-expensive banjos have tuners with gears that are housed inside the tuner's body itself. Although internal tuners tend to work better, tuners with external gears are fine on a beginner's banjo if they're in good working order. Both kinds are shown in Figure 13-5.

In either case, you want to check to make sure that the tuners move smoothly by tuning the strings up and down a bit and feeling the string movement through the peg. If necessary, have someone in the music store put the banjo back in tune for you after you experiment in this way!

Figure 13-5:
External (a)
and
internal (b)
geared
tuners.

a

b

Photographs courtesy of Elderly Instruments

I'm sure that you've already noticed that the banjo has a tuning peg that sits on the top part of the neck, almost right in the middle of the fingerboard. That's the 5th string's tuner. In order to cut corners, some manufacturers make inexpensive banjos that have a 5th-string tuner with no gears at all (see Figure 13-6). With this type of tuning peg (called a *friction peg*), the string fluctuates wildly up and down in pitch with just the slightest movement, making your attempt to get the string precisely in tune very difficult. These kinds of tuners are common on banjos that are over 100 years old, but on a new instrument, let your warning flags go up and avoid this banjo.

If you already own a banjo with this kind of tuner on the 5th string, don't toss the entire instrument! Have a knowledgeable music store replace it with a geared 5th-string tuning peg (shown in Figure 13-6). The cost of this kind of tuner plus the installation charge shouldn't run more than about $40. This amount of money is a small price to pay to save yourself hours of tuning frustration. Your loved ones will also be more appreciative of your practice sessions if you're playing in tune.

Figure 13-6:
Friction (a) and geared (b) 5th-string tuning pegs.

Photographs courtesy of Elderly Instruments

Help! I'm left-handed. Can I find a banjo for me?

Eight to 15 percent of the world's population is left-handed. A left-handed banjo player may naturally want to pick the strings with the left hand and fret with the right. On a guitar, this matter is simple because you can reset the strings so that they're in the proper low to high pitch relationship to your hands. (This is how Paul McCartney, who is perhaps the world's most well-known left-handed musician, plays both guitar and bass.) However, because the banjo has the shorter 5th string that sits on the top side of the neck, you simply can't flip the banjo around and immediately begin playing the banjo left-handed (well, you could, but it might not sound very good because the 5th string would be in the wrong place in relation to your picking hand).

To play left-handed, you have to have a banjo with a special neck that's a mirror image of a normal banjo neck so that the 5th string is on the top side of the instrument when you turn the banjo the opposite way. If you buy an entry-level banjo with a left-handed neck, you have a choice of just a few instruments and you may have to spend a bit more for this option. As you buy up to more professional-sounding banjos, your choices still remain limited, and you may have to have your necks custom built, which usually adds to the instrument's price.

Unless you already play another stringed instrument left-handed, I suggest that you try a regular right-handed banjo first. Try to make an arrangement with a music store to return your banjo in trade for a left-handed model if your experiment doesn't work out. If you feel extreme frustration after trying a right-handed banjo for a few weeks, consult with a local teacher or player to check your technique and ask his advice. If you both agree to try a left-handed instrument, then go for it.

Taking the plunge

If you've read the previous sections, you're now ready to make an informed decision on purchasing a beginner's banjo. The good news is that several banjos that combine all the necessary elements are available for under $400, giving you an instrument that plays well, sounds good, and is built to last until the time that you want to step up to something better. Check out banjos from the Deering, Gold Tone, Saga, and Epiphone companies, among others.

Don't worry too much about how these entry-level banjos look. These instruments don't have elaborate inlay patterns on the fingerboard or even a glossy finish, because the manufacturers are stressing good playability over fancy looks. These banjos also aren't going to sound as loud or as clear as more expensive instruments. However, they should *feel* like a higher-priced banjo and, at this point, that's the most important thing you need as a beginning player.

As a banjo teacher, every now and then I've witnessed new students who get so excited about their new hobby that they rush out and buy a professional-quality instrument that costs $2,000 or more before they're able to play a single song. For some reason, this kind of behavior seems to run rampant among middle-aged men like me! Although this impulse often works out to everyone's satisfaction in the long run, owning a professional instrument right off the bat can create too-high expectations of what you think you should be able to accomplish on the banjo. Remember, spending money doesn't make you a good banjo player — only practice can do that. Don't mistake the commitment of your financial resources with the commitment of the time that it takes to become a good banjo player.

The music store should offer to set up your banjo for free before handing it over to you and, in addition, may offer semiannual checkups. Take advantage of these services to keep your banjo in optimal playing condition (for more on maintaining your banjo, see Chapter 15).

Stepping Up to a Better Banjo

A good deal of complex psychology is involved in knowing when you're ready for a better (and higher-priced) banjo. Here's the most honest way of knowing that it's time: When you've reached the point in your playing where you honestly feel that your current instrument is holding you back from becoming a better player, consider it time to start looking for a better banjo.

If you hear greater clarity and volume as you play another instrument, then you're in the company of a potential new soul mate. A new banjo that's better than what you already have should also be easier to play and should sound good when you play up and down the neck. The high notes should sound bright and brilliant, and the low notes should be deep and penetrating. If the banjo is considerably more expensive than what you already own, it should look better than your current instrument and may have elaborate and beautiful inlays in the fingerboard and on the headstock. Also, a better banjo is likely heavier than your typical entry-level banjo.

In the following sections, you match your musical goals to your budget and personality. You train your eye to identify good components on a quality instrument, and you get acquainted with two more options: electric and vintage banjos.

Budgeting for a quality banjo

You have a number of different ways to think about an additional banjo purchase (your friends and loved ones may call these rationalizations, but you can pretend that this word is too big for you to understand). All of these various strategies have worked for me at different times as I've considered a new banjo purchase. See which of the approaches in the following sections is the best match for you.

I can't tell you how much to spend on your next banjo or which instrument you should buy. You have to figure this out on your own. However, keep in mind that banjos typically cost more than guitars for the same level of quality. Banjo players often spend $1,500 to $5,000 for a new, professional-quality, American-made instrument with a case. The more money you plan to spend, the more time you should spend researching your options. Don't forget to spend time talking with family and loved ones about your purchase plans. In this way, you may end up with a banjo that provides pleasure for the rest of your playing days and could also become a valuable family heirloom.

The gradual-upgrade approach

You're the sensible type. You never like to get into anything over your head, and you're slow and steady in regard to your long-range commitments. You started by playing on one of those entry-level banjos that costs around $400, but now you've got your eye set on the next most expensive banjo, which costs about $200 more than your current instrument.

In the long run, you'll be satisfied with this strategy only if you're really getting more instrument for your money. The potential downside is that you may feel compelled to make a new purchase every couple of years. However, when I was learning to play as a teenager, this buying strategy was the only one that I could afford, and it worked out fine for me! If you follow this path, you want to spend from $200 to $500 more for each step up to a better-sounding banjo.

The leap-frog approach

You're a bit more compulsive than the person described in the preceding section, but you've reached a sure conclusion that playing the banjo makes you happier than just about anything else in the world. You aren't getting any younger, and because you only go around once in life, you've decided not to wait to purchase an instrument that's close to the banjo of your dreams.

If you're interested in an open-back banjo, be ready to spend from $750 to $2,000 or more for a professional-grade banjo ready for old-time playing. Prices for professional-quality bluegrass banjos start at around $1,000 and quickly escalate up to $4,500 and above. Vintage collector's open-back and resonator banjos from the first decades of the 20th century have skyrocketed in value in recent years, costing from $3,000 to as much as $40,000 to $100,000 or more for the most coveted models (see the later section "Going vintage" for more details).

What have you got to lose with this approach? New banjos generally don't appreciate in value until they're several decades old, and vintage instruments are just downright expensive. Make sure with the leap-frog approach that you're buying an instrument from a respected and well-known builder or company so you can get back something close to your original investment if you and your banjo have to part ways.

The buy-something-different approach

You're a person who craves variety in life, and you don't limit yourself to enjoying and playing just one style of music. You love how various styles call for different banjo sounds and setups, and you may even be interested in starting a collection.

In this case, you want to purchase something that contrasts with what you already own by buying a banjo with a different sound or appearance or perhaps buying a bluegrass banjo if you already own an open back (or vice versa). With this approach, you can set a budget more flexibly based on your interest in the styles that you'll play on a different kind of banjo.

This approach is usually the domain of experienced players or collectors who are buying (or trading) professional-caliber instruments. In this case, the sky's the limit. But even new players can add variety to their lives by buying a different kind of entry-level instrument, like an electric banjo (which I discuss later in this chapter) to complement an acoustic resonator or open-back model. You can get away with spending as little as $400 to $500 with this approach if you're a beginner who craves variety in your banjos.

Knowing a quality banjo when you see it

Unlike a guitar, a banjo can be taken apart and put back together again with little more than an adjustable wrench. Many parts, such as necks, rims, tone rings, tuners, and even resonators, are interchangeable with other similar kinds of banjos. Therefore, knowing your components is crucial in selecting a quality instrument. The following sections discuss what to look for in terms of the internal parts when choosing a quality banjo.

A good banjo is the result of using well-made components that are matched and fit together with care. A *great* banjo comes from using the best components and fitting them together with the utmost skill and precision.

If you're in the market for a quality bluegrass banjo, be sure to check out the following builders: Bales, Huber, Gibson, Deering, Stelling, Nechville, Ome, Tennessee, Sullivan, Kel Kroyden, Osborne, Louzee, Gold Star, Bishline, and Recording King, among others. For a quality open-back banjo, don't forget to take a look at these makers: Chuck Lee, Wildwood, Bart Reiter, Chanterelle, Kevin Enoch, Jason Romero, Vega, Ome, and Recording King.

It's all in the wood: Banjo rims

Like the engine of a car, the rim and tone ring (see the following section) are the heart and soul of a banjo. The *rim* (or *shell*) is the ring-shaped piece of wood that, along with the tone ring, gives shape and definition to the banjo's sound. Banjo rims are usually made of maple, but beech, mahogany, and other woods are sometimes used. Most rims are made from pieces of wood laminated together and pressed into a circular shape. However, some rims are assembled from blocks of glued-together wood and are called, appropriately enough, *block rims*.

Rims are fairly standardized on quality bluegrass banjos, measuring 11 inches in diameter and around 3/4 inch in thickness. Most bluegrass players desire a dense, hard piece of maple for the rim because they feel that this type of wood conveys the banjo's sound more efficiently. You find much more variety in the sizes of rims used for open-back instruments, because open-back banjos come in many different sizes. Open-back rims can measure up to 12 inches in diameter but are typically thinner in width than a standard bluegrass rim.

The fellowship of the tone ring

The other vital part of the banjo pot is the *tone ring,* which sits on top of the wooden rim, increases the banjo's volume, and brightens its tone. On a more expensive banjo, the tone ring should be made from high-quality brass (often called *bell brass*), not aluminum. Bluegrass banjo tone rings come in the following two types:

- ✔ **Flathead tone rings:** Most banjos made today have flathead rings. Most bluegrass banjo players, including the first-generation masters Earl Scruggs and Don Reno, use this kind of ring. The flathead ring causes more surface area of the banjo head to vibrate, thereby giving the banjo a deeper tone.

- ✔ **Arch-top tone rings:** An arch-top ring is most common among banjos from the 1920s and 1930s but is also available as an option on many new instruments. This type of ring uses a different profile that causes less surface area of the banjo head to vibrate, resulting in a brighter tone. Bluegrass icon Ralph Stanley has long been associated with the sound of an arch-top bluegrass banjo.

As in the case of banjo rims, some builders have gone to great lengths to re-create the exact metal formulas found in banjo tone rings from the 1930s and 1940s, and these types of rings are found in some of the best new bluegrass banjos. Bluegrass tone ring sizes have become more or less standardized for new bluegrass banjos in the last 15 years, enabling players to experiment with their banjo's sound by swapping out one ring for another. A player may spend $2,000 to $3,000 on a new, professional-quality banjo, only to replace its tone ring somewhere down the line. These so-called pre-war formula tone rings range in price from $350 to $1,500, but can dramatically change the sound of an instrument.

You can find more variety in the kinds of tone rings used in quality open-back banjos, but also keep in mind that some old-time players prefer banjos with no tone ring at all (in this case, the head is simply stretched across the top of the wooden rim). Other old-time players prefer banjos that use a rolled brass hoop (called a hoop ring) for a tone ring. A *hoop ring* is a round, ring-shaped piece of brass that sits in a channel cut into the top of the rim with the head stretched across its top. The more muted tone of a hoop-ringed banjo is sometimes just right for the old-time sound, and, better yet, these instruments are usually less expensive than a banjo with a tone ring.

Some open-back banjos have tone rings that are virtually the same as those found on a matching model bluegrass banjo. However, new, high-end, open-back banjos are often fitted with specially made replicas, using tone-ring designs originally found on banjos dating back 100 years or more. The Tubaphone and Whyte Laydie styles of ring are two examples of replica tone rings found on many new, professional-grade, open-back banjos today (see Figure 13-7 to see all the different kinds of tone rings mentioned in this section).

Figure 13-7:
Banjo tone rings. From left to right: arch-top, flathead, Tubaphone, hoop.

Photograph courtesy of Elderly Instruments

Necks and resonators

Necks are typically made from maple (in either straight-grained or curly varieties), mahogany, or walnut. If the banjo has a resonator, its wood is almost always of the same kind as the neck. Most necks on high-end banjos are made from a single piece of wood and are called *one-piece necks.* Although these kinds of necks are preferred by most players, some builders prefer to outfit some instruments with a three-piece neck for additional stability and durability.

Builders and players alike agree that the type of wood used in the neck can have a significant impact on banjo sound, but actually describing these subjective differences can be very difficult! Generally speaking, walnut necks tend to impart the deepest tone of the three woods; maple necks add sweetness and clarity to the banjo's tone; and mahogany necks provide a more immediate response. However, the tone of any individual instrument is the result of many different factors acting together, including the mass of the neck itself. You can get a variety of banjo sounds from any of these kinds of wood.

Many players choose one type of wood over another based on appearance. You can make this factor the basis of your buying decision even on a professional-grade banjo, as long as all the other component parts are of high quality. Elaborately figured maple or walnut and deep-grained mahogany are each beautiful in their own way. Go with what makes the best impression on your senses — both visual and aural!

Radiused fingerboards

The *fingerboard,* or *fretboard,* is the thin strip of wood glued to the neck that serves as a mounting surface for the frets. When you fret a note with your left hand, you're pushing against the fingerboard. Most banjo necks have a flat fingerboard, but some players prefer a fingerboard that is curved across its playing surface. This kind of fingerboard is called a *radiused fingerboard* and is an option on more expensive instruments. Although you can expect to pay an extra $200 or more for a radiused fingerboard, if you're into more progressive bluegrass and jazz styles on the banjo, you may find that you can more easily strut your left-hand stuff on this type of neck.

Banjo bling: Inlays, plating, and engraving

Banjos are usually not only louder than guitars or mandolins, but they're also traditionally adorned with more ornate decoration — yet another reason why banjos rule! Aesthetic enhancements come in the form of elaborate inlay patterns in the neck and fingerboard, intricately carved neck heels, and engraved metal parts. Banjos with gold-plated or chrome metal parts may also grab your attention. These features not only brighten up the look of a banjo, but some players assert that gold plating also positively affects the banjo's overall tone by softening it.

For both open-back and bluegrass banjos, builders tend to decorate their banjos based on earlier tried-and-true designs. However, these days you can find planets, spaceships, peace signs, Buddhas, the family dog, and just about anything else you can think of to adorn a banjo fingerboard on a custom-built instrument.

Banjo bling can add to the cost of an instrument, but these decorative aspects of a banjo don't enhance its sound or playability. The overall worth of a banjo is determined by the quality of its component parts and how well these parts have been put together. For a more expensive banjo, the proof is always in the sound, not the bling. Don't get too carried away with appearance at the expense of good components, playability, and great sound.

Plugging in: Electric banjos

You can play just about any kind of music successfully on the banjo, and for those musicians who want to play in a rock, country, or jazz context or who just need the extra volume that comes with pickups and amplifiers, an electric banjo is just the ticket. These days, stylistic innovators such as Béla Fleck and Alison Brown are coaxing all kinds of exciting new sounds from electric banjos. Nothing is stopping you from forging your own bold musical horizons on an electric instrument, so check out some of your options in the sections that follow.

Adding a pickup to an acoustic banjo

If additional volume is the main concern, you can add an electric pickup to your regular acoustic banjo and be ready to take the stage at the next Banjo-palooza festival. Banjo pickups are attached to the coordinating rods inside the pot of the banjo and use a small piece of metal that's placed underneath one of the bridge feet as a pickup (see Figure 13-8). Installation is usually quick and easy. You can select from several different kinds of banjo pickups that range in price from $130 to $250 from EMG, Hatfield, McIntyre, and Fishman, among others.

Don't expect the sound of your banjo with an electric pickup to exactly (or even closely) resemble the acoustic sound of your banjo. Because of the placement of the pickup inside the pot and the physics of electric sound technology, you may be frustrated if you're expecting *great* banjo sound from this kind of setup. Remember, players elect to reinforce their banjo sound in this way to get more volume, not to get better tone!

Boldly going electric

If you're interested in getting all kinds of different sounds from an electrified banjo and you have your sights on being the first banjo rock star, you want to purchase a fully electric instrument. You need to budget from $700 at the low end to $4,000 or more at the high end for a top-of-the-line, custom-made banjo equipped with a *MIDI interface,* which essentially turns your electric instrument into a five-string synthesizer.

Figure 13-8:
A banjo
pickup
attaches to
the banjo's
coordinating
rods.

Photograph courtesy of EMG, Inc.

Electric banjos combine some of the structural features of banjos with the electronics and body shapes of electric guitars. Most electric banjos have a banjo head integrated into its body with two electric pickups positioned underneath the head. A toggle switch allows you to mix and match the different tones of the pickups to get a wider variety of sounds than you can find with an acoustic banjo outfitted with a pickup (and they also look really cool). Some instruments, like the Nechville Meteor, have small banjo heads and bodies that retain the circular banjo shape, but others, like the Deering Crossfire, have standard-sized heads and a larger body with the look of an electric guitar.

Because the sound is relayed from the bridge to the head just like on an acoustic banjo, these types of electric instruments retain the general sound quality of an acoustic banjo, but they aren't nearly as loud (until you plug them in, that is!). You can also get sounds out of these electric marvels that are very close to what you'd hear from an electric guitar, and the playability of these instruments is much closer to an electric guitar than a banjo as well. The strings feel light and fast underneath your fingers, and you can play with a lighter right-hand attack and still get a very big sound when you're amped up.

Some electric banjos dispense entirely with the banjo head and have only wood for their bodies. Called *solid body electrics,* this type of electric banjo comes even closer to the design and sound of an electric guitar (but doesn't sound like an acoustic banjo at all). Check out three options for electric banjos in Figure 13-9.

Figure 13-9: Three electric banjo options: the Nechville Meteor (a), the Deering Crossfire (b), and the solid-body Blue Star Banjo-blaster (c).

Photographs courtesy of Elderly Instruments

Finding many different types of electric banjos in one place may be difficult except at the largest of national acoustic retail outlets or at a major banjo camp or bluegrass festival (check out the later section "Finding the Right Music Store" for some tips on where to buy). If you make a purchase, find out whether you can return the instrument for an exchange or refund if you find that the banjo doesn't suit your needs after playing it for a day or two.

Electric banjos are way cool, big fun, and allow you to live out your rock-and-roll fantasies, but keep in mind that you can't be heard on an electric banjo in a jam session without plugging in to an amplifier. Even more important, electric instruments are usually not a welcome sight at your typical all-acoustic bluegrass, folk, or old-time jam session. The electric banjo is best viewed as an instrument that is designed for a different performance context than a regular banjo and should be used accordingly (or at least ask permission from the other musicians before plugging in and wailing away on "Tom Dooley").

Going vintage

If you explore the "used and vintage instruments" section of an acoustic specialty store's online inventory, your eyes may likely pop out at the high value of some older banjos. The most prized open-back banjos, such as an 1890s Cole Eclipse, can very easily change hands for $6,000 to $10,000 or more. A prized pre–World War II 1930s Gibson Mastertone flathead banjo with an original five-string neck can go for more than $100,000.

What's up with this? Well, you can't find anything like the beautiful craftsmanship of a 100-year-old, ornate, vintage, open-back banjo or the rich, booming sound of an old flathead Gibson banjo — in the eyes and ears of the right beholder, that is! Demand has fueled the market for vintage instruments of all kinds in recent years, which has caused resale prices to take a dramatic leap, not only for banjos but also for mandolins and acoustic and electric guitars.

One irony of this situation is that many of the best players, including those who make their living playing banjos, most likely can't afford these holy grails. These instruments tend to be purchased by amateur players or collectors with disposable income who often view vintage banjos as long-term investments.

Buying a very expensive vintage instrument without first thoroughly educating yourself about the history of banjo manufacturing, knowing which instruments players and collectors treasure, and getting a handle on the ever-changing state of the market is unwise. A good way to begin is to read up on banjo history and visit those Internet sites of stores carrying vintage inventories (see the following section for a list of these stores). Track resale prices on those instruments that interest you most and start saving for a *big* future purchase!

Finding the Right Music Store

The first store you think to visit on your banjo quest may be the local branch of one of those large national music outlets designed to serve customers more interested in rock music. As you enter through the front door, you're blasted by a shriek of heavy metal electric guitar. You gradually regain your hearing as Music Store Dude, a teenaged sales clerk dressed in black from head to toe with piercings in various parts of his anatomy, approaches you.

You meekly ask, "Do you have any banjos?" Music Store Dude sneers, shrugs, and raises his eyes to the ceiling, leaving you to explore the deep recesses of the cavernous store. If you're lucky, you may find a dust-covered beginner's instrument sitting forlornly in a corner, but you can't tell what it sounds like because the banjo's sorely out of tune. Even if the banjo were playable, you couldn't hear it anyway because of the young Jimi Hendrix wannabe wailing over in the next aisle. Consider it time to leave and find a music store better fitted for your needs (and your hearing).

In the following sections, I help you find a store that can provide you with quality service and banjos — either in person or online.

Buying from an acoustic specialty store

Banjo music is *real* music made by *real* musicians. You don't have synthesizers, lip-synching, or wardrobe malfunctions in the styles of music you play on the banjo (well, alright, there was that *Beverly Hillbillies* episode where Lester Flatt's city-raised wife shrunk his clothes by boiling them in Granny's iron kettle, but that doesn't count). When you go looking to buy a banjo, you should start with a retail outlet that specializes not only in acoustic music, but whose staff also knows something about banjos. If that store has a variety of different banjos and the sales staff can offer advice as to which banjo is going to be best suited to your musical aspirations, then you can feel confident that you've found a good place to shop. If the store hosts weekly jam sessions and has a banjo teacher on staff, even better!

Even if it takes you a couple of hours to drive to the closest acoustic specialty store, it's worth it. By taking the time to get to know the folks who work at this store, you can not only have access to their expertise, but you can also likely get lots of good advice regarding teachers, jam sessions, concerts, festivals, and workshops in your own immediate area.

If you're considering a purchase of a professional-quality instrument — a banjo that could easily cost $2,000 or more — your visit to an acoustic specialty store is practically mandatory. Whether you're buying a beginner's instrument or the best that they have in stock, you want to actually see and play as many different banjos as possible. As you compare each banjo's sound, construction, craftsmanship, and playability, don't be afraid to ask a lot of questions of the banjo specialist at the store.

Buying online

The Internet is a great place to buy some things, but what about a banjo? If you're a new player and don't have a more experienced banjo-playing friend or a teacher to help you, I advise against it. Internet buying usually requires a knowledgeable buyer, and if you're new to banjos, you may not be able to make the best purchase on your own. Take the stress off yourself and make that personal connection with the acoustic specialty store to find just the right instrument for you and your budget. You support your regional acoustic music scene and aren't at the mercy of the dreaded Music Store Dude!

If you're already playing and looking to step up to a better-sounding instrument, shopping on the Internet can be a positive experience. The key is knowing what you're looking for and being an educated buyer in regard to that particular instrument (check out "Stepping Up to a Better Banjo" earlier in this chapter for help in how to begin your banjo search).

Many of the best regional music stores maintain an active presence on the Internet and update their inventory daily on their websites. Several of these retail outlets have a true international reach and are very dependable places to buy both new and used instruments and accessories.

Be sure to check an Internet store's return policy before you purchase. Don't buy from anyone who won't allow you to return a banjo that you don't like after you've had it for a couple of days. And for now, I'd totally avoid online purchases from individual buyers, unless you've been able to establish direct phone contact with a seller and come to total agreement on a return policy, method of payment, and how the instrument is to be shipped.

Getting you started: A banjo store directory

Here's a short list of some of the best regional and national stores that specialize in new and used resonator and open-back banjos. Each store is a brick-and-mortar, walk-in establishment as well as a retail outlet providing excellent Internet and telephone customer service. Inventory varies at each store depending upon what's in stock:

- Acoustic Vibes Music (Phoenix, Arizona): www.acousticvibesmusic.com
- Banjo.Com (Atlanta, Georgia): www.banjo.com
- Denver Folklore Center (Denver, Colorado): www.denverfolklore.com
- Dusty Strings (Seattle, Washington): www.dustystrings.com
- Elderly Instruments (Lansing, Michigan): www.elderly.com
- First Quality Music (Louisville, Kentucky): www.fqms.com
- Greg Boyd's House of Fine Instruments (Missoula, Montana): www.gregboyd.com
- Gruhn Guitars (Nashville, Tennessee): www.gruhn.com
- Gryphon Stringed Instruments (Palo Alto, California): www.gryphonstrings.com
- Hatfield Music (Pigeon Forge, Tennessee): www.hatfieldmusic.com
- Janet Davis Acoustic Music (Bella Vista, Arkansas): www.janetdavismusic.com
- Mandolin Brothers (Staten Island, New York): www.mandoweb.com
- Mass Street Music (Lawrence, Kansas): www.massstreetmusic.com
- McCabe's Guitar Shop (Santa Monica, California): www.mccabes.com
- McPeake's Unique Instruments (Mt. Juliet, Tennessee): www.cmcpeake.com
- The Music Emporium (Lexington, Massachusetts): www.themusicemporium.com
- Music Folk (St. Louis, Missouri): www.musicfolk.com
- Picker's Supply (Fredericksburg, Virginia): www.pickerssupply.com
- Turtle Hill Banjo Company (Bryantown, Maryland): www.turtlehillbanjo.com

If your banjo does meet unfortunate circumstances in transit, immediately contact the store or buyer from which you made the purchase. The store will arrange for the shipping company to come and inspect the banjo. Then, they either take the instrument with them or have you return it. Be sure to save all packing materials, because they're crucial evidence in the shipping company's determination of damages. A reputable music store either sends a replacement or arranges for a repair as soon as the damaged banjo is received.

Chapter 14

Getting the Right Stuff: Banjo Gear

In This Chapter
▶ Acquiring the essentials
▶ Choosing accessories that make practicing more fun

*B*anjo players are real "gear heads." They keep up on the latest products that help get banjos from one place to another with greater ease, and make practicing and playing more productive and fun. Join me for a voyage to the Island of Banjo Gear in this chapter, where you encounter items (like cases, strings, picks, straps, capos, and tuners) that are just about essential for happy picking and other items (like metronomes and computer software) that can improve your playing or just make playing a lot more fun. (Are you still in the market for a banjo? If so, sail on back to Chapter 13 for a complete banjo buyer's guide.)

If the significant others in your household start to complain about how long your banjo gear wish list has become after you complete this chapter, feel free to go ahead and put the blame on me!

Picking Up the Stuff You Really Need

Whether you're practicing at home or playing in a jam session at a festival, all banjo players need to have certain pieces of equipment — in addition to the actual banjo, of course. The following sections provide the vital info on the stuff you don't want to be without, either at home or on the road.

At the top of this list is a banjo case (after all, you won't enhance the reputation of banjo players very much if you carry your banjo around town without something to put it in — and no brown paper bags, please!). Although most new instruments come with a case, you may want to grab a lightweight gig bag to make walking around the festival campground a breeze or consider a deluxe flight case so you can take your banjo with you on your next vacation (won't *that* make your loved ones happy!). Check out the following sections for the total lowdown on banjo storage and transport.

Cases: Becoming King of the Road

Most banjos stand up pretty well to the rigors of changing temperatures and humidity in a house, but even so, you want a good case for keeping your baby safe when you aren't practicing and for providing secure transport to your next lesson, rehearsal, or gig (yes, banjo players occasionally *do* get work).

Cases come in four basic varieties: hard-shell, soft-shell, gig bag, and flight cases. Each of these cases has a time and a place, but keep in mind that the primary purpose of a case is to protect your instrument. Usually, the more you invest in a case, the better that protection is. If you plan on traveling a great deal with your banjo, including taking your banjo with you on an airplane, choosing the right case for a quality instrument is an important decision — a decision I help you make in the following sections.

Cases or bags usually aren't included in the purchase price of most entry-level banjos. Although you can go through life without proper storage for your instrument, it makes good sense to budget an extra $50 to $70 for a simple case or bag for your first instrument. In addition to providing some basic protection for your banjo, a case gives you a pocket or two to store some of your other accessories, like picks, a tuner, and a capo.

Hard- and soft-shell cases

Hard-shell cases are the most common case option and usually accompany most intermediate- to high-quality banjo purchases (see Figure 14-1). *Hard-shell cases* are made of either wood that's covered with nylon or fabric (I especially like the vintage tweed look myself), or molded fiberglass (giving your banjo case that ever-stylish Stormtrooper look). A hard-shell case is fine for day-to-day use, as long as the banjo fits in it well. With proper care, this case should last for many years. Expect to pay from $100 to $250 for one of these, if you're purchasing the case separately.

Soft-shell cases are usually made of cardboard. Although they prevent your banjo from getting wet if some overenthusiastic audience member spills her beer while requesting "Wagon Wheel" for the umpteenth time, keeping your banjo dry is about all these cases are good for. At around $40, they're an inexpensive option and are lightweight, but they don't offer much protection for your instrument. If you paid more than $400 for your banjo, go for broke and invest in a hard-shell case or a well-padded gig bag.

Photograph by Anne Hamersky

A banjo is usually damaged while inside a case due to a loose fit that allows the banjo to move inside the case when it meets an impact. If you're purchasing a hard-shell case separately, look for the tightest fit possible between the inside of the case and the instrument. Padding on the inside top of the case and plenty of support for the neck are characteristics of a case that provides good protection. If you can see or feel the banjo move within the case when you gently shake it, the case isn't doing its job. Keep looking for something that fits your banjo more snugly. Look to these brands, among others, for good quality in hard-shell cases: Ameritage, Golden Gate, American Vintage, Canadian/TKL, Superior, and Gold Tone.

Gig bags

Many musicians prefer the soft, padded *gig bag* either as their main case of choice or as an alternative way of getting around when weight and portability are important considerations (check out the gig bag look in Figure 14-2). Gig bags range from $70 to $250 for nylon models with backpack style straps, or you can spend $400 or more for a hand-tooled leather bag. With rugged fabrics and reinforced, padded construction, some of the newer gig bags offer almost as much protection as a hard-shell case (short of driving a tour bus over it).

Figure 14-2:
A light-
weight gig
bag.

Photograph by Anne Hamersky

Gig bags are lighter than hard-shell cases and are great when you need to walk with your banjo over considerable distances at a banjo camp or blue-grass festival. Higher quality gig bags have more padding, thereby offering more protection for your banjo, and they offer greater storage capacity for picks, strings, banjo tools, and sometimes even a small laptop computer.

Check out the following brands, among others, when you're shopping for qual-ity gig bags: Reunion Blues, Superior Trailpak, Gold Tone, and Boulder Alpine.

Flight cases

If you ever plan on flying with an expensive banjo or you just want to pile all of Aunt Myrna's heaviest luggage on top of your banjo case in the trunk of your car without fear, a flight case may be in your future. *Flight cases* are the Hummers of the banjo-case world; they offer the utmost in protection for your instrument (see Figure 14-3). Made from molded fiberglass or carbon fiber, flight cases are watertight, offer extensive protection from movement inside the case, and have generous inside storage and functional external locks. One case should last a lifetime.

Figure 14-3:
Flight cases offer the best protection for your banjo.

Photograph by Anne Hamersky

I bet you can already predict one of the negatives of this type of case. Yes, you guessed it: price. You can expect to pay $695 or more for a top-of-the-line case, and you may have to be on a waiting list for a few months to get one in your favorite exterior and interior color combination. Carbon fiber cases are the newest high-tech entry into the flight-case world. At $900, they're a considerable investment, but they're lighter in weight than fiberglass models, which can weigh from 10 to 15 pounds. After you put a 10-pound bluegrass banjo in one of these, you're carrying around as much as 25 pounds of music. Believe me, you'll start to feel this somewhere between Concourse A and Concourse D!

Flight cases are the way to go if you're looking for the best protection available for your instrument. Check out Hoffee, Price, and Calton deluxe banjo cases if you're looking to buy the best.

Come fly with me: Banjos on a plane!

Whether you're headed to your next vacation spot or your destination is halfway across the country to attend a music camp or festival, sooner or later you'll want to take your banjo with you on an airplane. I fly with my most valuable instrument frequently and although I've never had an instrument damaged in transit (as I write with fingers crossed), I know many other musicians who've had pegheads snapped, necks broken, and flanges busted on their way to or from a show or music camp.

Even in the best of conditions, you can never be entirely sure how you'll be able to store your banjo on an airplane, and this unpredictability can be maddening. Despite this state of affairs, here are a few valuable strategies that I've picked up over the years in dealing with banjos at 30,000 feet. All of these tips are directed toward the primary goal of getting your banjo on board with you as carry-on luggage:

✔ **Travel with a flight case.** No matter what happens, you're still offering your instrument the best protection possible with a flight case. Taking your banjo in a gig bag is an alternative option that works for many of my traveling banjo player friends. A big advantage to this mode of travel is that gig bags are small enough to squeeze into the overhead compartments of both commuter and jumbo jets, while many hard-shell cases are just ever-so-slightly too big. But the idea of using gig bags on a plane has always made me nervous. If you're one of the last to board a full domestic flight and the overhead compartments are full, you'll have to surrender your banjo to a flight attendant for storage down below. If this happens to you and your banjo is in a gig bag, your banjo won't have close to the same kind of protection a flight case offers.

✔ **Know your airlines, figure out their boarding procedures, and choose routes with as few changes of planes as possible.** In my experience, Southwest Airlines is the most accommodating of all carriers for allowing banjos on board, but the good news is that many other airlines are welcoming banjo players and their instruments these days (as long as they don't play in the aisles during flights, that is). I've successfully carried my banjo on board United, American, Air Canada, Jet Blue, and Delta flights in the last few years. Boarding procedures vary by airline, by type of plane, by airport, and seemingly by the mood of the airline workers on that day. Despite these obstacles, see what you can do to figure out how to be in one of the first boarding groups. Apart from the individual airline's policy, the key to getting your instrument on board is getting yourself on the plane while overhead and closet space is still available for storage.

✔ **Don't draw attention to your banjo while checking in and boarding.** Act like taking your banjo on board as a carry-on is a natural thing, and it will be! If you approach an airline representative saying "I have a banjo with me. What should I do with it?" you could be asking for trouble, especially if the representative hasn't had enough morning coffee.

✔ **Don't try to preboard with your banjo.** Unless you have an otherwise valid reason, carrying a banjo with you usually isn't deemed a good enough reason to earn membership in the preboarding group. For every time this strategy has succeeded, I've been stopped an equal number of times by an airline representative.

✔ **Be friendly, cooperative, and creative in order to get your banjo onboard.** If you're courteous and exercise some creative thinking, you'll be treated with respect in return from the flight attendants and the other passengers whose help you're going to need to get your banjo on board. If you make a request with kindness, you'll likely receive the same in return.

✔ **Remove items from your case that won't get through the security checkpoint.** Although some of these restrictions have relaxed in the last few years, I move items such as string cutters, screwdrivers, banjo wrenches, and other tools from my banjo case to my suitcase before heading to the airport. In my experience, it's fine to keep fingerpicks, tuners, and capos in the case as you take your banjo through security.

Strings: You can't pick without 'em

You've probably figured out by now that you need all five strings on your banjo to make good music (if not, you may want to start with the first chapters of this book!). Although your banjo was hopefully equipped with all of its strings when you got it, these strings aren't lifetime guaranteed; it isn't unusual for a string to break every now and then while you're tuning or playing, and sooner or later all strings wear out, becoming hard to tune and sounding dull. When this moment arrives, you need to be ready with the right kind of replacement string on hand to continue playing.

The most economical way to buy strings is to purchase a set that contains all five strings. String sets aren't expensive; you should expect to pay from $6 to $12 for a good, name-brand set, and getting a discount for purchasing multiple sets isn't uncommon. You also can buy individual strings from most music stores. If you need to replace one string on your banjo more frequently than the others (for most players, it's the 1st string), you should purchase several extras of this particular string so that you don't have to constantly break up entire sets.

Most players keep one or more extra string sets on hand to replace broken strings on the spot. Many players replace an entire set of strings when they sound dull, build up a lot of grit and grime, or become difficult to tune (visit Chapter 15 for a step-by-step guide on to how to change strings). Be sure to throw one or two sets in your case, along with a small pair of wire cutters to slice off the unneeded string ends.

Your string choice should be determined by the kind of banjo you play, the sound you want to get, and how you want the strings to feel when you play them. The following sections share the secrets of making good string choices.

Loop-end and ball-end strings

Banjo strings come in *loop-end* and *ball-end* varieties, as shown in Figure 14-4. You use one or the other depending on the design of your banjo's tailpiece (the *tailpiece* holds one end of the strings at the pot end of the banjo):

- ✔ **Tailpiece for loop-end strings:** This tailpiece has finger-like attachments made for grabbing the loops that you can find at one end of loop-end strings. The great majority of banjo tailpieces feature this design, and most of the strings you'll find available are loop-end strings. Nylon and gut strings (see the following section) require you to tie your own looped ends to the banjo's tailpiece.

- ✔ **Tailpiece for ball-end strings:** If your tailpiece has only small holes at its end, you need ball-end strings for your banjo. The round ball at the end of the string prevents it from feeding itself back through the small tail-piece hole.

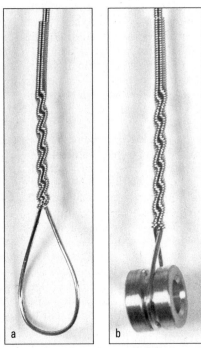

Figure 14-4:
Loop-end (a)
and ball-end
(b) strings.

Photographs courtesy of Elderly Instruments

Nickel-plated, stainless-steel, nylon, and gut strings

Practically all bluegrass players and most clawhammer players (see Chapters 5 through 9 to discover these ways of playing banjo) use nickel-plated or stainless-steel strings. These two kinds of *steel string sets* include a wound 4th string, which has additional wire wrapped around its core to add thickness and mass to the banjo's lowest-pitched string. Both kinds of metal strings produce the bright, ringing sound that is associated with the banjo and are appropriate for all kinds of playing at any ability level.

Steel string sets differ according to the kind of material used as a wrap around the 4th string. Fourth strings can be wound with bronze, stainless steel, nickel, or monel (a nickel alloy). Each type of winding provides a slightly different tonal quality:

- ✔ Bronze and stainless-steel 4th strings tend to produce a brighter sound.
- ✔ Monel produces a darker tone.
- ✔ Nickel falls somewhere in the middle.

Some open-back banjo players prefer to use nylon or gut strings on their banjos. These strings produce a more authentic sound for clawhammer, classic, and minstrel styles. (Yes, I do mean *gut* strings, as in a totally carbon-based, once-was-a-life-form product. Visit Chapter 11 to find out more about classic and minstrel styles).

A new type of string has recently caught the ear of many old-time, minstrel, and classic players: a synthetic string called *nylgut,* which combines the durability and affordability of a nylon string with the preferred "natural" tone of a gut string. It's a great alternative to both nylon and gut, and you should try it if you want that organic sound without having to actually harm any living thing in the process.

You need to search out an acoustic specialty store to find the relatively rare types of strings such as nylon, gut, and nylgut. If you want an alternative to steel strings, try them all and see which one best suits your banjo and your way of playing.

String gauges: Light, medium, or heavy

String thickness is expressed in terms of *string gauge* and is measured in thousandths of an inch, believe it or not! A light-gauge string set has slightly thinner strings (and smaller gauge numbers) than a medium- or heavy-gauge set. Your preference in strings should be determined by your playing style, your banjo, and the kind of sound you want to produce with your instrument.

You can find a wide variety of string sets available today (an example is shown in Figure 14-5), but the most important thing to remember is that designers put string sets together according to whether they're loop- or ball-end, the diameter of the strings, and the kind of wrap used around the low 4th string.

Figure 14-5:
A typical
five-string
banjo string
set.

Photograph by Anne Hamersky

My own string preferences have evolved over the years. These days, I prefer lighter-gauge strings because they sound the best to me on my banjo, and they enable me to play *fast* as I creep into middle age! For bluegrass playing, I prefer to use a string set with the following string gauges: .010, .011, .013, .020w, and .010. Now let me translate! My 1st string is 10/1,000 of an inch thick; my 2nd string is 11/1,000 of an inch thick; and so on. My fourth string measures 20/1,000 of an inch thick and is a wound string (hence the *w*). You name the 5th string last; it's almost always the same gauge as the 1st string. This is how catalogs and store websites describe string sets. (I bet you never associated the banjo with such precision!)

Many others, especially clawhammer players, prefer medium-gauge string sets because of their tone and playability. A typical medium-gauge set may have the following gauges: .011, .012, .014, .022w, and .011. As you can see, these strings feature variations of only a couple thousandths of an inch compared to a light set, but you can definitely feel and hear the difference as you play. The heavier the gauge of the string, the stiffer it feels against your fingers and the darker its sound is. Unless they're playing a banjo with a long neck or are experimenting with tuning the banjo below normal pitch, most players don't use heavy-gauge strings. However, they're available as individual string options from acoustic specialty retailers.

I can't identify a single best set of strings — this is something that you figure out over time. You should try different gauges and types of strings to see what works best for you. Don't be surprised if your choices change many times over the years as you continue to play banjo.

Here's a short list of some of the most popular string brands: GHS, American Made Banjo Company, D'Addario, Elixir, Gibson, John Pearse, Black Diamond, LaBella, Martin/Vega, Chris Sands (for classic nylon strings), and Aquila (for gut and nylgut strings).

Picks: Giving your fingers playing power

A thumbpick and one or more fingerpicks give you the ability to play with more volume, greater dynamics, and a more forceful attack. Whether or not you need picks is dependent upon the style of music you're making and your personal taste in how you want your music to sound. Many players feel that clawhammer and other old-time styles sound best when played with the bare fingers of your right hand, and most all classic- and minstrel-style players go pickless in their playing. However, the bluegrass style pretty much requires the use of a plastic or metal thumbpick along with two metal fingerpicks shaped to fit the player's index and middle fingers.

Although the feel of the picks on the ends of your digits can be uncomfortable at first, in the long run they'll give you more volume and power for the styles that need it.

Numerous choices of thumbpicks and fingerpicks patiently await you at your local acoustic music store or online. These range in price from a couple bucks to $35 or more for a pair of hand-crafted, stainless-steel fingerpicks or polymer blade thumbpicks.

Clawhammer technique requires either real or artificial fingernails to properly execute the downward stroke that's a central characteristic of this way of playing. If you aren't able to grow real nails that are long and strong enough for all of those vigorous down strokes, check out artificial nails or several kinds of fingerpicks made especially for clawhammer playing.

You should try as many different kinds of picks as you can to hear what makes your banjo playing sound the best. Check out Chapter 5 for detailed information on selecting picks that are right for you and for tips on how to fit them on your fingers.

Straps: Take a load off!

A quality banjo weighs up to ten pounds, so using a comfortable strap can save wear and tear on your back, shoulder, and neck. And banjo players don't use straps only to play while standing up. If the banjo neck is heavier than the banjo pot, which is the case on most entry-level instruments (see Chapter 1 for more info on banjo parts), you should use a properly fitted strap even while sitting down. This helps balance the weight of the banjo and frees up your left hand for gymnastic feats of fretting.

Banjo straps range in price from $8, for a simple nylon or woven-fabric strap, to $80 or more, for a fancy, handmade, leather beauty. I prefer a simple and sturdy leather strap that has little to no decoration; these cost around $45. You also may want to explore dual-shoulder-strap models and straps with shoulder pads, because these types of straps help cushion the impact of the banjo on your body.

Don't try to fit a strap by attaching one end of it to the banjo peghead. Banjo straps attach to the tension hooks of your banjo pot by using metal or plastic clips or with the strap ends fastened to the banjo with Chicago screws (see Chapter 2 for detailed help with fitting a strap on your instrument).

If you have an extra guitar strap around your house, you can turn it into a serviceable temporary strap for a lighter banjo; just attach shoelaces to each end and securely tie the shoelaces around the banjo's tension hooks.

Capos: Playing easily in different keys

Capo is shorthand for the Italian word *capotasto,* which, unfortunately, doesn't refer to the latest variety of flavored cappuccino drink. It literally means "head of fretboard." A capo (pronounced *kay*-po) is an adjustable tension clamp that shortens the effective length of the fingerboard of your banjo (the *fingerboard* is the flat surface of the neck that's used by the left hand to fret the strings). In so doing, the capo also shortens the length of your strings (which causes them to sound higher in pitch). A capo allows you to play in different keys by transferring the chords, licks, and songs you already know how to play to a new place on the banjo neck. A capo is a required piece of musical gear to take along whenever you may be playing music with others.

Banjo capos are designed to fret the 4th to the 1st strings on your banjo, but not the short 5th string. Because the 5th string needs to be raised the same number of frets as the other strings when using a capo, it gets its own special equipment to raise its pitch when you use a capo on the other strings. Raising the pitch of the banjo to play in a new key is a two-step process: First, you apply the capo to raise strings 1 through 4, and then you work with the 5th string to adjust its pitch.

The following sections explore capo options, how to properly use a capo, and the equipment you can use to raise the 5th string's pitch.

Choosing a capo

Banjo capos cost between $15 and $150 or more. Your choices range from inexpensive elastic-band models to spring-loaded capos to fancy, professional, hand-tooled, stainless-steel capos in velvet cases (really, I'm not kidding!). Figure 14-6 shows a variety of capos that you can choose from.

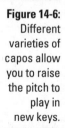

Figure 14-6:
Different
varieties of
capos allow
you to raise
the pitch to
play in
new keys.

Photograph courtesy of Elderly Instruments

A banjo player uses a capo a lot, so it doesn't make sense to cut corners with this purchase. Fortunately, you can find perfectly good capos for under $20. Although some players prefer spring-loaded capos for quick installation and removal, I use a capo that wraps all the way around the banjo's neck and attaches to the banjo using a quick-release button lock. I control the amount of tension that the capo applies to the strings by loosening or tightening a thumbscrew in the back. One advantage of this kind of capo is that you can place it out of the way behind the nut when you aren't using it (the *nut* is the white strip below the first fret that guides the strings from the fingerboard to the headstock).

Using a capo

Here's a step-by-step guide to hassle-free, thumbscrew-style capo use:

1. **Bring the edge of the capo just behind (but not on top of) the fret on the banjo neck where you want to place it (see Figure 14-7a).**

2. **Slowly tighten the adjustment screw a few turns while maintaining pressure on the top of the capo with your other hand (check out Figure 14-7b).**

3. **When you think that the capo is tight enough, try playing a few notes with the right hand.**

4. **Continue to tighten the adjustment screw just until all the fretted strings sound clear with no buzzing.**

    Don't apply any more pressure than is needed because this causes the strings to sound sharp.

5. **Experiment with capo placement.**

Some capos may apply just the right amount of pressure if they're a slight distance away from the fret instead of right up against it (as shown in Figure 14-7c); however, in most cases, you'll stay in tune more easily and your banjo will sound better with the capo positioned as close to the fret as possible.

Figure 14-7:
Placing the
capo right
up against
the fret (a);
tightening
the capo
(b); using
an alternate
placement
for the
capo (c).

Photographs by Anne Hamersky

Tuning with a capo

It's not uncommon to find that the banjo has gone just a bit out of tune with the capo on, even if it was in very fine tune without it. When this happens to you, don't retune by using the tuning pegs — if you do, your banjo will be out of tune when you take the capo off again. Here's what you should do:

- ✔ **If the string is sharp** (which it usually is when using the capo), try pushing down on the string on the bridge side of the capo (as shown in Figure 14-8a).

- ✔ **If the string is flat,** press down on the string at the peghead (see Figure 14-8b). This slick maneuver equalizes the tension of the string on both sides of the capo, and the string should still remain in tune when you remove the capo.

Some spring-loaded capos grip the strings with such force that they cause the strings to fret sharp and the banjo to go out of tune. Be sure to select a capo with adjustable tension to deal with this common problem.

The 5th-string capo and spikes: Going along for the ride

If you place a capo at the 2nd fret, you also need to raise the pitch of your 5th string the same number of frets so that all your banjo strings are in the same relationship as before you used the capo. How does that work? In this case, the 5th string is so special that it gets its *own* equipment to raise its pitch. Check out the following options to achieve this miraculous 5th-string feat:

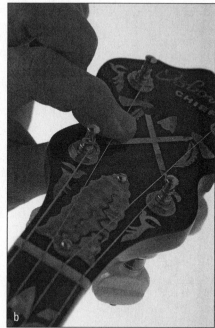

Figure 14-8: Pushing down on a string near the bridge to lower a string's pitch (a); pushing down at the headstock to raise its pitch (b).

a

b

Photographs by Anne Hamersky

✔ **Slide-mounted 5th-string capos:** The distinguishing characteristic of this capo is the long, slim, metal bar that is attached with two small screws to the banjo neck (see Figure 14-9a). You slide the capo along the bar to the fret you want to use, and then lower the capo against the string by tightening the thumbscrew. Because the hand-screw controls the amount of tension against the string, the 5th string stays in better tune with this kind of capo. Disadvantages? The metal bar adds just a bit of width to the neck and your left hand may have to move around the capo screw when moving up and down the neck. However, this kind of capo works well for many players.

✔ **Fifth-string railroad spikes:** Another ingenious solution to the problem of raising the 5th string's pitch is to use the small railroad spikes from the train tracks of an HO gauge model train set. The spikes are gently nailed into the banjo fingerboard above the 5th string with the hook of the spike remaining just high enough off the fingerboard to hook the 5th string behind the appropriate fret (see Figure 14-9b). Hey, I know this sounds strange, but I'm completely serious here!

Luckily, you don't have to ruin your neighbor's model train display by hiring a bunch of miniature John Henrys to steal the spikes right off the track. This operation is best left to a good repair person, but if you insist on doing this yourself, you can buy a package of spikes with instructions from most acoustic specialty stores. The spikes are installed at the frets where you want or need them. Most players have just two spikes installed for the 5th string at the 7th and 9th frets for playing in the keys of A and B, but some players prefer having additional spikes at other frets.

The more spikes you want on your banjo, the more you need to have a professional repair person do this installation work for you. Placing the spike in just the right place so that it doesn't get in the way of your left-hand fretting fingers or any other spikes when in use is important.

If you have 5th-string spikes already installed on your banjo, look to see which way the hook is pointed. Most spikes are installed so that the hook points down toward the 1st string. If this is the case, you can hook the 5th string underneath the spike by pushing the string down and underneath the hook (as I show in Figure 14-9b). At first you may need both hands pushing down on the string on either side of the spike to do this, but after a few tries, you should get the hang of it.

Your 5th string will probably be sharp after it's underneath the spike, so take a moment to tune it to the rest of your banjo. Now you're ready to pick!

Figure 14-9:
Using a slide-mounted 5th-string capo (a) or a railroad spike (b) to raise the 5th string's pitch.

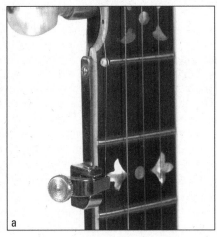

Photographs by Elderly Instruments and Anne Hamersky

Electronic tuners: Getting by with a little help

I'm not sure how banjo players survived in the era before portable tuners! Although these amazing little devices never replace a good ear, they have made getting the banjo in tune a lot easier by adding a visual reinforcement to what you hear. Tuners especially come in handy at a festival, a jam session, or even onstage — where you sometimes have so much noise around you that using your ear alone to tune the banjo is difficult. Just about everyone carries a portable tuner, and you should too.

You want to choose a chromatic tuner. Unlike a guitar or bass tuner, a *chromatic tuner* gives you all the notes available in Western music (what more could you ask for?). Believe it or not, you'll eventually need most, if not all, of these reference points for tuning your banjo, especially if you're an old-time player.

Tuners give an astounding amount of information to help you get in tune. When you pick a string, the tuner responds by indicating which note you're closest to and a moving needle tells you just how sharp or flat you are from that note. As you tune the string up or down in pitch, the meter responds accordingly, letting you know when you've tuned your string exactly to the correct pitch. Tuners also work equally well whether or not you're using a capo (but don't forget, if you're tuning with a capo in position, you'll get different note readings than you would if the banjo were in an open position).

There are two main varieties of portable tuners:

✔ **Internal microphone tuners:** These tuners (one is shown in Figure 14-10) have a built-in microphone that picks up the sound of your banjo if the tuner is placed on a nearby music stand, table top, or even resting on your knee. These tuners are affordable at $30 or more and are durable (I have a Boss tuner of this type that's lasted over 20 years). On the downside, although these tuners can be accurate in a quiet room, they experience problems if another musician is playing nearby or if the room has too much ambient noise.

✔ **Clip-on tuners:** Portable clip-on tuners made a huge splash on the acoustic scene when they were introduced about 15 years ago, and now it's hard to imagine living without one. These types of tuners attach directly to your banjo at the peghead (see Chapter 2) or on the pot and focus only on the sound of your instrument, excluding whatever noise is around you. This feature is a real lifesaver if you're trying to tune while other musicians are playing or if you're in a workshop with 15 other players, who are all using their clip-on tuners to tune at the same time! One disadvantage of these tuners is that sometimes they aren't as accurate as the internal microphone variety of tuner. Some of the cheapest clip-on tuners don't work well for very long, especially after you've dropped them a few times, so don't be afraid to spend a bit more on something that you'll use every time you start to play your banjo. Clip-on tuners begin at $10 and climb to $70.

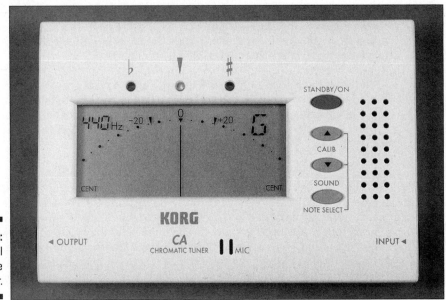

Figure 14-10: An internal microphone tuner.

Many tuners have a backlight that allows you to see the tuner's readout in a dim or dark environment. You pay more for this feature, but you may be surprised at how often this little light comes in handy around a festival campfire or waiting in the backstage wings for your *American Banjo Idol* audition.

Collecting More Cool Tools to Help Your Playing

From banjo mutes to string winders and from finger exercisers to torque wrenches, there's no end to the available accessories promising to make you a better player. Although buying everything in sight is tempting, you want to know about a few items that can actually enhance your playing and make your banjo sound its best.

Metronomes and drum machines

Keeping a steady rhythm is essential to great banjo playing and figuring out how to play with a metronome or drum machine is a good way to develop this important musical skill.

A *metronome* maintains a steady beat at whatever tempo you choose while a *drum machine* goes to the next level by providing realistic drum sounds for different styles and rhythms at different speeds. In either case, it's difficult for most players to jump right in and start playing along. In the following sections, I show you different kinds of metronomes and provide a practical guide to using these tools in your daily practice routine.

How they work

The metronome has come a long way from the pyramid-shaped wooden box with the moving pendulum that used to sit on top of your grandmother's piano all those years ago (although there's no question that these retro models are still very cool). Today's metronomes use digital technology to combine a myriad of features in increasingly small packages (see Figure 14-11a). Although they all share the primary function of allowing you to control the speed of a clicking beat, most electronic metronomes also provide a visual component, with small lights and arrows providing additional cues for playing in rhythm.

The more expensive the metronome, the more bells and whistles you get (and I mean this quite literally!). You can find metronome and tuner combos, tiny in-ear metronomes, as well as deluxe models that allow you to stack rhythms one on top of another. Expect to shell out from $25 to $180, depending upon which bells and whistles suit you best.

Drum machines do everything that metronomes can do, but they're also capable of emulating hundreds of percussion sounds (see Figure 14-11b). Most models have presets that instantly give you satisfying jazz, country, funk, and rock backing rhythms, but you can create your own drum sounds as well. Turn it on and set the speed and the preset, and you've got an instant drummer cooking underneath your banjo playing! Many professional players prefer practicing with a drum machine, and if you follow in their footsteps, you'll spend from $180 to $300 for a current model.

Figure 14-11:
Metronomes of different shapes and sizes (a); a drum machine (b).

a

b

Photographs courtesy of Elderly Instruments

Playing along with the metronome

I rely on my trusty metronome to assist me in checking my rhythmic accuracy and to help me increase speed. Unfortunately, metronomes don't come with instructions on how to use them, and figuring out how to get started on your own isn't easy. Here's a step-by-step guide to playing with the metronome with examples oriented toward the bluegrass player (for more on bluegrass banjo, see Chapters 5, 6, 7, and 9):

1. **With banjo in hand, set the metronome to around 66 beats per minute.**

   If your metronome has the option of accenting a particular beat, turn this feature off for now.

2. **Start counting in a cycle of four beats, saying one number for each metronome click: one, two, three, four, and repeat.**

3. **Because bluegrass roll patterns have eight notes in them, play two of these roll notes for every metronome click.**

   Pick one note when you hear the click and the second note exactly halfway between one click and the next.

4. **Use an alternating thumb roll to get started; continue until you've reached the end of the roll pattern.**

   If you play 3-2-5-1-4-2-5-1 as your string sequence, play the 3rd string at the same time as a metronome click, play the 2nd string between that click and the next, and play the 5th string on the next click. Congratulations! You've successfully played with the metronome.

5. **Now try the same roll pattern, repeating the sequence as many times as you can without stopping while staying with the metronome beat.**

   You want to go from the end right back to the beginning of the roll without missing a beat.

   If the metronome is set too fast for you to keep up, gradually adjust it to a lower number setting until you find a tempo where you can play along. If the metronome is too slow, increase the speed by moving it to the next highest number.

   After you're comfortable playing this first roll with the metronome, try playing other rolls or an easy song that you already know well.

Even the best musicians have trouble following the beat of the metronome. If this happens to you, don't worry. Stop playing, find the beat, and start over again. If you're still having trouble getting started, listen to the beat of the metronome and imagine what your roll pattern should sound like against that beat. After you can hear this rhythmic pattern in your head, try again.

After you're able to play an exercise or song effectively all the way through at one metronome setting, adjust the tempo to the next-highest setting and try it again. This is a great way to gradually increase your speed and accuracy. You'll find that at some tempo settings you'll hit a roadblock and find it difficult to play what you just played at a slightly slower tempo (and these roadblocks can be different for each song). Just keep practicing, and you'll soon be able to move on to the next higher metronome setting.

As you continue to increase speed, the metronome may end up beating so fast that it becomes a frantic distraction at 140 beats per minute or more. At this point, it's a good idea to change the note value that the click equals from two roll notes to four. Because you're now going to play four roll notes instead of two for every metronome click, you need to adjust your metronome accordingly. If you left the metronome setting at the same number as before, you'd now be playing twice as fast, so go ahead and back the metronome down 30 or 40 beats per minute and try playing once again with the metronome in this new way. If you try the alternating thumb roll again, this time you'll play *four* notes for every metronome click instead of two.

Because of the banjo's robust volume, you may have trouble hearing the beat of your metronome above the beautiful sounds of your own playing. If you're thinking about purchasing an electronic metronome, make sure it has a headphone jack. You can then use an external set of headphones to more easily hear the beat. Better yet, try hooking up a set of external speakers like the ones on a desktop computer to your metronome's jack. This way, you get as much sound as you need.

Do you practice near a computer? If so, try using a metronome or drum machine application that can be downloaded for free off the Internet (type the words *metronome* or *drum machine* into an Internet search engine and see what turns up). Most of these programs have just a small learning curve and work about as well as a stand-alone metronome.

Your computer and the banjo

In addition to metronome and drum machine applications (see the preceding section), a host of other computer programs and websites can enhance your banjo-playing experience. I go into more detail about how your computer can be one of your banjo's best friends in the following sections.

Many valuable banjo resources on the Internet are completely free, including websites with tablature, downloadable MIDI files, and lively discussion groups (begin your hunt by checking out www.banjohangout.org, www.bluegrassbanjo.org, and https://banjonews.com, the website for *Banjo Newsletter* magazine).

Slow-downer programs

Perhaps the most useful type of computer aid for banjo playing is one of several applications that slow down the tempo of a digital music source without changing its pitch, called a *slow-downer* program. These programs make it easier to play along or to understand a particular piece of music. I use one of these programs all the time when I really want to dig deep into another player's work to get every note and nuance.

Although you can buy a special stand-alone CD player that performs these same functions, you can save $200 or more by going the computer-application route. Two of the most popular slow-downer programs are Transkriber, available at most music stores, and the Amazing Slow Downer, which is available for purchase only via download at www.ronimusic.com. Although these apps are available for either your computer or a smartphone, the phone apps are cheaper, so investigate this option before your purchase. You can also find no-cost options out there as well. Windows Media Player has a slow-downer feature already built into its interface, and several Macintosh freeware programs also do the trick. However, getting a dedicated program with special looping and mixing features that can isolate the specific licks you want to learn is worth the cost.

After opening a slow-downer application, you choose the music track you want to work with and then set the tempo (which is usually expressed as a percentage of normal performance speed). You can also control the pitch of what you're listening to and work with various mixing options to hear the banjo more clearly through your computer's speakers.

Recording software

Applications such as Apple's *GarageBand* and *Audacity* allow you to record directly into the computer (so you can hear how good you *really* sound), and programs such as *Band in a Box* (for both Macs and PCs) provide you with a digital bluegrass band accompaniment. *GarageBand* is for Macs only, while *Audacity* is available as a free Internet download for either Macs or PCs. *Band in a Box* is now available in a special bluegrass edition that provides realistic-sounding bluegrass backup along with 50 bluegrass song arrangements.

YouTube

These days, YouTube is an essential resource for any banjo player. In addition to watching old performance video jewels from such great players as Pete Seeger, Don Reno, Earl Scruggs, and other banjo legends, you can also catch highlights of your favorite band's performance at last weekend's festival or concert. In addition, more and more instructional material is available at YouTube — if you're looking to learn a particular song, don't hesitate to type a title into the search engine and see what comes up.

Chapter 15

Taking Care of Your Baby: String Changing and Basic Maintenance

In This Chapter

▶ Putting on new strings

▶ Discovering how to set the bridge

▶ Fine-tuning your banjo's head tension

▶ Cleaning your banjo

▶ Taking your banjo to a professional

▶ Access the audio tracks and video clips at www.dummies.com/go/banjo

*B*anjos are the mechanical wonders of the acoustic-instrument world. To the uninitiated, a banjo appears as a complex and intimidating hybrid of wood and metal with a bit of plastic (the banjo head and your tuning peg's buttons). However, for those of you who know your way around a banjo, the instrument offers endless potential for adjustment and tinkering. Of course, knowing what you're doing before you start going crazy with a wrench and wire cutters is always good!

Part of being a good banjo player is knowing how to keep your instrument in top shape. In this chapter, I start you down the road to becoming a banjo-adjustment expert by introducing several basic things you can do now to keep your banjo sounding its best. You discover how to take off your old strings and put on new ones, how to properly set the bridge so that all the fretted notes stay in tune, and how to adjust head tension. You also figure out how to keep your banjo looking its best, and I discuss when you need to seek professional advice on repairs and maintenance.

The type, quality, and workmanship of the main components of your banjo — the wooden rim, the metal tone ring (if you have one), and the neck — determine the basic sound of your banjo. However, that basic sound can be altered in ways that you can easily hear by using different kinds of strings or

by making adjustments to such components as the bridge and head. The art of banjo adjustment, which consists of matching the playability and sound of the instrument to the preferences of an individual player, is called *setup*.

Replacing Banjo Strings

Like checking the oil in your car, shining your shoes, or balancing your checkbook, changing your old banjo strings for new ones is one of those slightly annoying tasks that's always possible to put off for another day. Although you don't do any damage to your banjo by continuing to play with worn-out strings, you'll feel much better about your banjo and your playing after you've installed a slick, shiny set of new strings. Your instrument will sound great and be easier to play, and you may be inspired to practice even harder.

If you've never changed strings on an instrument before, replacing the strings for the first time should take you no more than 30 to 40 minutes if you follow the instructions in this section. After you have the hang of it, you should soon be able to change all your strings in 15 minutes or less. The only tools you need to have on hand are a pencil and a wire cutter. A couple handy tricks make string-changing a much less onerous task. I cover everything you need to do in the next sections.

Deciding when your strings need a changin'

Some banjo players are able to play on the same set of strings for months at a time, but other players change strings as frequently as once a week. Body chemistry and climate have a lot to do with how fast strings wear out. In either case, the stickier and dirtier the immediate environment for your banjo, the quicker your strings collect dust and grime — and the more frequently you should change them.

Because a set of strings costs about as much as a latte these days, claiming poverty probably isn't a good reason for not keeping them fresh and new. However, if you live in a moderately humid climate, you keep your hands relatively clean when you play, and you wipe your strings down with a soft rag at the end of each practice session, your strings should last for a good, long time — as long as three to six months. Here are a few telltale signs that you need to think about making a change:

 ✔ The banjo becomes more difficult to tune; the strings especially sound out of tune when fretted up the neck.

 ✔ The strings feel rough to the touch, and you can see signs of grit, grime, and corrosion.

✔ A string breaks! You definitely need to replace the broken string. If you haven't changed strings for a while, go ahead and change all of them. (By the way, if the *same* string breaks consistently, you may have a problem with your nut or bridge, in which case you should consult your local acoustic music store repair person.)

Make sure you've figured out whether your banjo is designed to take loop- or ball-end strings (the great majority of banjos use loop-end strings). Take a moment to read up on this topic in the section on strings in Chapter 14 so you can make an informed string purchase. While you're at the store, go ahead and buy more than one set so you have plenty of extra strings on hand (stores often offer a discount on multiple sets too, so don't be afraid to ask!).

Changing strings 1 through 4: A step-by-step guide

Some folks like to place the banjo on a table to change strings, while others simply hold the banjo in a normal playing position. Either way, the process of replacing old strings with new ones is the same.

The bridge isn't glued to the head. It stays attached to the banjo with the tension of the strings. If you were to remove all the strings at one time, the bridge would come off, and you'd have to reposition it while installing your new strings. For this reason, I recommend changing just one string at a time. It doesn't really matter in what order you change strings, as long as you can remember which ones you've changed and which ones you haven't after you've started.

In the following sections, I give you the steps to change your 1st string. Follow the same steps to change the other strings on your banjo — with one important exception. The 3rd- and 4th-string tuners rotate clockwise to raise the pitch of a string and counterclockwise to lower it. This direction is opposite from how the 1st- and 2nd-string tuners raise and lower strings. Remember that all four strings are threaded so that they wrap around each tuning post from the center of the peghead. Check out Video Clip 40 for a demonstration.

Step 1: Figuring out which string is which

Your new strings most likely come packaged in a plastic pouch. Inside this pouch, you find each string stored in a separate paper envelope. The five envelopes are labeled either with the numbers 1 through 5 indicating which string is which (1 for 1st string, and so on), or they have numbers indicating the width of the string, measured in thousandths of an inch (0.010, 0.012½, for example). If the latter is the case, the outside packaging indicates which width goes with which string. The widths of the 1st and 5th strings should be the same; they're the smallest numbered strings in your set. The 2nd, 3rd, and 4th strings are consecutively larger.

Step 2: Removing the old string

Before you can put a new string on, you have to remove the old one. This step isn't rocket science. Begin by changing the 1st string. Simply turn the 1st string peg counterclockwise until the string is completely slack. Carefully pull the string through the hole in the tuning peg at the headstock to free it from that end of the banjo. Then take a moment to observe how the string is threaded through the tailpiece at the pot end of the banjo before removing it, so that you can retrace these steps when you attach the new string.

Step 3: Attaching the string to the tailpiece

Before you unravel the new string and install it on your banjo, take a sharpened pencil and gently rub its point back and forth a few times in the grooves of both the bridge and the nut, blowing off the excess. The graphite provides lubrication for the string at these two points of contact, which makes keeping the string in tune easier. You can also use the pencil to widen the loop end of the string to secure it to the banjo more easily (both of these steps are shown in Figure 15-1).

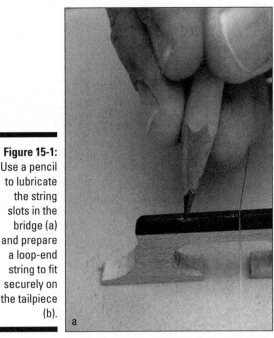
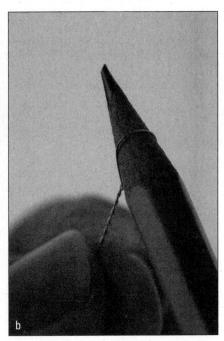

Figure 15-1:
Use a pencil to lubricate the string slots in the bridge (a) and prepare a loop-end string to fit securely on the tailpiece (b).

a

b

Photographs by Anne Hamersky

You always want to attach the loop end of the string first onto the banjo's *tailpiece* (the claw-shaped object attached to the edge of the head that holds the strings at the opposite end of the banjo from the tuning pegs). Most tailpieces have five finger-like hooks or knobs that are designed to hold this end of the string. Tailpieces on bluegrass banjos often have covers, in which case you need to lift the cover up to find the attachments. Take note of how the old string is fastened to the tailpiece and install your new string in the same way. Figure 15-2 shows the string fit on two kinds of tailpieces typically found on open-back and bluegrass banjos.

Figure 15-2:
Loop-end
string fit on
old-time
(a) and
Presto-style/
bluegrass (b)
tailpieces.

 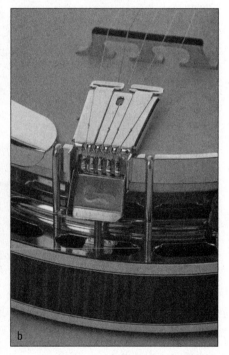

Photographs by Anne Hamersky

REMEMBER

Most bluegrass banjo tailpieces are designed so that the string comes out from under the front edge of the tailpiece. Check to see that you've threaded the string so that it emerges from the tailpiece in the same way.

Step 4: Fastening the string to the tuning post

Now you must attach the other end of the 1st string to the tuning peg's post. Note that the post has a small hole in it. Thread the end of the string through this hole from the center of the peghead, pushing the string out through the hole toward the peghead's outer edge. Then pull the string through the hole so that you have just a bit of slack in the string along its entire length — enough for you to wrap around the tuning shaft no more than three or four times. See Figure 15-3 to see how this process looks.

Figure 15-3: Attach the 1st string to the tuning post from the center of the peghead (a); pull the slack of the string through the tuning peg hole before winding it around the post (b).

Photographs by Anne Hamersky

Make sure that the string is seated in the proper 1st-string notch in the bridge. The loop end of the string may occasionally slip out from the tailpiece, so use this time to check that the string is still secure at that end of the banjo.

Step 5: Winding the string around the tuning post

Things get a little tricky with the next two steps. While holding the string with the right hand, use your left hand to create a crease in the excess string pointing toward the center of the headstock (see Figure 15-4). This kink prevents the string from moving back through the post when you begin to tighten it.

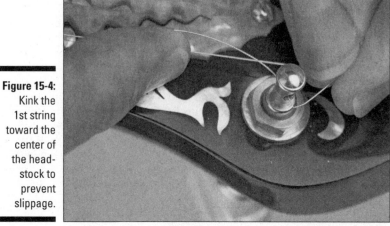

Figure 15-4:
Kink the 1st string toward the center of the headstock to prevent slippage.

Photograph by Anne Hamersky

Now tighten the 1st string around the post by turning the peg in a clockwise direction. Try feeding the string through your right-hand thumb and index finger. As you continue to turn the peg with your left hand, guide the string so that it wraps in downward circles around the post, in the direction of the headstock (see Figure 15-5).

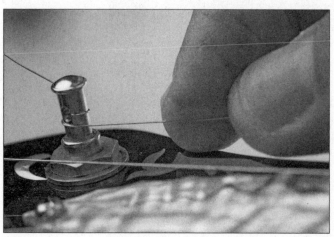

Figure 15-5:
Wrap the string in downward circles around the post while guiding it with the right hand.

Photograph by Anne Hamersky

Step 6: Securing the string to the tuning post

Remember the crease you put in the string in Step 5? Most of the time, this crease prevents the string from slipping back through the hole in the tuner. However, many players also pin the excess string against the tuning post to insure that the string won't slip back through the hole.

Here's how to do this: Wrap the excess part of the string back around the post toward the center of the headstock and bring it underneath the string just in front of the tuning post. Now pull the excess string up and wedge it between the string and post. As you continue to tighten the string with the tuner, the excess string will be pinned against the post, preventing it from slipping out of the hole (both steps are shown in Figure 15-6).

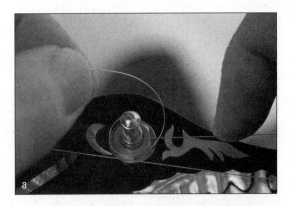

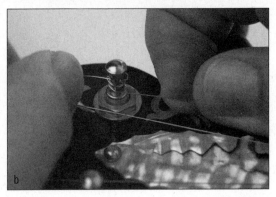

Figure 15-6: Wrap the excess part of the string back around the post (a) and wedge it against the post to avoid slippage (b).

Photographs by Anne Hamersky

Step 7: Bringing the string up to pitch

You're almost finished! Continue to turn the peg clockwise to tune the 1st string up to a D note, making sure that the string is sitting in the 1st-string nut slot. Use your electronic tuner to tune the 1st string or use the 2nd string fretted at the 3rd fret as a reference pitch. (For more instructions on tuning, see Chapter 2.)

You'll find that you'll have to spend a bit more effort keeping a new string in tune as the string gets used to being stretched. You can speed up this adjustment process by taking a moment now to stretch the string by gently pulling on it a couple of times. This will save a lot of future retuning and insure that the new string is attached correctly. Don't forget to retune the stretched string! Trim the excess string as close to the tuning post as you can using your wire cutters, and you're done!

Replacing the 5th string

Most banjos have a *geared* 5th-string tuning peg, meaning that the tuner has internal gearing to assist in more accurate tuning, like your other tuners. With this kind of peg, the tuning post emerges from the side of the peg, making the string installation process a bit different. Here's a step-by-step guide:

1. **Remove the old 5th string, observing carefully how it is wrapped around the tuning post and attached to the tailpiece.**

2. **Turn the tuning peg so that the hole in the tuning post is parallel to the direction of the other four banjo strings.**

3. **Secure the new 5th string at the tailpiece and thread the string through the hole in the tuning post, leaving just a bit of slack.**

   Check to see that the string is seated in the bridge notch for the 5th string.

4. **Turn the peg counterclockwise.**

   This step also causes the post to move counterclockwise as the string begins to wrap around the tuning post.

5. **Crease the excess part of the string in a clockwise direction and move it around the back of the tuning post and underneath the string to pin it against the post.**

   Doing this after the string has wrapped around the peg with one full revolution may be easier.

6. **Because the 5th string has its own nut or a small spike to guide it to the peg, make sure that as the string tightens, the string is seated in the 5th-string nut.**

7. **Tune the string up to pitch (G for G tuning), and trim the excess string with a wire cutter.**

   That's all there is to it! If you need some help tuning your 5th string, you can use an electronic tuner or check out the tuning instructions in Chapter 2.

A few inexpensive banjos have 5th-string tuners without gears. The big difference between geared and non-geared tuners is that the string's pitch goes up and down much more dramatically with only a slight movement from a tuner without gears. Generally, it's easier to get the precise note you need with a geared tuner. The process of changing the 5th string with a non-geared peg is the same as the steps I outline in this section, except that you wrap the string counterclockwise around a vertical tuning post (see Chapter 13 for more on geared and friction 5th-string tuning pegs).

Setting the Bridge

Unlike a guitar, the bridge on a banjo is movable. However, the bridge needs to be positioned on just one spot on the banjo head so that your strings sound in tune when fretted up and down the neck.

Even though the tension of the strings usually keeps the bridge firmly in place, over time the bridge may drift from its original position or may even fall over if bumped the wrong way (this scenario is typically a moment of high drama accompanied by a loud cracking sound, but usually no permanent damage is done). You may also decide to try different kinds of bridges on your banjo to see how they affect the sound.

For these reasons, you need to know how to properly set the bridge. For this procedure, you don't need three hands — just your two ears and the help of an electronic tuner, if you have one. Finding the correct bridge placement involves playing harmonics and comparing the sound of these notes to the sound of a fretted string, which I explain how to do in the following sections.

When in doubt about bridge placement, consult your friends at your local acoustic music store. They should be more than glad to set the bridge as well as get you on the road to making this adjustment yourself without the stress and hassle.

Discovering harmonics

Harmonics (or *chimes*) are one of the natural physical byproducts of a vibrating string. When you pick a string, it vibrates not only along its entire length, but also in fractional sections of 1/2, 1/3, 1/4, and so on. These additional, shorter-length vibrations add color and tone to the sound of the string.

If you very lightly touch a string directly above a fret at one of the points where the string length can be evenly divided and play that string, you hear the bell-like sound of a harmonic. Harmonics are a central feature of such bluegrass favorites as "Bugle Call Rag" and Earl Scruggs's "Foggy Mountain Chimes." For the 4th to the 1st strings on your banjo, harmonics are found directly above the 5th, 7th, 12th, and 19th frets. Because the 5th string is a different length than your other banjo strings, its harmonics are found at the 10th, 12th, and 17th frets.

It can take some practice (and some time) to get your banjo harmonics sounding good. The key is to find the exact location over the appropriate fret with the left hand and to use the lightest touch possible. Move the finger slightly back and forth along the string to find the exact spot that allows the string to ring at its best.

Using harmonics to set the bridge

After you have a feel for how to play harmonics, you can use them to help you set your bridge. Try playing the harmonic that's found at the 12th fret of the 1st string (see Figure 15-7). Remember that creating a harmonic takes a very light touch and that your left-hand finger has to be positioned directly over the fret instead of behind it as you would when normally fretting a note. After you're able to sound the harmonic (you'll know it when you do), you can enhance the bell-like effect by raising your left-hand finger off the string just after you strike it with the right hand.

Compare the pitch of the 12th-fret harmonic to the pitch of the string when fretted at the 12th fret. If your bridge is placed correctly, these two notes should sound the same. However, if you can hear a difference in pitch, you need to reposition the bridge in the following ways:

- ✔ If the fretted note sounds higher than the harmonic, move the bridge away from the neck, towards the tailpiece.

- ✔ If the fretted note sounds lower than the harmonic, move the bridge towards the neck, away from the tailpiece.

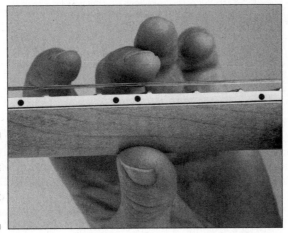

Photograph by Anne Hamersky

Usually only very small movements — fractions of an inch — are required to find the right position for the bridge. Grab one end of the bridge with each hand and firmly but gently push it just a bit along the head in the proper direction to get the string in tune.

After moving the bridge, you need to retune the banjo and try this procedure again. Getting the bridge in the best position may take several tries to get the harmonic in precise tune with the fretted note (your tuner can help you here).

After you've matched the pitches for the 1st string, try the same exercise on the 4th string. The 4th-string side of the bridge may need to be positioned slightly closer to the tailpiece in order to match the pitch of the harmonic to the fretted note.

Adjusting Head Tension

Tweaking the tightness of the banjo head is another basic skill that makes a difference in the tone and volume of your instrument. The *head* is the drum-like skin that's stretched across the top of your banjo's round pot. When you play a note, the energy from the moving string is transferred through the bridge to the surface of the head, which amplifies and colors the sound of the string across its entire surface. The tightness of the head affects how bright and loud your banjo sounds and can also contribute to the playability of your instrument along with its ability to stay in tune.

In the following sections, I discuss the relationship between the tightness of your head and your instrument's tone and show you how to make adjustments to the head to bring out the best from your banjo.

Relating head tension to banjo tone

In general, the looser your banjo head is, the mellower your banjo sounds. A looser heads adds more low (or *bass*) tones to the banjo and somewhat reduces the volume of the instrument. Conversely, the tighter the banjo head, the brighter and louder the instrument is. Although adjustments or changes in bridges and tailpieces can also affect the tone of your banjo in similar ways, changing head tension is the best — and easiest — thing you can do to brighten the sound of your banjo (or take a bit of the edge off in order to stop attracting the pets in your neighborhood).

The philosophy of banjo setup is usually to find a middle ground within a range of adjustment to bring out the best tonal qualities of a particular instrument. In regard to banjo heads, when you hear players talk about loose or tight heads, they're usually splitting hairs and talking about small adjustments in head tension. If the head is *really* loose, keeping the banjo in tune is next to impossible and its tone is very muddy. If the head is *really* tight, the banjo sounds like a tin can, or the tension may even cause the head to break. Although beauty is in the ear of the beholder, most players feel that a banjo responds best and has the best tone when the head is "medium tight." When pushing against the head with your thumb close to the bridge, a medium-tight head should offer a good deal of resistance against your thumb but should depress slightly against this pressure.

Tightening the head

A new head, whether on a brand-new banjo or as a replacement head on an old instrument, stretches and needs some retightening once or twice in the first couple of weeks of use. For this reason, bringing a new banjo home from a music store with a loose head isn't unusual. After the first weeks of using your banjo, the head should remain stable and only need a slight adjustment once every three to four months or when temperature and humidity significantly change.

The head is stretched tightly across the top of the banjo by the tension hoop, and everything is held in place by the brackets that ring around the pot. Banjos vary in the number of brackets that they have. Most bluegrass banjos have 24 brackets, but minstrel banjos have far fewer brackets, and some open-back instruments have even more. Figure 15-8 shows the side view of a bluegrass banjo pot as it appears when looking down on it while playing.

Figure 15-8: The banjo pot.

Head
Tension hoop
Side of head
Tone ring
Bracket
Resonator screw
Resonator

Photograph by Anne Hamersky

To check to see whether your banjo's head is loose, try pushing against the head near the bridge with your thumb. Does the head bend under this pressure and cause the bridge to sink with it? If so, you need to try tightening it by using the instructions in the following sections.

Using your banjo bracket wrench

Your banjo likely came with a bracket wrench tucked in the pocket of your case. *Banjo bracket wrenches* are sized to fit securely over the ends of the *bracket nuts,* which are the nuts that are attached to the long, slender metal rods (called *brackets*) that hold the banjo head tightly to the pot (see Figure 15-9). Make sure you use the right size wrench for this adjustment. In a pinch, an adjustable conventional wrench works for quick fixes, but this type of wrench can be difficult to work with in the close quarters of the banjo pot — and inadvertently cause you to strip out the bracket nuts. Consult your local acoustic music store or acoustic Internet retailer to find a wrench that's designed for your banjo. They usually cost around $5.

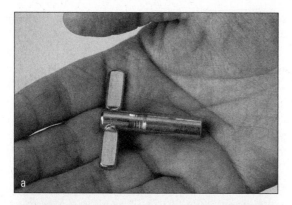

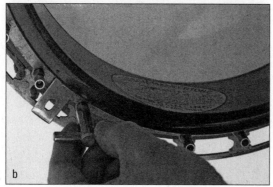

Figure 15-9:
A banjo bracket wrench (a); using the wrench to adjust the bracket nuts (b).

Photographs by Anne Hamersky

If you have a resonator on your banjo, you need to remove it to find the bracket nuts. Most resonators are attached to the pot with three or four screws that are easily visible and can be unscrewed by hand. Some entry-level banjos use small Philips head screws to hold the resonator. In this case, you'll need to dig through your garage tool kit for a screwdriver that will provide a proper fit.

After the resonator is off your banjo, use your banjo bracket wrench to tighten the head by turning the nuts clockwise, and loosen the head by turning in a counterclockwise motion. For more specific instructions on how tightly or loosely to adjust your banjo head, you can "head" to the next section.

Making small adjustments

The key to having a well-adjusted and happy banjo head is to make gradual adjustments and to keep the pressure as uniform as possible around the tension hoop. Here's a step-by-step guide to tightening the head:

1. **Before you go to work with the banjo wrench, make sure that each bracket is finger tight.**

   Having one or two brackets work themselves completely loose isn't unusual if the head hasn't been adjusted for some time or at least since the banjo was in the showroom. Feel each bracket with your fingers, tightening each one as needed by hand, before tightening with a wrench.

2. **Fit the banjo wrench onto the end of the bracket that's closest to the neck of the instrument and tighten no more than 1/4 of a turn or until the wrench meets some additional resistance; tighten the other brackets in the same way.**

   Monitor the resistance you feel in the banjo wrench as you tighten each nut and try to match the tightness of the other brackets as you move around the pot.

   Some players tighten *opposite* brackets when installing a new head, moving consecutively to the bracket that's 180 degrees across the rim near the banjo tailpiece and proceeding around the circle in this way. If you're doing only a slight adjustment to the head, you don't need to do this. Just move to the adjacent bracket and go around the circle.

After moving around the banjo pot to uniformly tighten all the brackets, take a moment to retune your instrument and try playing a few chords or tunes. As you tighten the head, you should hear a brighter and clearer tone and more volume, but if the head gets too tight, the sound of the banjo becomes thin and wiry. If your head was very loose to begin with, the bridge should rise in response to the tighter head, causing the string action to become higher (in this case, your banjo is now likely to be closer to factory specifications).

Exercise caution in tightening the head — it's possible to break it if you tighten it too much. The adjustments I suggest here should be very minor ones, where you're tightening or loosening the head tension by up to 1/2 of a turn of the bracket. When in doubt, head to your local acoustic music store for professional help getting the best setup for your instrument.

Maintaining uniform tension is key to having a good banjo sound, whether your preference is for a mellow or a bright tone. Take a moment to visually inspect the tension hoop; it should appear level around the pot and parallel to the tone ring and the top of the rim. If the tension hoop has one side pulled lower than the other at any point around the circle, the hoop is providing uneven pressure to the head. In this situation, loosen the head to even the pressure and begin the tightening process again.

Keeping Your Banjo Looking Its Best

Keeping your banjo looking sharp should be a part of your regular maintenance routine. Banjo players tend to go off the deep end in everything that they do related to the instrument, including cleaning. I try to practice moderation in this aspect of banjo maintenance. With a brand-new banjo, I try to keep it clean and shiny for a while, but sooner or later, especially after the first weekend festival of the summer, the plating inevitably begins to show signs of wear.

At that point, I resort to spot cleaning the banjo every now and then when the mood strikes me, leaving a complete and thorough polishing of the metal parts for those times (maybe once every couple of years) when I have the banjo disassembled (to install a new head, for instance).

If you keep up with regular cleaning rituals, your instrument will be easier to play, you'll have to change strings less often, and you'll preserve the wood finish and metal plating longer. So be sure to follow these few simple maintenance guidelines:

- ✔ **Rub the strings down with a cloth after each playing session to dramatically increase the life of your strings.** A cloth diaper or flannel rag is just right for this job.

- ✔ **After cleaning off the strings, gently rub the back of the neck with the cloth to remove smudges and hand oil from the neck.** Keeping the wooden surfaces of your banjo free from dirt and hand oil preserves the finish and keeps your banjo shining for years to come.

- ✔ **Take a moment to wipe off fingerprints, smudges, and whatever else may have accumulated on the metal plating of your banjo.** If your banjo has nickel plating (which is silver in appearance), that cloth diaper or soft rag can once again work wonders.

    Even the softest rags can scratch fancy gold plating. For gold, try an eyeglass cleaning cloth and spray. Together, they remove smudges without scratching the delicate plating.

- ✔ **Wipe off your armrest with a soft cloth to remove any sweat or other grime and dirt.** The plating on your armrest is especially susceptible to tarnishing. Sooner or later, you'll likely just give up and let the power of biochemistry take its course, but some extra attention with the cloth keeps nature at bay for a while.

    Wearing a wristband on your right arm while playing is an even better solution if you want to keep your banjo in like-new condition for as long as possible. You may look a little silly, but you'll have the cleanest arm-rest in town!

- ✔ **Every month or two, use a guitar polish to bring luster back to the wood finish on the resonator and neck.** Most high-quality polishes are applied with a damp, soft cloth and are buffed using a clean, dry, soft cloth. If your banjo has a resonator, take it off the banjo to make polishing it easier.

When cleaning plated parts, use the softest cloth you can find and don't apply too much pressure. The idea here is to gently remove stains from the surface of the plating, not to rub off the plating itself! Some folks recommend using silver polish every now and then on nickel- or chrome-plated parts (never use silver polish on gold plating!). I stopped doing this kind of housekeeping on my banjo some years ago when I realized that what was left on my polish cloth used to be the plating that was on my banjo! Although metal polishes such as Simichrome Polish can make the metal parts of your banjo shine like nothing else can, keep in mind that metal polishes are actually removing your plating in very small increments to create that shine. Metal polishes are best for very occasional use (once or twice a year).

Sooner or later, I always forget to move my belt buckle to the side, and I put a few scratches into the back of the resonator. No big deal! Your banjo is meant to be played, and a scratch here and there or some tarnished plating isn't going to hurt your instrument or make it sound worse. The point is to have fun playing and not spend too much time worrying about keeping your banjo in showroom condition.

Knowing When to Consult a Professional

You may have gotten the impression from the discussion in the preceding section that a banjo is a delicate flower of an instrument, susceptible to damage by just breathing the wrong way on it. Of course, nothing could be further from the truth. Banjos are hardy creatures, and if you have a well-made instrument, it should provide years of enjoyment with no significant repairs of any kind needed.

However, you may have occasions when consulting a repair person for help on things that you shouldn't try to fix yourself is your best option. These problems include the following:

- ✔ **Cracks:** Repairing cracks in any part of the wood or metal — anywhere on your banjo, inside or out — is a job best left to the pros.

✔ **A severely twisted or bowed neck:** Minor neck adjustments can be made by tightening or loosening the metal truss rod that runs under the fingerboard. For banjo necks with more severe problems, heat can be applied to bend the neck back into its proper position. But don't try this yourself — let a good repair person do this work!

✔ **Worn frets:** Over time, the frets develop gouges where they come into contact with the strings. A repair person will first even out the frets (this is called *dressing the frets*). This gives them a couple years of additional use, at which point you'll want to replace your old frets with new ones (a process called *refretting*).

✔ **A broken head:** After you've been playing a while, you can learn how to install a new head yourself. For now, leave this task to your trusted repair person.

✔ **Tuner, tailpiece, or nut problems:** With more experience, you can fix some of the problems that arise from these parts. For now, however, consult a repair person before replacing or working on any of these parts yourself.

Part V
The Part of Tens

 You'll have more fun playing with others after you check out ten essential things you need to know before you head to your first jam session at www.dummies.com/extras/banjo.

In this part...

✔ Maximize your banjo practice time and progress more quickly with ten useful tips and suggestions.

✔ Meet the greatest and most influential banjo players of our time and become familiar with their incredible music.

Chapter 16

Ten Tips to Make Practicing More Fun

Practice. Ugh. For many people, just the word itself conjures up bad memories of traumatic mandatory childhood music lessons. (I'm reminded of my piano teacher who used to threaten me with a ruler unless I played my scales perfectly. Ouch!) You've probably realized by now that if you're going to make progress on the banjo, you have to practice just about every day if you can, but I don't want you to view this as a chore. Practice should be something that you look forward to every time you pick up the instrument. You gotta do it, so try to find ways to make it as much fun as possible.

In this chapter, you find ten practical and useful tips you can use right now that will keep you coming back to your banjo time and time again . . . to practice!

Practice Regularly

This is the tough one! You lead a busy life without a whole lot of available time for banjo playing, and setting aside even 30 minutes a day for practicing can seem impossible, right? Here's my secret to practicing success: If you can't schedule a consistent time of day for a longer practice session, ramp down your expectations and play for just five minutes, several times a day if you can. Regular daily practice, even if each session is for a short amount of time, leads to quicker progress than cramming in long sessions on your few days off from work.

When my daughter Corey was learning to play piano a few years ago, she came up with an interesting practice regimen: She would play for five or ten minutes three or four times almost every day, approaching the piano to play whenever the urge struck her. Similarly, when he's at home, banjo virtuoso Béla Fleck also practices several times a day in short intervals. Don't talk yourself out of playing today because you don't have that 30 minutes available; play for just five minutes if you can, in between household chores or preparing dinner, and have fun while you're doing it. As you maintain that daily connection to your banjo, you'll become a better player.

If you can play for a little while almost every day *and* find one or two days a week when you can settle in and play for a couple of hours at a time, all the better. Keep in mind that the more skilled you are as a player, the more practice time you need to advance to the next level.

 Take the banjo out of its case and keep it on an instrument stand in your practice area (but out of the way of dogs, cats, and young children who may inadvertently tip it over). Then, when you're ready to spend a few minutes playing, your instrument is right there waiting for you.

Set Goals

Setting short-, medium-, and long-range goals keeps your practice routine on the right track and helps you to assess your overall progress. Your goals are unique to you. If you've never played a stringed instrument before, your first goal may be to successfully play a few simple songs for your friends. A little farther out in time, you may aspire to hold your own in a beginners' jam session. If you're feeling even more ambitious, someday you may want to play in a local amateur band or organize your family to make music together.

Your long-range goals (where you want to be one to three years out in time) determine your medium-range goals (6 to 12 months out in time). These medium-range goals help you to focus on what you should be practicing in the next one to two weeks (your short-term goals). Reevaluating and adjusting your goals every once in a while is fine. They're there to inspire you to keep scaling to ever-greater banjo-playing heights, not to take all the fun out of playing.

 If you're taking lessons, work with your teacher to create a set of realistic, achievable goals that you can put in writing. You can even do this on your own. After you write down your goals, check back every month or two to see whether you're still on track.

Warm Up

Athletes warm up with stretching routines, and you can do the same in your practice sessions. Warming up is a very important part of your overall practice as it prepares you mentally and physically for what comes next. When you warm up, work on aspects of your playing that you don't have time to think about after you start playing faster.

For instance, you can devise warm-up exercises to isolate and work on specific right-hand picking patterns or left-hand techniques apart from songs. Your warm-up is also the time for you to focus on your tone, your rhythm, and the clarity of your left-hand fretted notes, making adjustments when necessary. Try playing a few of your favorite songs, listening carefully to the clarity and fullness of each note and checking your overall technique as you play. Chapters 5 and 6 cover the fundamentals of banjo technique and contain excellent exercises for your warm-up.

Although some players may need to warm up for only a few minutes before they're ready to move on (which is the case with some experienced players), you may want to stay in this warm-up mode for up to 30 minutes or more before moving on to work on specific tunes. That's fine! Practicing "within your zone" is better than wasting time playing things that are too difficult for you. If you're picking up the banjo several times a day but for short intervals (as suggested in the earlier section "Practice Regularly"), you can make all of your warm-up exercises your first short session, or play a brief warm-up each time you pick up your banjo — go with what works for you and keeps you enjoying your playing the most!

Use Tablature Sparingly

Although *tablature* (written music) is a wonderful resource that allows quick access to hundreds of tunes and also allows you to study closely the subtleties of a master player, use it in small doses. Tablature is great for showing you the left- and right-hand mechanics of how something is done, but don't confuse the ability to read and play tab with really being able to play banjo. Try to internalize the *sound* of what you're playing as quickly as possible so that you're concentrating on what you're hearing, rather than what your eyes are following on the tab page. (For more tips on how to read tab, see Chapter 4.)

Using tab in a jam session can be a significant breach of custom. You can begin to break the tab habit now by working on your accompaniment skills and playing with other musicians at your level as much as possible. Think of tablature as a road map, not a destination! (For more ideas on accompanying others, turn to Chapter 10.)

Get the Right Hand First

For adult learners, one of the most difficult aspects of banjo playing is putting the right- and left-hand techniques together and using both hands at the same time to play smoothly without interrupting the even flow of notes. If you're also experiencing this problem, try playing the right-hand part by itself on the banjo's open strings. After you have the rhythm and the mechanics of the right hand down, begin to add the left-hand techniques, bit by bit if necessary. Using this building-block approach may feel a bit mechanical at first, but it can cut your learning time in half. Plus, this method is a good way to check whether you're playing something correctly.

Your right-hand technique communicates a lot about you as a player — your tone, your rhythm and drive, your volume, and even your mood! When playing with others, staying in rhythm is much more important than getting every note fretted correctly. Great players spend a lot of time working on right-hand technique. If you do the same, you'll be a great player some day too!

You can work on right- and left-hand techniques in Chapters 5 through 9.

Gradually Increase Your Speed

Playing slowly until you master a technique or song is a tough guideline for banjo players to remember, because they all want to play as fast as they can as soon as possible. However, if the song doesn't sound right when played slowly, the tune isn't going to get any better when played fast (trust me on this one!). After you're warmed up, use your practice time more efficiently (and enjoy it more in the process) by practicing at a speed that's slow enough to allow you to maintain control of what you're playing. Keep in mind that this tempo may be different for each piece you're working on.

After you're comfortable playing at a slower pace, you may decide that you want to crank the speed up a notch. Regular practice with a metronome can help you to play faster. First, find a tempo where you're playing a song well and get comfortable playing along without getting out of sync. Now try increasing the tempo on the metronome to the next-highest setting and start playing again. The increase in speed is sometimes so gradual that you may not notice a difference in the tempo at first. However, sooner or later you'll hit a bump in the road where you find one or two parts of a tune that give you problems. Work on just those sections at the new tempo, and after you've mastered them, start playing the entire tune again. You'll soon be playing effectively at a faster tempo. Head to Chapter 14 for a complete explanation of how to use a metronome in your banjo practice regimen.

Be patient with your progress in this area — speed is a function of time spent with your instrument and is measured over months or even years. Especially if you're an older player or if you've never played a fretted instrument before, speed may be the last element that falls into place as you're learning to play. Banjo music is virtuosic stuff — think of it in the same way you would if you were an organist or a sax player approaching a piece by J. S. Bach or Charlie Parker. You wouldn't expect to pick up *that* kind of music overnight, would you? Just keep playing as much and as often as you can, and you'll reach your goals.

Take Songs One Measure at a Time

Tablature enables you to play a song from beginning to end without really knowing what you're playing. However, when you go to actually internalize something that you just played from tab, you need to work on memorizing each note and phrase and be able to move comfortably from one part to the next without stopping. The best way to do this is to start at the beginning (hey, what a concept!) and play the first measure or two over and over until you've got it without looking at the tab. If you're learning by ear, you want to be able to play these measures by hearing them first in your head.

Listen to the sound of several measures played together and try to identify the musical phrases of your song (think of a musical phrase like you would a line of verse from a lyric — a *phrase* is a complete musical thought that usually consists of a couple of measures of music). After you've mastered the first phrase, move on to the second phrase. After you've got the second phrase down, spend a few moments playing the first and second phrases together, remembering not to rely on the tablature. Keep building in this fashion to the end of the song, remembering to work each new phrase into the entire tune as you go along.

You'll likely encounter some repetition along the way, so after you have the first section of a tune down pat, the second section usually takes less time. (See Chapter 4 for an introduction to the anatomy of a song.)

Play the Right Repertoire

If your goal is to play music with others, work on the tunes that they like to play. Luckily, almost all bluegrass and old-time musicians learn a basic shared set of tunes at one time or another. The musicians at your local jam session may also play a few personal favorites, including some tunes that may be unique to your part of the country. Keep in mind that more advanced players share a different set of tunes than beginning-level players, bluegrassers have a different repertoire than old-timers, and younger musicians may play some different tunes than the older folks play.

In Chapters 7, 8, and 9, you can play tunes that are jam standards, using both bluegrass and clawhammer techniques. These examples give you a good place to start in terms of building up your repertoire. After you've mastered a few basic pieces and you feel you're ready to try a beginner's jam session, find out what tunes these musicians like to play. Attend the session and make a list of the songs you hear or bring a digital recorder along to record the pieces you don't know (with the permission of the other musicians), so that you can work on them at home.

The Internet can also be of assistance as you search for tunes. Banjo player Pete Wernick has lists of bluegrass jam session favorites at www.drbanjo. com. You can also find several archives of old-time music; visit the homepage of the Friends of Old Time Banjo (www.oldtimebanjo.com) for links to the Digital Library of Appalachia at Berea College and other archival resources. Banjo Hangout at www.banjohangout.org has hundreds of free tabs in both bluegrass and old-time styles, contributed by users.

Listen Actively

Actively listening to your favorite banjo music on CD or to other musicians at concerts and jam sessions makes you a better player. Before you even start to work on a new song, find a recorded version of it first and try to pick up the song by ear. As you listen to great playing, you're internalizing what the banjo is supposed to sound like, the finer details of the style you're learning, and how the instrument fits in a group setting. Active listening also helps you to remember a song's chord progression and gives you ideas on how to accompany others when you aren't taking a solo.

Keep in mind that there's a time and a place for active listening. To keep the peace at home, carve out time when you can listen alone or in a way that doesn't disturb others (here's where headphones can come in handy). If you feel compelled every once in a while to expose your friends to your favorite banjo music, be aware that they may not want to listen to "Whoa Mule" 20 or 30 times in a row (I'm not sure why, however . . .).

Keep Track of Your Progress

Most players keep a tune list in the front pocket of their music notebook. You can group tunes any way you like. Some players group by key or tempo, whereas others create a list of tunes they already know, a list of tunes they're working on right now, and another list of tunes they want to learn in the near future. A tune list comes in handy when you're comparing what you know with another musician, but you suddenly can't recall a thing about any of the tunes you know (believe me, it happens, even with professional players).

If you're working hard at building up speed with the metronome, write the tempo settings down in pencil for each tune you're working on so that you know what tempo to start at during your next practice session. You may also want to maintain a practice diary where you can keep some brief notes about some of the things you worked on that day and also remind yourself about what needs more work the next time your pick up the banjo — which will be just after you put down this book today, or tomorrow at the latest, right?

Chapter 17

Ten Great Banjo Players You Need to Hear

. . . .

In This Chapter

▶ Getting to know the banjo's most influential stylists

▶ Listening to and collecting essential recordings and videos

. . . .

These ten players have made a difference in the world of the banjo. They're stylistic trendsetters who have developed new techniques of playing the instrument and inspired players from all over the world. Some have expanded the musical potential of the banjo with innovative playing techniques, while others have brought new audiences to the instrument. I end this chapter with a list of additional great players you should check out if you have the time.

Earl Scruggs (1924–2012)

Earl Scruggs is not only the most influential banjo player of all time but also one of the most important musicians in the history of American music. His blazing-fast, three-finger technique is the most copied banjo style in the world and has been the defining characteristic of bluegrass music for the last 70 years (for more on bluegrass banjo, see Chapters 5, 6, 7, and 9).

Scruggs helped popularize the banjo and bluegrass music with a large national audience in the 1950s and '60s through folk festival and television appearances (*The Beverly Hillbillies*) and movie soundtracks as the banjo-playing half of Lester Flatt, Earl Scruggs, and the Foggy Mountain Boys (Earl's unforgettable showpiece "Foggy Mountain Breakdown" was featured in *Bonnie and Clyde*). Hundreds of thousands of banjo players cite him as a primary influence. Check out *The Essential Earl Scruggs* album (Sony) and *The Best of the Flatt and Scruggs TV Show, Vol. 2* (Shanachie) for some of the best of his music.

Pete Seeger (b. 1919)

In the 1940s through the 1960s, Pete Seeger placed the banjo front and center in the American folk-song revival as part of a long and prolific career as a singer, songwriter, author, and political and environmental activist, and he's still going strong! Pete's self-published 1948 book *How to Play the 5-String Banjo* was the first instructional book on American folk banjo styles. This book reveals his musical eclecticism, with chapters devoted to blues, Spanish, and South American music in addition to clawhammer, old-time, bluegrass, and his own traditionally-based style. (Get to know Pete's style in Chapter 8.)

On the head of his trademark long-neck banjo is written "This Machine Surrounds Hate and Forces It to Surrender." That about says it all, doesn't it? Give a listen to his album *Darling Corey and Goofing Off Suite* (Smithsonian Folkways) for a generous helping of Pete's banjo style, and check out the DVD *Pete Seeger: The Power of Song* (Genius Products; also available in Amazon Instant Video) for a career overview.

Béla Fleck (b. 1958)

Béla Fleck emerged from the progressive bluegrass scene in the 1980s to blaze trails and set new standards for the banjo within contemporary rock, jazz, classical, and world music. He's the premiere banjo player in the world today, bringing a staggering technical ability and lyrical musicality to the music he creates with his band, Béla Fleck and the Flecktones, and through collaborations with such diverse artists as Chick Corea, Marcus Roberts, Zakir Hussain, Edgar Meyer, Tony Trischka, and others. I recommend listening to the bluegrass-oriented *Tales from the Acoustic Planet* (Warner Brothers), the classical recording *Perpetual Motion* (Sony), and *Across the Imaginary Divide* with the Marcus Roberts Trio (Rounder) to experience today's most influential player.

Bill Keith (b. 1939)

The banjo's innovative Renaissance man, Bill Keith helped to develop the melodic style of banjo playing, enabling banjo players to play scales while still using familiar three-finger roll patterns. This widely adopted technique empowers the player to reproduce note-for-note versions of everything from a fiddle tune to a Bach invention and has significantly enhanced the banjo's musical potential. (For more on the melodic style, see Chapter 9.)

Keith is also responsible for the Keith "D" tuner, which allows the player to quickly and accurately move from one pitch to another within a song, and he was one of the first college-educated, Northern musicians to play bluegrass in Bill Monroe's band, helping to break down the banjo's geographical and cultural barriers. To dive in deeper to Keith's music, you can explore *Something Auld, Something Newgrass, Something Borrowed, Something Bluegrass* (Rounder) for Bill's ingenious playing on bluegrass and jazz tunes.

Mike Seeger (1933–2009)

Mike Seeger (Pete's half-brother) devoted his life to singing, playing, and documenting traditional music made by American southerners in the first decades of the 20th century. With over 25 field recordings to his credit, Mike preserved the diversity of southern folk banjo styles while exposing historically important players such as Dock Boggs to wider audiences. As a member of the old-time string band The New Lost City Ramblers, Seeger spread the sound of old-time and clawhammer banjo to folk audiences who lived far outside the American South (see Chapter 8 for more on these styles).

As a player, Mike uses old-time music as a wellspring for his own creative and personalized fusions, forming a model for contemporary artistic expression within this genre that has influenced hundreds of other old-time players. *Southern Banjo Sounds* (Smithsonian Folkways) is essential listening. Also be sure to catch *Always Been A Rambler*, a New Lost City Ramblers documentary (Arhoolie).

Don Reno (1927–1984)

Around the same time Earl Scruggs was learning to play in nearby North Carolina, Don Reno developed his three-finger approach to banjo playing in South Carolina. As his professional performing career blossomed in the 1950s and '60s, Reno separated himself from Scruggs's sound by bringing a new set of playing techniques to bluegrass banjo, adopted from his extensive knowledge of country guitar playing. From jazzy chordal licks to virtuosic single-string runs, Reno's playing offered an alternative to Scruggs's approach within bluegrass. Reno's *Founding Father of the Bluegrass Banjo* (CMH Records) is a compilation of some of his best late-career work, while *The Very Best of Don Reno & Red Smiley* (Goldenlane Records) is a good overview of the '50s recordings. (See Chapter 9 for an introduction to Reno's single-string playing technique.)

J. D. Crowe (b. 1937)

Considered the most influential banjo player of bluegrass music's modern age (1970s to the present), J. D. Crowe brings a forceful right-hand attack and a bluesy intensity to his Scruggs-based bluegrass banjo playing. With crisp, aggressive pull-offs and ideas borrowed from early rock 'n' roll and country guitar, Crowe is also a superb and influential band leader. The mid-1970s version of his band, The New South, featuring mandolin player Ricky Skaggs, guitarist Tony Rice, and dobro player Jerry Douglas, set the standard for the sound of modern bluegrass, absorbing contemporary country and folk influences. In 2013, Crowe announced his retirement from touring but he still occasionally performs in various bluegrass all-star collaborations — catch him if you can! *J.D. Crowe & the New South* and *The Bluegrass Album* (both from Rounder) are essentials for any banjo player's music collection.

Tony Trischka (b. 1949)

Tony's reputation as the first avant-garde bluegrass player was established in the 1970s through a series of groundbreaking recordings filled with startling original compositions. Luckily, the rest of the banjo world has finally caught up to him. Today, in addition to being at the forefront of the boldest of banjo explorations, Tony is known as a master of a wide variety of traditional and historical banjo styles. He is an outstanding instructor who has influenced thousands of players through his books, DVDs, and online banjo school. Count such players as Béla Fleck, Chris Pandolfi, and yours truly among his dedicated students. Check out the albums *Double Banjo Bluegrass Spectacular* (Rounder) and *Territory* (Smithsonian Folkways) for a sampling of music from this very influential player.

Alison Brown (b. 1962)

Count this Nashville-based banjoist at the top of the list of today's most influential progressive players. Combining influences from jazz, folk, Latin, bluegrass, Irish, and world music, Brown's work on electric and acoustic banjo (and guitar) is lyrical, warm, and virtuosic — all at the same time (a rare accomplishment for a banjo player)! She fronts the Alison Brown Quartet, a jazz-tinged ensemble featuring drums, piano, and bass, and she also heads up her own record label, Compass Records. Check out *The Company You Keep* and *Stolen Moments* (both from Compass Records) for listening adventures in progressive acoustic and jazz fusion styles.

Jens Kruger (b. 1962)

The future of banjo playing goes international in the hands of the phenomenal Swiss musician Jens Kruger. For the last decade, Jens has made North Carolina his home base, performing with his guitar-playing brother Uwe and bassist Joel Landsberg as the Kruger Brothers. While Jens's technical mastery is awe-inspiring, his musicality and emotional expression have connected strongly with audiences all over the world. In addition to being at home with all three-finger styles, he's an awesome clawhammer player (which frankly, just isn't fair to the rest of us!). Check out *Appalachian Concerto* (Double Time Music) featuring a string quartet and *Best of the Kruger Brothers* (Double Time Music) for a complete musical banjo feast.

Other banjo players you should hear

In case you want to go a little further in your exploration of the ever-expanding universe of banjo sounds and styles, I've provided the following lists of banjo players I think you need to check out:

- **Clawhammer and old time:** Virgil Anderson, Danny Barnes, Riley Baugus, Mac Benford, Carroll Best, Dock Boggs, Laura Boosinger, Hank Bradley, Kate Brislin, Paul Brown, Samantha Bumgarner, Gaither Carleton, Bob Carlin, Maybelle Carter, Fred Cockerham, John Cohen, Mary Z. Cox, Kyle Creed, Rufus Crisp, Dwight Diller, Cousin Emmy, Cathy Fink, Dan Gellert, Alice Gerrard, Roscoe Holcomb, Mark Johnson, Grandpa Jones, Buell Kazee, Walt Koken, Jens Kruger, Lily May Ledford, Frank Lee, Brad Leftwich, Dan Levenson, Bertram Levy, Charlie Lowe, R. D. Lunceford, Joel Mabus, Reed Martin, Steve Martin, Michael Miles, Bruce Molsky, Lynn Morris, Joe Newberry, Molly O'Day, Tom Paley, Ken Perlman, Charlie Poole, Dirk Powell, Ola Belle Reed, Dink Roberts, Ivan Rosenberg, Mark Schatz, Lee Sexton, Morgan Sexton, Wayne Shrubsall, Matokie Slaughter, Will Slayden, Hobart Smith, Richie Stearns, Jody Stecher, Kirk Sutphin, Molly Tenenbaum, Suzanne Thomas, Odell Thompson, Leroy Troy, Stephen Wade, Abigail Washburn, Doc Watson, Oscar Wright

- **Bluegrass:** Tom Adams, Eddie Adcock, Danny Barnes, Terry Baucom, Kristin Scott Benson, Ron Block, Dennis Caplinger, Cia Cherryholmes, Pat Cloud, Noah Crase, Charlie Cushman, Doug Dillard, Steve Dilling, Joe Drumright, Ben Eldridge, Tony Ellis, Bill Emerson, Emily Erwin, Tony Furtado, John Hartford, Casey Henry, Murphy Henry, John Hickman, Steve Huber, Kenny Ingram, Snuffy Jenkins, Courtney Johnson, Vic Jordan, Jens Kruger, John Lawless, "Little Roy" Lewis, Greg Liszt, Keith Little, Ned Luberecki, Rudy Lyle, Steve Martin, Rob McCoury, John McEuen, Jim Mills, Lynn Morris, Joe Mullins, Alan Munde, Mike Munford, Alan O'Bryant, Sonny Osborne, Chris Pandolfi, Herb Pedersen, Noam Pikelny, Don Wayne Reno, Butch Robins, Sammy Shelor, Allen Shelton, Avram Siegel, Craig Smith, Fred Sokolow, Ralph Stanley, Ron Stewart, Don Stover, Dave Talbot, Bobby Thompson, Scott Vestal, Eric Weissberg, Pete Wernick

Part VI
Appendixes

Go to www.dummies.com/cheatsheet/banjo to access the Cheat Sheet created specifically for *Banjo For Dummies,* 2nd Edition.

In this part...

- ✔ Discover just about all the chords you will ever need and name the notes on your banjo neck.

- ✔ Find out what audio tracks and video clips are available to access online to help you hear and see the concepts presented in this book.

Appendix A

Banjo Chords and Notes

. . . .

Chords come in a couple of different varieties: major for when you're feeling good; minor for when the mood is a bit more introspective; and 6ths, 7ths, and 9ths for when you need to jazz it up a bit. Chords are made up of individual notes, and knowing where to find both notes and chords on your banjo neck comes in handy in all sorts of ways. Don't try to learn all these positions at once; instead, absorb them one at a time as you need to use them in new songs. In this way, you'll soon be the master of your own banjo chord universe.

Chords

In Figures A-1 and A-2, I give you 57 chord diagrams for the major, minor, 7th, and minor 7th chords found in the first position on the banjo neck (frets 1 through 5) along with five chord shapes used for 6th and 9th chords.

I include a movable banjo chord position chart, Figure A-3, which shows the positions of the G, C, and D movable major, seventh, minor, and diminished chords on the first 12 frets of the banjo. A movable chord position requires the left hand to fret strings 1 through 4 of your banjo. The advantage of movable chords is that they can be easily shifted up and down the neck to fret new-letter-name chords.

To find other letter-name chords using these same positions, shift the movable chord position up or down according to the order of notes that follows:

G / G♯ *or* A♭ / A / A♯ *or* B♭ / B / C / C♯ *or* D♭ / D / D♯ *or* E♭ / E / F / F♯ *or* G♭ / G

For example, if you fret the F-shape G chord that's found at the 5th fret (and shown on the upper-left chart in Figure A-3), and you move this chord up two frets, you'll be playing an A chord. Note that the A note is located two notes above the G note, as shown in the preceding list. Each adjacent note corresponds to a one-fret change up or down on your banjo neck.

REMEMBER

Some chords and notes (for example, G#/A♭) have two names but are found in exactly the same place on your banjo neck. Called *enharmonic equivalents,* these chords and notes are called either by one letter name or the other depending upon what key you're playing in.

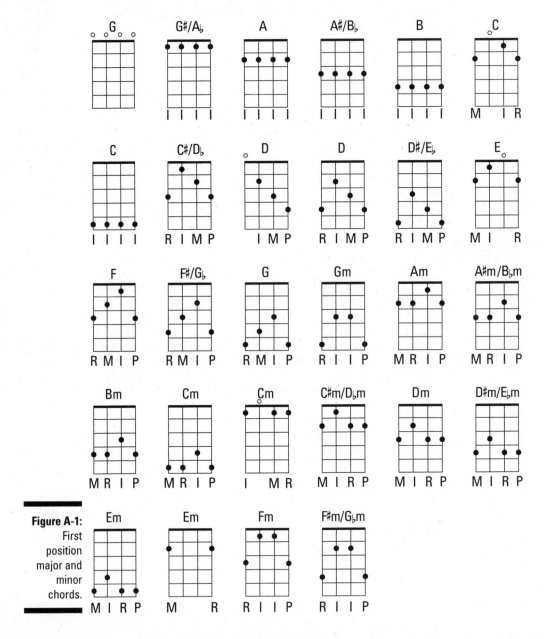

Figure A-1: First position major and minor chords.

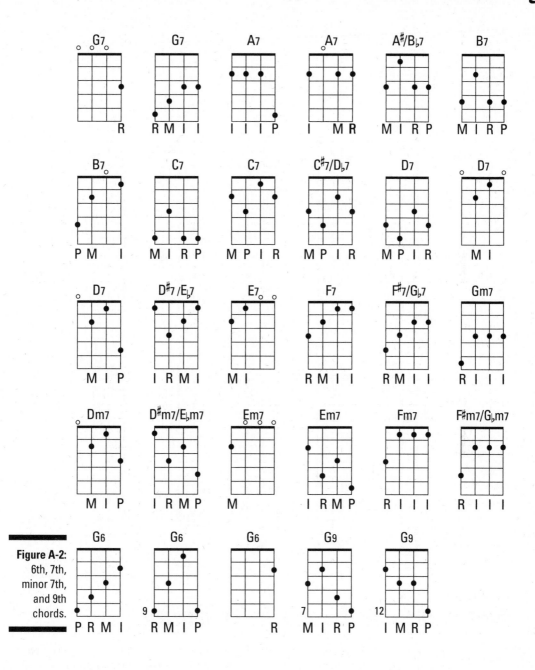

Figure A-2: 6th, 7th, minor 7th, and 9th chords.

F-shape: ●

D-shape: ■

Barre-shape: ◆

□ = not necessarily fretted, but may be

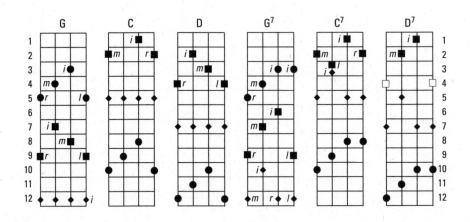

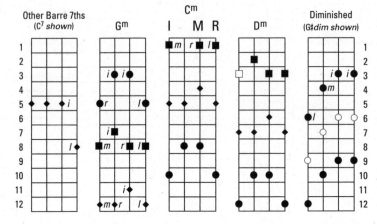

Figure A-3:
A movable
banjo chord
position
chart.

Notes on the Banjo in G Tuning

Figures A-4 through A-8 show you the names of the notes on the banjo finger-board in G tuning. Knowing these names can be useful in building chords and for locating melody notes on your banjo. Each figure lists the names of the notes on an individual string.

Figure A-4:
1st string:
Open D.

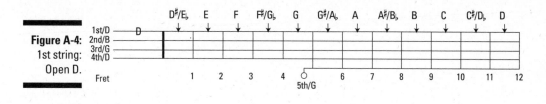

Figure A-5:
2nd string:
Open B.

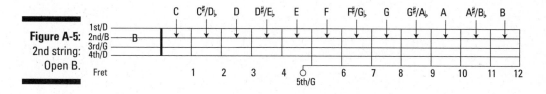

Figure A-6:
3rd string:
Open G.

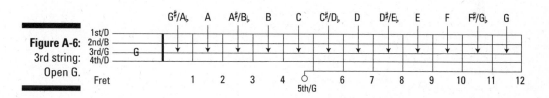

Figure A-7:
4th string:
Open D.

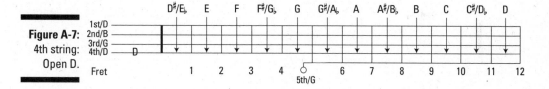

Figure A-8:
5th string:
Open G.

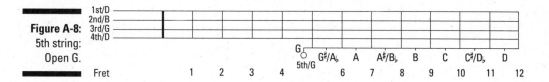

Appendix B

Audio Tracks and Video Clips

· ·

Sometimes, reading about a concept and trying to practice it just doesn't cut it — you need to see or hear it, too. Wherever you see the "Play This!" icon, you find references to audio tracks and video clips that demonstrate various banjo tunes and techniques. I also provide a few audio tracks that you can use as backing tracks to play over to make your practice sessions more fun and interesting. This appendix provides you with a handy list of all the audio tracks and video clips referenced throughout the book.

If you've purchased the paper or e-book version of *Banjo For Dummies,* 2nd Edition, you can find the audio tracks and video clips — ready and waiting for you — at www.dummies.com/go/banjo. (If you don't have Internet access, call 877-762-2974 within the U.S. or 317-572-3993 outside the U.S.)

Discovering What's on the Audio Tracks

Table B-1 lists all the audio tracks that accompany each chapter, along with any figure and tab numbers if applicable. You also find several backing and play-along tracks to help you with your practice.

Table B-1		Audio Tracks
Track Number	Chapter	Description
1	2	G Tuning Reference Notes
2	3	Strumming "She'll Be Comin' Round the Mountain" (Figure 3-11)
3	4	G-Major Scale (Figure 4-3)
4	4	D-Major Scale (Figure 4-4)
5	4	G-Major Scale, Beginning on Open 4th String (Figure 4-6)

(continued)

Table B-1 *(continued)*

Track Number	Chapter	Description
6	4	"Frère Jacques"
7	4	"She'll Be Comin' Round the Mountain" (Full Version)
8	4	Tab Rhythm Exercise (Tab 4-6)
9	4	Pinch Patterns with G, C, and D7 Chords (Tab 4-7)
10	4	"She'll Be Comin' Round the Mountain" with Pinch Patterns (Tab 4-8)
11	4	"Worried Man Blues" with Pinch Patterns (Tab 4-9)
12	4	"Man of Constant Sorrow" with Pinch Patterns (Tab 4-10)
13	5	Clawhammer Melody-Note Exercise #1 (Tab 5-1)
14	5	Clawhammer Melody-Note Exercise #2 (Tab 5-2)
15	5	Clawhammer Brush Exercise (Tab 5-3)
16	5	Clawhammer Brush and 5th-string Exercise (Tab 5-4)
17	5	Basic Clawhammer Technique Exercise #1 (Tab 5-5)
18	5	Basic Clawhammer Technique Exercise #2 (Tab 5-6)
19	5	Clawhammer Technique with G, C, and D7 Chords (Tab 5-7)
20	5	"Boil Them Cabbage Down" with Clawhammer Accompaniment (Tab 5-8)
21	5	"Worried Man Blues" with Clawhammer Accompaniment (Tab 5-9)
22	5	Right-Hand Thumb Bluegrass Exercise (Tab 5-10)
23	5	Right-Hand Index and Middle-Finger Bluegrass Exercise (Tab 5-11)
24	5	Bluegrass Alternating Thumb Roll with G, C, and D7 Chords (Tab 5-12)
25	5	Bluegrass Forward-Reverse Roll with G, C, and D7 Chords (Tab 5-13)
26	5	Bluegrass Forward Roll with G, C, and D7 Chords (Tab 5-14)
27	5	"Boil Them Cabbage Down" Singing and Guitar with Mixed-Roll Accompaniment (Tab 5-15)
28	5	"Worried Man Blues" Singing and Guitar with Forward-Roll Accompaniment (Tab 5-16)
29	6	3rd-string Slides (Tab 6-1)

Track Number	Chapter	Description
30	6	4th-string Slides (Tab 6-2)
31	6	1st-string Slides (Tab 6-3)
32	6	Open-string Hammer-ons (Tab 6-4)
33	6	Fretted Hammer-ons (Tab 6-5)
34	6	Open-string Pull-offs (Tab 6-6)
35	6	Fretted Pull-offs (Tab 6-7)
36	6	Choke, Choke and Release, Pre-choke (Tab 6-8)
37	6	Basic Clawhammer Technique with G, C, and D7 Chords (Tab 6-9)
38	6	Bluegrass Roll Review: Alternating Thumb, Forward-Reverse, and Forward Rolls (Tab 6-10)
39	6	Clawhammer 3rd-string Slides (Tab 6-11)
40	6	Clawhammer 1st-string Slides (Tab 6-12)
41	6	Clawhammer 4th-string Slides (Tab 6-13)
42	6	Clawhammer Open-string Hammer-ons (Tab 6-14)
43	6	Clawhammer Fretted Hammer-ons (Tab 6-15)
44	6	Clawhammer 4th-string Pull-offs (Tab 6-16)
45	6	Clawhammer 3rd-string Pull-offs (Tab 6-17)
46	6	Clawhammer 1st-string Pull-offs (Tab 6-18)
47	6	Clawhammer Special Pull-off (Tab 6-19)
48	6	Foggy Mountain Choke in Clawhammer Banjo (Tab 6-20)
49	6	Bluegrass Alternating Thumb Rolls with Slides (Tab 6-21)
50	6	Bluegrass Forward-Reverse Rolls with Slides (Tab 6-22)
51	6	Bluegrass Forward Rolls with Slides (Tab 6-23)
52	6	Bluegrass Alternating Thumb Rolls with Hammer-ons (Tab 6-24)
53	6	Bluegrass Forward-Reverse Rolls with Hammer-ons (Tab 6-25)
54	6	Bluegrass Forward Rolls with Hammer-ons (Tab 6-26)
55	6	Bluegrass Alternating Thumb Rolls with Pull-offs (Tab 6-27)
56	6	Bluegrass Forward-Reverse Rolls with Slides and Pull-offs (Tab 6-28)

(continued)

Table B-1 *(continued)*

Track Number	Chapter	Description
57	6	Bluegrass Forward Rolls with Hammer-ons and Pull-offs (Tab 6-29)
58	6	Bluegrass Forward Rolls with Chokes (Tab 6-30)
59	7	"Worried Man Blues" Melody in Clawhammer Style with Guitar Accompaniment (Tab 7-1)
60	7	"Worried Man Blues" Melody in Bluegrass Style with Guitar Accompaniment (Tab 7-2)
61	7	"Worried Man Blues" Melody Using Left-Hand Techniques, Clawhammer Style with Guitar Accompaniment (Tab 7-3)
62	7	"Worried Man Blues" Melody Using Left-Hand Techniques, Bluegrass Style with Guitar Accompaniment (Tab 7-4)
63	7	"Boil Them Cabbage Down" Clawhammer Melody with Guitar Accompaniment (Tab 7-5)
64	7	"Boil Them Cabbage Down" Bluegrass Melody with Guitar Accompaniment (Tab 7-6)
65	7	"Cripple Creek" Clawhammer Melody with Guitar Accompaniment (Tab 7-7)
66	7	"Cripple Creek" Bluegrass Melody with Guitar Accompaniment (Tab 7-8)
67	7	"Goodbye Liza Jane" Clawhammer Melody with Guitar Accompaniment (Tab 7-9)
68	7	"Goodbye Liza Jane" Bluegrass Melody with Guitar Accompaniment (Tab 7-10)
69	7	"Ground Hog" Clawhammer Melody with Guitar Accompaniment (Tab 7-11)
70	7	"Ground Hog" Bluegrass Melody with Guitar Accompaniment (Tab 7-12)
71	8	1st-string Clawhammer Pull-offs (Tab 8-1)
72	8	Clawhammer Double-Thumbing Technique (Tab 8-2)
73	8	"Old Joe Clark" Using Double-Thumbing and 1st-string Pull-off Techniques (Tab 8-3)
74	8	"Soldier's Joy" in Double C Tuning (Tab 8-4)
75	8	"Cluck Old Hen" in Modal Tuning (Tab 8-5)
76	8	"Last Chance" (Tab 8-6)

Track Number	Chapter	Description
77	8	Seeger Basic Strum (Tab 8-7)
78	8	"Swing Low, Sweet Chariot" Using Seeger Stroke (Tab 8-8)
79	8	"Little Birdie" Using Seeger Stroke (Tab 8-9)
80	8	"Pretty Polly" Using Old-Time Fingerpicking Techniques (Tab 8-10)
81	8	"Coal Creek March" from Pete Steele, Using Old-Time Fingerpicking Techniques (Tab 8-11)
82	9	Scruggs-style Roll Patterns: Alternating Thumb, Forward-Reverse, Forward, the "Lick" Roll, Foggy Mountain, Backward, Middle-Leading, Index-Leading (Tab 9-1)
83	9	G Licks (Tab 9-2)
84	9	C Licks (Tab 9-3)
85	9	D Licks (Tab 9-4)
86	9	G Fill-in Licks (Tab 9-5)
87	9	Creating a Bluegrass Solo Using Licks, G-C-D7 Chord Progression (Tab 9-6)
88	9	"Everyday Breakdown" Bluegrass Banjo with Guitar and Mandolin Accompaniment (Tab 9-7)
89	9	"Shortening Bread" Bluegrass Banjo with Guitar and Mandolin Accompaniment (Tab 9-8)
90	9	"Banjo Cascade" Melodic Banjo with Guitar and Mandolin Accompaniment (Tab 9-12)
91	9	"Turkey in the Straw" Melodic Banjo with Guitar and Mandolin Accompaniment (Tab 9-13)
92	9	"Blackberry Blossom" Melodic Banjo with Guitar Accompaniment (Tab 9-14)
93	9	Single-String Right-Hand Exercises (Tabs 9-15 to 9-17)
94	9	Single-String Scale Exercises (Tabs 9-18 to 9-21)
95	9	D Scale (Tab 9-22)
96	9	"Red Haired Boy" Played in Single-String Style with Guitar Accompaniment (Tab 9-23)
97	9	"Arkansas Traveler" with Guitar Accompaniment (Tab 9-24)
98	9	"Reno's Rag" with Guitar Accompaniment (Tab 9-25)

(continued)

Table B-1 *(continued)*

Track Number	Chapter	Description
99	9	"Winston's Jig" with Guitar Accompaniment (Tab 9-26)
100	9	"The Distance Between Two Points" Combining Three-Finger Techniques (Tab 9-27)
101	10	G-C-D with Barre Shape (Tab 10-1)
102	10	G-C-D Chords with F Position (Tab 10-2)
103	10	G-C-D with D Shape (Tab 10-3)
104	10	G-C-D Moving from F to D Shapes (Tab 10-4)
105	10	Moving Back and Forth between G Major and G Minor Chords (Figure 10-4)
106	10	Playing a G Major Chord and Moving to an A Minor Chord (Tab 10-5)
107	10	Moving Back and Forth between E Major and E Minor Chords (Figure 10-5)
108	10	Playing a G Major and an E Minor Chord (Tab 10-6)
109	10	Shifting from a D Major Chord to a D Minor Chord (Figure 10-6)
110	10	G-C-D Progression with F-Shape Vamping (Tab 10-7)
111	10	Vamping to "Red River Valley" Using F and D Shapes (Tab 10-8)
112	10	Vamping to "Blackberry Blossom" Using F and D Shapes with Guitar Accompaniment (Tab 10-9)
113	11	"Pompey Ran Away" African Banjo Tune (Tab 11-1)
114	11	"Juba" 19th-Century Minstrel Banjo Tune (Tab 11-2)
115	11	"Hard Times" 19th-Century Minstrel Banjo Tune (Tab 11-3)
116	11	"Colorado Buck Dance" Early 20th-Century Classic Banjo Piece (Tab 11-4)
117	11	"Banjoisticus" Early 20th-Century Classic Banjo Piece (Tab 11-5)

Looking at What's in the Video Clips

Table B-2 lists all the video clips that accompany each chapter.

Table B-2		Video Clips
Clip Number	**Chapter**	**Description**
1	2	G Tuning, Low to High
2	3	Fretting and Changing Chords
3	3	Strumming and Changing Chords
4	4	Playing the Pinch Pattern
5	4	Playing "Worried Man Blues" Using a Pinch Pattern
6	5	Clawhammer Banjo: Right-Hand Position and Basic Strum
7	5	Clawhammer Banjo: "Boil Them Cabbage Down" Using Basic Strum
8	5	Bluegrass Banjo: Fitting Fingerpicks
9	5	Bluegrass Banjo: Right-Hand Position
10	5	Bluegrass Banjo: Alternating Thumb Roll
11	5	Bluegrass Banjo: Forward-Reverse Roll
12	5	Bluegrass Banjo: "Worried Man Blues" with the Forward Roll
13	6	Left-Hand Techniques: Slides
14	6	Left-Hand Techniques: Hammer-ons
15	6	Left-Hand Techniques: Pull-offs
16	6	Left-Hand Techniques: Special Clawhammer Pull-off
17	6	Left-Hand Techniques: Chokes
18	6	Using Both Hands in Clawhammer Banjo
19	6	Using Both Hands in Bluegrass Banjo
20	7	Clawhammer Banjo: "Worried Man Blues"
21	7	Bluegrass Banjo: "Worried Man Blues"
22	7	Clawhammer Banjo: "Cripple Creek"
23	7	Bluegrass Banjo: "Cripple Creek"
24	7	Clawhammer Banjo: "Ground Hog"

(continued)

Table B-2 *(continued)*

Clip Number	Chapter	Description
25	7	Bluegrass Banjo: "Ground Hog"
26	8	Clawhammer Banjo: Double Thumbing
27	8	Clawhammer Banjo: "Old Joe Clark"
28	8	Clawhammer Banjo: Double C Tuning and "Soldier's Joy"
29	8	Clawhammer Banjo: Modal Tuning and "Cluck Old Hen"
30	8	Clawhammer Banjo: "Last Chance"
31	8	Old-Time Banjo: The Seeger Stroke
32	8	Old-Time Banjo: D Tuning and "Coal Creek March"
33	9	Bluegrass Banjo: "Everyday Breakdown"
34	9	Bluegrass Banjo: "Blackberry Blossom"
35	9	Bluegrass Banjo: Single-String, Right-Hand Exercises
36	9	Bluegrass Banjo: Playing Single-String Scales
37	9	Bluegrass Banjo: "Red Haired Boy" in Single-String Style
38	11	19th-Century Banjo: "Hard Times"
39	11	Classic Banjo: "Banjoisticus"
40	15	Changing Strings on Your Banjo

Customer Care

If you have trouble downloading the companion files, please call Wiley Product Technical Support at 800-762-2974. Outside the United States, call 317-572-3994. You can also contact Wiley Product Technical Support at `http://wiley.custhelp.com/`. Wiley Publishing will provide technical support only for downloading and other general quality control items.

To place additional orders or to request information about other Wiley products, please call 877-762-2974.

Index

• P •

Pandolfi, Chris (single-string style), 183
pattern adjustments, melody notes, 133
patterns, right- and left-hand, 19
peghead, neck component, 14–15
Perlman, Ken (banjo instruction), 227
phrase (musical idea), 212, 317
piano, reference tuning, 31
pickers, 131
Picker's Supply website, 267
picking, string striking motion, 26
picks. *See* fingerpicks; thumbpicks
pickups, electric, 261–262
Pikelny, Noam (single-string banjo), 183
Pilhofer, Michael (*Music Theory For Dummies,* 2nd Edition), 186, 218
pinch patterns, 68–72
pitch
  5th-string characteristics, 9
  five-string banjo versus guitar, 9–10
  G tuning, 24–25
  order of notes, 29
  reference tuning, 27
  repeated, 103
  string adjustment, 17–18
plating, 260–261
plectrum banjos, 10–11
polishing banjo, 308
"Pompey Ran Away" song, 213
position. *See* body position
pot
  armrest, 16
  banjo element, 12
  beginner-level banjos, 248
  brackets, 16–17
  bridge, 16
  coordinating rods, 16
  flange, 16–17
  head, 15, 17
  resonator, 16
  resonator screw, 16
  rim, 15, 17
  tension hoops, 16
  tone ring, 15–17
practice sessions
  active listening, 318
  goal-setting, 314

length, 313–314
progress-tracking, 319
regular, 313–314
repertoire, 317–318
right-hand focus, 316
song measures, 317
speed increases, 316–317
support, 20
tablature, 315
warm-up routines, 315
pre-choke, 116
"Pretty Polly" song, 158–159
private lessons
  anxiety, overcoming, 224
  costs, 226
  group classes, 226–227
  one-on-one/group, 223–224
  reasons for, 224
  teachers, 224–227
progress-tracking, 319
Propik
  fingerpicks, 91
  thumbpicks, 90
pull-offs
  bluegrass techniques, 127–128
  clawhammer techniques, 114, 121–124, 146–147
  fretted, 113–114
  left-hand techniques, 111–114
  open-string, 112–113
purchasing guide. *See* banjo buying guide; gear buying guide
push-offs. *See* pull-offs

• Q •

quality banjo. *See* better-quality banjo

• R •

radiused fingerboards, 260
railroad spikes, 5th-string capos, 283
rapping. *See* clawhammer
Recording King banjos, 258
recording software, 290
"Red Haired Boy" song, 190

• S •

• *V* •

Notes

Notes

Notes

Notes

About the Author

Bill Evans is not to be confused with the deceased jazz piano legend or the very-much-living jazz saxophone player (or the Austin, Texas, real estate agent). *This* Bill Evans is an internationally known five-string banjo performer, teacher, scholar, recording artist, and composer who brings a deep knowledge, intense virtuosity, and contagious passion to all things banjo, with music fans and banjo students from all over the world in a career that spans over 35 years.

Bill has taught thousands of people to play the five-string banjo through his instructional DVDs and books and in one-on-one lessons and appearances at music camps and workshops throughout the United States, Canada, and Europe. His own events, the NashCamp Banjo Camp, a three-day workshop outside of Nashville, Tennessee, and the California Banjo Extravaganza, a series of concerts and workshops held throughout northern California, bring together banjo players from all over the world.

Bill's CDs *In Good Company, Bill Evans Plays Banjo,* and *Native and Fine* have topped folk and bluegrass charts and made many "Best of" lists. He tours regularly with his solo show *The Banjo in America,* presenting over 250 years of music on a variety of vintage instruments. He has shared the stage with the San Francisco Symphony, Dry Branch Fire Squad, and Fletcher Bright, among many others, and has appeared on *A Prairie Home Companion with Garrison Keillor.*

To find out more about Bill, visit www.billevansbanjo.com.

Dedication

It would not be possible for me to devote my life to the banjo without the support and love of my family: my wife Kathy and my children Jesse and Corey. Thank you! I dedicate this book to you.

Author's Acknowledgments

I'd like to thank Jody Stecher, Brad Leftwich, Mac Benford, and Eli Kaufman of the American Banjo Fraternity for their advice and assistance in the preparation of the clawhammer and classic banjo sections of this book.

I am indebted to Stan Werbin and photographer Dave Matchette from Elderly Instruments for providing many of the photos used in this book and to Janet and Greg Deering, Carolina Bridges, and David Brandrowski of Deering Banjos for the wonderful cover shot. Thanks also to photographer Kelsey Vaughn at Gruhn Guitars for supplying photos of the Osborne Chief banjo and to Erin Inglish, Michelle Haft, Max Schwartz, and Jody Stecher, my photogenic banjo models. The rest of the photos used in this book were taken by Anne Hamersky. Thanks, Anne, for your inspirational work!

Thanks to Adam Traum for his expertise with the video that accompanies this book and to Dix Bruce and Jim Nunally for their help with the audio tracks. Thanks also to Ann Jefferson, Larry Cohea, Cindy Sinclair, Sonny Osborne, Tony Trischka, Fletcher Bright, Ron Thomason, and Alan Munde for their constant friendship, support, and musical inspiration.

I am grateful to my Wiley team who cheerfully and patiently dedicated themselves to this project: David Lutton, David Hobson, Elizabeth Rea, Christy Pingleton, and Paul Chen; to my agent Carole Jelen at Waterside Productions; and to Earl Scruggs, who inspired so many of us to play this wonderful instrument.

Publisher's Acknowledgments

Assistant Editor: David Lutton

Project Editor: Elizabeth Rea

Copy Editor: Christine Pingleton

Technical Editor: Kara Barnard

Art Coordinator: Alicia B. South

Project Coordinator: Rebekah Brownson

Project Manager: Paul Chen

Photographer: Anne Hamersky

Cover Image: ©Jamie Latty/Deering Banjo Co.

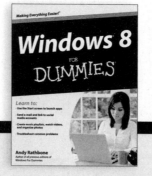

Math & Science

Algebra I For Dummies,
2nd Edition
978-0-470-55964-2

Anatomy and Physiology
For Dummies,
2nd Edition
978-0-470-92326-9

Astronomy For Dummies,
3rd Edition
978-1-118-37697-3

Biology For Dummies,
2nd Edition
978-0-470-59875-7

Chemistry For Dummies,
2nd Edition
978-1-1180-0730-3

Pre-Algebra Essentials
For Dummies
978-0-470-61838-7

Microsoft Office

Excel 2013 For Dummies
978-1-118-51012-4

Office 2013 All-in-One
For Dummies
978-1-118-51636-2

PowerPoint 2013
For Dummies
978-1-118-50253-2

Word 2013 For Dummies
978-1-118-49123-2

Music

Blues Harmonica
For Dummies
978-1-118-25269-7

Guitar For Dummies,
3rd Edition
978-1-118-11554-1

iPod & iTunes
For Dummies,
10th Edition
978-1-118-50864-0

Programming

Android Application
Development For
Dummies, 2nd Edition
978-1-118-38710-8

iOS 6 Application
Development For Dummies
978-1-118-50880-0

Java For Dummies,
5th Edition
978-0-470-37173-2

Religion & Inspiration

The Bible For Dummies
978-0-7645-5296-0

Buddhism For Dummies,
2nd Edition
978-1-118-02379-2

Catholicism For Dummies,
2nd Edition
978-1-118-07778-8

Self-Help & Relationships

Bipolar Disorder
For Dummies,
2nd Edition
978-1-118-33882-7

Meditation For Dummies,
3rd Edition
978-1-118-29144-3

Seniors

Computers For Seniors
For Dummies,
3rd Edition
978-1-118-11553-4

iPad For Seniors
For Dummies,
5th Edition
978-1-118-49708-1

Social Security
For Dummies
978-1-118-20573-0

Smartphones & Tablets

Android Phones
For Dummies
978-1-118-16952-0

Kindle Fire HD
For Dummies
978-1-118-42223-6

NOOK HD For Dummies,
Portable Edition
978-1-118-39498-4

Surface For Dummies
978-1-118-49634-3

Test Prep

ACT For Dummies,
5th Edition
978-1-118-01259-8

ASVAB For Dummies,
3rd Edition
978-0-470-63760-9

GRE For Dummies,
7th Edition
978-0-470-88921-3

Officer Candidate Tests,
For Dummies
978-0-470-59876-4

Physician's Assistant Ex
For Dummies
978-1-118-11556-5

Series 7 Exam
For Dummies
978-0-470-09932-2

Windows 8

Windows 8 For Dummie
978-1-118-13461-0

Windows 8 For Dummie
Book + DVD Bundle
978-1-118-27167-4

Windows 8 All-in-One
For Dummies
978-1-118-11920-4

Available in print and e-book formats.

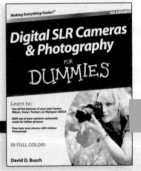

Available wherever books are sold. For more information or to order direct: U.S. customers visit www.Dummies.com or call 1-877-762-2
U.K. customers visit www.Wileyeurope.com or call (0) 1243 843291. Canadian customers visit www.Wiley.ca or call 1-800-567-4797.

Connect with us online at www.facebook.com/fordummies or @fordummies

Take Dummies with you everywhere you go!

Whether you're excited about e-books, want more from the web, must have your mobile apps, or swept up in social media, Dummies makes everything easier .

Dummies products make life easier

- DIY
- Consumer Electronics
- Crafts
- Software
- Cookware
- Hobbies
- Videos
- Music
- Games
- and More!

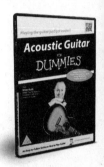

For more information, go to **Dummies.com**® and search the store by category.

FOR
DUMMIES
A Wiley Brand